TO A DIFFERENT DRUM

by Dr. Pauline G. Hamilton
AN AUTOBIOGRAPHY

AN OMF BOOK

Helen J. Slater

PORTKNOCKIE

© OVERSEAS MISSIONARY FELLOWSHIP
(formerly China Inland Mission)
Published by Overseas Missionary Fellowship (IHQ) Ltd.,
2 Cluny Road, Singapore 1025,
Republic of Singapore

First published 1984
Reprinted ....1984, 1985(thrice), 1988

OMF BOOKS are distributed by
OMF, 404 South Church Street,
  Robesonia, Pa 19551, USA
OMF, Belmont, The Vine,
  Sevenoaks, Kent, TN13 3TZ, UK
OMF, PO Box 177, Kew East,
  Victoria 3102, Australia
and other OMF offices.

ISBN 9971-83-839-7

Printed in Singapore

Contents

Foreword

"The princes and princesses of the church" is the name we give our missionaries at Park Street Church on the Boston Common, where I served as pastor for 33 years. Jolly, humble, intelligent, down-to-earth Pauline, a beloved missionary of Park Street Church, would not accept such a title; but as you read the trials and triumphs of this remarkable lady I am sure you will be aware of His glory showing through.

She is a person of faith. A twentieth-century woman who achieved her goals in the area of science and became a professor at Smith College, she dedicated her talent and abilities to God without reserve. Refusing to accept an appointment to a Chinese university, she offered herself as a missionary and went out under the China Inland Mission. For her, God is a reality, an omnipotent sovereign, a Father, and a guide in all things. He is a God who can be trusted.

God called her to be His own when she was on her way to commit suicide. He stopped her. She in turn dedicated her life entirely to Him to go anywhere at any time.

At times in her career she was assigned to distasteful tasks. At other times she was tempted to abandon her calling. But always she remembered her dedication and was obedient to assignments. It took many years for her to arrive at the work for which she was called, mainly with students and young people, from which she reaped a rich harvest.

She was exemplary as a missionary, with strong convictions yet always willing to obey the Lord as He made His will known to her through fellow missionaries and the circumstances of life.

I commend this book to you as a witness to the faithfulness of God. It will encourage you in your Christian walk.

HAROLD J. OCKENGA.

1
Blow-Out

"Hon! Hon! Come back! Hon, come back!"

Mother was calling to me as I pulled away from the cottage in my sister's gray convertible coupé. I could see her petite figure in my rearview mirror. Mother was not very tall, only a bit over five feet. Her beautiful white wavy hair blowing softly in the summer breeze was framing her face, today etched with lines of worry. Her hands were gripping the porch railing as though she were steadying herself. I swallowed hard, but just ignored her calls. Pushing my foot harder on the accelerator, I sped away. The car was a fairly new one Sis was letting me use while she was traveling in Europe, and on that hot summer afternoon I had the top down, not to enjoy the breeze blowing my long brown hair, but so that everything would go according to plan.

I had only one intention. Although that graveled mountain road was one of my favorite drives, I was not out for a pleasure drive. No, not today. All I could think of was to reach the hairpin turn at the open mine at

Cornwall and go flying over the cliff to put an end to my miserable existence.

No one would know I had gone over intentionally. There was no guard rail to stop me, and accidents there were frequent. Besides, I had to take this route to go for the bottled gas we needed. At last the opportunity I had hoped for for weeks had come, and in such a way that no one would guess I meant to take my own life. Mother was not able to go with me as our hired girl could not be found, and Mother had to be at the cottage when the girl returned. I had not left any suicide notes for anyone. My going over the cliff would be considered just one of those tragic accidents.

Life could not continue as it was. Everything I had ever wanted, hoped for, and worked for was gone — my future destroyed. And it seemed that no one cared.

From the time I was a small girl I had wanted to study medicine, and I had worked hard toward that dreamed-of goal. Two years of medical school were already behind me. How I had looked forward to the vigorous, fulfilling years ahead in my career, and eventually to having a happy home of my own. But now, in the space of just a few weeks, hopes for both career and home had all been shattered.

The first blow had come in the form of a letter from the medical school informing me that I had a secondary lesion of tuberculosis in the right lung and must take a year out from my studies. I was supposed to be going into my clinical year! I wasn't prepared for anything like this. I was aware that lately I hadn't had my previous strength and energy, but I thought it was just the usual end-of-year weariness.

On receiving this news my parents hurried me off to our little vacation home in the Pennsylvania mountains, as the only therapy for pulmonary tuberculosis in those days was rest, fresh air, and nutritious food. The cottage was close enough to our hometown for Dad to commute to work every day.

My brothers and sisters, all older than I, were away, and had no idea what I was going through. Nor could I have shared this turmoil with them in any case. I felt no one could possibly understand.

Following the doctor's orders I had tried to rest, but I couldn't. At night sleep wouldn't come. I would lock myself in my bedroom and pace the floor into the wee hours. It just seemed that the bottom had fallen out of everything! But that was only the beginning.

The second blow came the day I told my boyfriend, a student in another medical school, about the tuberculosis. My parents objected to this boy, and I guess because they objected I had come to like him more than ever. In fact, we were secretly planning to elope sometime that summer. But since I had seen the x-rays myself and knew how serious the disease was, I felt it was only fair to explain the situation to him. He came to see me, and we decided together that our relationship had to end. But I could never forget the unfeeling way he said, "Well, I guess we'd better part company; you're as good as dead." That cut me deeply, especially since I had thought he really loved me. Not knowing how serious our relationship was, my parents couldn't know what this new hurt meant to me. They were just relieved, I guess, that it was all finished. Then several weeks later that wound was opened up again when word came from a friend that this boy I had hoped to marry had eloped with my best girl friend! But the worst was still to come.

A second letter arrived from the medical school. This time it contained the statement of my dismissal from the school. Under no condition could I return to continue my training. I guess I deserved dismissal as my behavior had hardly been above reproach! But it was blow upon blow! It was more than I could take.

And so every night I continued to lock my bedroom door and pace the floor. And each night Mother stood outside, pleading with me to talk things over with her, trying to assure me that they could understand and that they did not blame me. I wouldn't listen. How could she and Dad understand when they had never experienced anything like this? I took so many sleeping pills that I should have died, but instead they just envigorated me and left me sleepless. I could think of nothing worth living for.

And now suddenly the opportunity had come to end my anguish. As I was tearing up the road with the accelerator pushed to the floor, familiar landmarks flashing by me, a kind of mad exhilaration possessed me. I had neither the time nor the inclination to reassess things now. I just wanted to reach my destination. Numbing my sense of feeling, I didn't let myself think of Mother as she had looked, calling after me in her fear, or that she had called me "Hon," the family's name of endearment for me.

I was almost at the open mine — just two more turns to make. Suddenly there was a terrific *bang* and the car careened out of control, nearly flipping over on that narrow gravel road. Somehow reining the shiny convertible to a stop, I got out, saw the skid marks and then spotted the blown-out tire on the left front wheel.

As I stared at the ragged hole in that tire, I didn't hear any heavenly voices, but I knew that God had done this. Right there on that skid-marked mountain road the Spirit of God brought back to my mind things I must have learned many years before in Sunday school. The first words that came to me were, "He cares!" And then, in a marvelous way He continued to show me how much He loved me. I knew the verse He was using — John 3:16 — I had learned it as a child. But this time it had my name in it: "God so loved Pauline Hamilton, that if Pauline Hamilton believes in Me, she shall not perish, but have everlasting life."

I began to reason: obviously God cared enough to stop me on that road, stop me from taking my own life — but why? I had turned my back on Him many years before, and refused to give Him any place in my life and my plans. What reason could He have to care about me? But He did, and the realization of that love broke me.

I crouched down on the road with all the necessary tools beside me to attempt changing the tire, but instead I found myself weeping before the Lord, He speaking to me and I to Him. I didn't know much about prayer then — my praying up to that time had been little more than "Now I lay me down to sleep," or "Lord, give me this or that." Today it was different. Though neither formal nor beautiful, my prayer came from the heart. It ran something like this: "God, You win. I've made an awful mess of things. Lord, if You can do anything with this mess, here I am. You take over."

Something happened there on that hot, dusty road that I can't explain scientifically; but it changed my life completely. I wasn't even sure the words that came to my heart were from the Bible — yet I felt they had to be. "Be strong and of good courage," God said to me. "Be not afraid, for I am with you." How I needed those words — and what comfort they brought to my heart!

Minutes after I had handed the mess of my life over to the God who cares, a car came into sight from the opposite direction. The driver, a man who was also living at the mountain resort, stopped when he saw my predicament and asked kindly if he could help. As he changed my tire, he didn't ask any questions, probably thinking my tears were brought on by the blow-out.

After the spare tire was at last securely in place, I slowly backed the car around and headed for home. Oh, I was dirty! My face was streaked, dust having mixed with perspiration and tears to make mud. Quickly slipping into the house I announced simply to Mother that I had had a blowout, and ran to my room to clean up. Wisely, my parents never asked any questions. I don't know how they prepared supper that evening without any gas — I wasn't hungry and didn't go down. I was still pretty well shaken by all that had happened and wanted to be alone to think over the events of the afternoon. Amazingly, the old burden and heaviness of heart seemed to have gone!

That night I didn't lock my bedroom door nor pace the floor. Instead I pulled down my old Bible from the shelf, dusted it off and began searching for those life-transforming words the Lord had spoken to my heart. It was hard going, as I didn't know where to look for anything. However, as I leafed through the pages, one passage caught my attention. Jesus was asking His disciples, "What do you want?" "What do you want?" I felt as though God was now directing that question to me personally. Quick as a flash I thought of the verse Mother had quoted to me many times: "Seek first the kingdom of God and His righteousness, and all these things shall be added unto you." I hunted high and low for those words until finally I found them in Matthew's Gospel — chapter 6, verse 33.

Can you believe I continued turning over the pages of my Bible most of that night? The time passed quickly, and I felt exhilarated, as it seemed that every place I opened, God had something to say to me personally. Finally I came to the passage where God said to Joshua: "As I was with Moses, so I will be with you; I will not fail you or forsake you. Be strong and of good courage ... This book of the law shall not depart out of your mouth, but you shall meditate on it day and night, that you may be careful to do according to all that is written in it; for then you shall make your way prosperous, and then you shall have good success. Have I not commanded you? Be strong and of good courage; be not frightened, neither be dismayed; for the Lord your God is with you wherever you go" (Joshua 1). I knew that this was God's promise and His instruction to me. What a promise! What a challenge!

When I first opened my Bible that night, a slip of paper had fallen out of it onto the floor. I didn't pick it up, however, until hours later when I was ready to go to bed. I don't know where it came from, but on that piece of paper was written this verse: "As you go step by step, I will open up the way for you." I knelt down and prayed simply and sincerely, "All right, Lord, You open the way, and I will follow." His response to me was from the fiftieth Psalm: "Call upon Me in the day of trouble; I will deliver you, and you shall glorify Me." I went to bed marveling.

By the time I lay down on my bed, it was nearly five o'clock in the morning. I was absolutely exhausted, both nervously and physically. I slept, and I slept and I slept — so much so that on the second day my worried parents called the doctor. "Let her sleep," were his instructions once he was sure that my problem was simply exhaustion.

I slept for about two and a half days. I awoke a new creature in Jesus Christ. This was evident as I found old habits dropping away, habits that I hadn't been able to break in my own strength. I never again smoked. I stopped drinking. My dependence on drugs was gone. It really was the beginning of a new life for me, a life of simply following step by step.

Throughout this experience my parents never tried to pry into my privacy, never asked any questions, though I am sure they were dying to know what had happened. They simply hung on for me in prayer. And, as far as I know, they never mentioned a word about those days to any of my brothers or sisters. It was our secret.

2
Now what?

Now what? was the basic question on my mind. *Where do we go from here?* I was at a dead-end in my life and was impatient for the Lord to do something to show me the path ahead. But instead He left me sitting out a rest-cure in the Pennsylvania hills. Healing was gradually coming, aided I'm sure by my brightened outlook, not to mention my having given up smoking, getting off drugs and alcohol. But daily I cried to Him with impatience, reminding Him of His promise to lead me.

If God does guide, I wondered, *how does He do it? How do I know it is God and not my own idea?* As I had more questions than answers, I began to study God's Word just as I studied my scientific books, digging into the text and keeping notes and making outlines. And every day for exercise I went out walking in the low wooded mountains. I loved to be alone so that I could think things through and try to understand what God was saying and what was happening.

Seeing myself and my situation in a new light, I began searching for reasons for what had happened to me. Why, for instance, had I developed into such a self-willed individual? And why did I find it so hard to confide in others?

As I pondered these things, I began to understand that many of my problems probably had roots in my childhood. As the youngest child of five, I had come in for a lot of teasing. How I resented teasing and hated being laughed at! And so early I had learned to keep my own counsel. I hated always being told that I was too little to do things with others. *I'll show them*, I decided. *If I'm too little to do what they do, then I'll do better than they.* I remember on report-card day digging out my brothers' and sisters' old report cards to prove to my father that I had done better than they did when they were in that year of school. I longed for praise. I guess this underlay much of my proud bullheadedness as I grew up.

As for my rebellion against God, I remembered all too clearly when it was I shut the door on Him. I was about nine. Mother had come to my bedroom to talk to me about "opening my heart to the Lord Jesus." "Will — be in Heaven?" I asked smartly. I hated this person bitterly, for I felt she had wronged me in many ways.

"I suppose so, Hon," Mother answered with some doubt in her voice. "She says she is a Christian."

"Well, if she is going to be in Heaven, I don't want to go there." My answer was simple and to the point. The door had not only been shut, but shut tightly. But now it was open. I had God on my side, and He had promised to lead me step by step. Even though I didn't know what the future held, I felt a new sense of adventure as I looked forward to seeing how God would lead.

One day as I was walking out on the mountains, I happened to meet my former physiology professor from medical school. She called over to me, "What's happened to you? Why aren't you returning to school? Is it because of your health?" Others had been asking the same embarrassing questions.

"No, it's not because of that," I replied, glancing awkwardly away as she came toward me. "I've really just about recovered, but the school has said I couldn't return under any conditions."

"Have you thought of appealing their decision?" she asked with concern.

"No, I guess I had it coming. I don't question that they were right in dismissing me." As a matter of fact, eight of us had been dismissed that year, more for our way of life than because of low grades or anything else.

"Well, what are you going to do now?" she asked kindly.

"I... I don't know," I hesitated. "In fact, I don't have the vaguest idea where to turn. No place would have me now."

"But you can't say that!" she exclaimed. "Why don't you go over to the University of Pennsylvania to see Professor H.? I could give you a letter of introduction if you need one."

Though I had not met this professor, I knew of him. He was well known for his work.

"After all," she reminded me, "you were more interested in doing research than in practising medicine."

I laughed bitterly and said, "You want me to go to a better school than the one I was kicked out of? Not a chance!"

With that my professor friend started to walk away, throwing one last comment over her shoulder. "Nothing ventured, nothing gained. You can at least give it a try."

As I walked on in the late afternoon sunshine, I

pondered about our chance meeting and this conversation.

Why yes, I suddenly concluded to myself, *I've got nothing to lose but my face, and I don't have any face left anymore, so I might just as well go and see that professor.*

Back at the cottage I surprised my mother, who was out in the kitchen, with "How.would you like to go to Philadelphia tomorrow?" Mother was always ready to go whenever the car was going.

"Sure," she answered brightly. "What do you want to go to Philly for?"

The words started tumbling out about my chance conversation with the physiology professor. By the time I had finished, Mother was quite excited about our adventure.

Next day when we arrived at the university, I went off in search of the Department of Zoology, where I was told I could probably find Professor H. All kinds of doubts and questions were going around in my head — such as *Is this just a wild goose chase?* — when I was told by his secretary that Professor H. just happened to be in his office that day. I knocked on his door and waited.

"Come in," the professor called pleasantly.

I caught the surprised look on his face that he tried to suppress as I walked in. He obviously wasn't expecting a complete stranger. Impressive with his bushy hair and square jaw, the professor asked, not unkindly but in a puzzled tone, "Who are you, and why do you want to see me?"

He listened attentively as I told him that I was very interested in studying with him and in doing work toward a Master's degree. I told him also, quite honestly, about my dismissal from medical college. When I had finished the professor looked right at me with his steel-blue eyes and said, "I hate women. Women should not study science. I don't have any women in my classes, and I don't intend to start taking them now ..."

Well, that was enough said. While his remarks were sharp and totally unexpected, I did not sense any harshness or animosity toward me personally. Fortunately, I am not the kind that cries easily. I guess that's because I grew up alongside two brothers who felt they had won if I cried when they teased me. Anyway, now I managed to reply as calmly as I could, "Thank you. I appreciate the time you have given to me." I wasn't about to waste any more of the man's time by pleading for mercy.

I grasped the doorknob to make my escape — but before I could open the door, he called to me. "Come back!" he cried. "You don't look so bad to me. I'll give you a chance. See what you do this first semester."

After stopping at the student health building for a chest x-ray (which showed nothing but a healed T.B. scar) I raced over to the graduate school office and with heart pounding presented Professor H.'s letter of explanation to make late registration. It did seem that, although God was testing me, He was fully in control.

It was anything but flattering to enter into the graduate program like this. I was embarking on a new course of study under a man who avowedly hated women in his classes. But not only was I the lone woman, I was also the only committed Christian in a class of about 25 male science students. It hardly seemed a promising start for a new Christian just picking up the pieces after failure.

But that wasn't all. Going down the list of rooming places for students given me by the school office, Mother and I discovered the professor wasn't the only one who had a thing about women. After a string of polite refusals we almost gave up. But the very last name on the list had just one vacancy left, and welcomed me. Gratefully I moved in the next day.

It was several weeks before I discovered the Lord had pulled a fast one on me — I was living in the home of a pastor! It really was good for me. In the midst of all my heavy studies I learned a lot of other lessons from that family and met many wonderful people in their church. The result was that I began to grow in the Lord in a new way, as a member of the body of Christ. God had begun to pick up the pieces of a life that just months before had seemed hopelessly wrecked.

3

Ph.D. by faith

Daily I was facing the challenge of being the only committed Christian in my class with those 25 sharp fellows. It was good for me, though. It forced me to dig into God's Word and to come up with reasons for my faith.

The Lord didn't leave me to struggle on alone, however. A professor who attended my landlord's church told me about a Christian group that met in the university. Inwardly suspecting that this would be a bunch of "duds," I finally went along one day to see for myself. What I discovered, to my surprise, was a gathering of very down-to-earth people, some of the most brilliant students in the university. I began to attend these meetings regularly and was soon participating in their good times of fellowship.

I worked hard at my studies, and in no time at all the first semester came to an end. I felt that I had done well but I kept remembering that my prof. had said, "We'll see what you can do the first semester." I was at a loss to know what to do now. I continued to remind the Lord

that He had promised to open up the way before me —
step by step. Now, what about the next step? Did I
stay, or did I go?

I was beginning to grapple with some practical
dilemmas in my life as well. Since I had wasted so much
of my father's money already in the fiasco of medical
school, I felt that I could not accept any more money
from him for my studies. I determined now to trust the
Lord for everything. I didn't know anything about
living by faith. I hadn't read about Hudson Taylor of
the China Inland Mission and his life of faith — as a
matter of fact, I had never even heard of him. But
somehow I knew that God would have me trust Him for
all my needs. The little bit of personal money I had at
the beginning of the first semester was now used up,
so even if I could stay on I still had the problem of where
to get the money to pay my tuition. Yet as I prayed, I had
a peaceful heart.

On the last day of registration for the next semester,
I received one of those long business envelopes from the
Dean's office in the mail. *Now what?* I thought as I
unfolded the crisp stationery and began to read. I
couldn't believe my eyes. The letter stated that Pauline
Hamilton was hereby granted a full tuition scholarship
and a living stipend!

This can't be mine! I thought as I stared at the
information. *This letter can't be for me — I didn't apply for
any scholarship!*

I grabbed my coat and hurried right over to the
Dean's office. "I received this letter," I said breathlessly,
handing the letter to the secretary, "and there must be
some mistake."

"Are you Pauline Hamilton?" she asked as her eyes
scanned the page.

"Yes, I'm Pauline Hamilton."

"Are you studying physiology in the Department of Zoology?" She was looking up at me now, smiling.

"Yes," I said, my heart pounding and my throat dry.

"Well, then, the letter was meant for you," she laughed kindly.

"That can't be," I argued. "I haven't applied."

"No," she explained, "you didn't apply. Professor H. applied for you."

The professor who hated women in his classes, this fine scholar who had only known me for one semester, had submitted my name for scholastic help! I was incredulous, but delighted. Now I knew that Professor H. was behind me, and not only that, but I could complete the year's studies without financial worry. The Lord had indicated the next steps very clearly.

From that time on throughout my studies, right up until I received my Master's degree, as time drew near each year to apply for scholarships and fellowships I would say to the Lord, "Well, now, what about it? Should I apply this time?" And every time it seemed that the answer was, "I can provide the money for you without your applying for it, if this is where I want you to be." This way I gained both my guidance and my finances.

As I neared the completion of my Master's degree program, I began wondering how to go about securing employment. Never having looked for a job in my life, I was just about to go and talk it over with my professor when he instead came looking for me in the laboratory. His words bowled me over.

"How would you like to continue your studies for a Ph.D.?" he asked.

"Oh!" I said, regaining my composure, "that sure would be nice, but I haven't dared to dream of that."

"Well," he continued, "I have a certain amount of money allocated to me from a Rockefeller Foundation grant, and I would like to delegate it to you to continue the research problem you did for your Master's degree. I feel there is something there, and I'd like to see you go deeper into it and then get your Ph.D."

"Well, you know," I said with a twinkle in my eye, "I'll have to pray about this." He was Jewish and seemed to understand a bit about my queer ways. He said nothing more.

Several weeks later he called me into his office and asked, "What about it?"

"What about what?" I asked.

"Well, about staying on with me?" His eyebrows were drawn together in a slight frown.

"You weren't serious, were you?" I said rather lightly.

"Why shouldn't I be serious?"

"Do you realize what day it was when you asked me to stay on?" I was beginning to feel just a bit uncomfortable.

"No, what day was it?"

"It was April Fools' Day! I thought you were just making a joke out of me."

We had a good laugh over the whole thing, but Professor H. had indeed been quite serious. Thus in a remarkable way God made it possible for me to go for my Ph.D. But today I still say that the Ph.D. doesn't stand for Doctor of Philosophy but for Praising Him Daily! While my friends ended up with degrees plus debts, I ended up with degrees and money in my pocket because I had dared to trust a God who kept His promise to guide me step by step.

It was during those years at the University of Pennsylvania that I was first called by my longstanding nickname "Grandma." I was a graduate student, and so I was older than most of the other students in the Christian group. They began to come to me for advice and looked on me as someone with whom they could share their problems. Sometimes the group met in my laboratory. We had a lovely relationship with each other. I was beginning to sense ways I could serve the Lord with my gifts.

Occasionally I went with this group to a place called Keswick in southern New Jersey for student weekends and Bible conferences. Some of the girls waited on tables in the dining hall to pay their expenses. On one occasion when the dining room staff was short a waitress, they asked me if I could help out. As I had pinch-hit like this before, I agreed. This time I was assigned to wait on the speakers' table, where all the "bigwigs" were. There was a big turnout for this conference, and the dining room was full and bustling with activity.

Everything went just fine until the very end of the meal when I was serving the coffee. I don't know exactly how it happened, but somehow I spilled hot coffee right down the back of one of the speakers. It was an awful moment. He was a big man and very dignified, but so pleasant. Though I had slopped coffee all over him, it was he who apologized to me, and graciously took all the blame for the accident. Covered with confusion and embarrassment, I didn't know what to do. Hastily I retreated to the kitchen.

"Who is that man?" I asked as I related my tale of woe to the other waitresses. "He won't even let me wash his shirt for him!"

"Well," teased one of the girls, "maybe he thinks that if you can't even handle a cup of coffee, you can't wash a shirt either!"

"But, who is he?" I persisted. "Do any of you know him?"

"Why, he's just the Home Director of the C.I.M.!" volunteered one of the others, enjoying my predicament to the full.

"C.I.M.?" I queried. "I never heard of it."

"C.I.M. is short for China Inland Mission — you haven't heard of it? It's the biggest interdenominational and international mission that works in China. It's a faith mission, founded by an Englishman named Taylor, Hudson Taylor. Haven't you ever read his biography? You should; it's really thrilling."

At the first opportunity that afternoon I went over to the bookroom. They seemed to have lots of books on the China Inland Mission. I guess I bought the lot. I began reading through the stack and was greatly blessed, particularly by *Hudson Taylor's Spiritual Secret*, which has come to mean more and more to me down through the years. Before I had finished reading, I understood more than ever before what it meant to "live by faith." I soon became a donor to the C.I.M. and then a prayer partner. A spilled cup of coffee and a very Christian gentleman were God's unique way of giving me my introduction to the C.I.M.

In my own life I was discovering that living by faith means more than just trusting God for finances or direction; it also means trusting Him when all does not go well. While I was working toward my doctorate,

I developed a very strange illness. Calcium was being released from my bones and being deposited in the tissues. Both the disease and the treatments were very painful.

Eventually the doctors told me that there was little or no hope of recovery and that if I lived I would probably be crippled for life! For a 26-year-old this was not a very bright prospect.

I had plans to spend the summer on Cape Cod doing research at the famous Marine Biological Laboratories at Woods Hole, Massachusetts. It was a privilege to be able to work there, and as I felt it was wise to keep busy I decided to go, regardless of failing health.

That summer on Cape Cod the Lord zeroed in on my commitment to Him. He used a passage in 1 Corinthians 6: "Do you not know that your body is a temple of the Holy Spirit within you, which you have from God? You are not your own; you were bought with a price. So glorify God in your body." And He continued to challenge me with Philippians 1:21 — "For to me to live is Christ, and to die is gain." I was forced to ask myself if I really believed that. Was I willing for God's will if it meant dying?

After my return from Cape Cod I was visiting a pastor friend and his wife. His mother was there too. They all knew that I had just been to see the specialist, and they were asking me about the interview. I told them that the specialist had said quite frankly that there was nothing more that could be done medically. After some moments the pastor's mother said to me, "Well, Pauline, I'm sure you are *ready* to die — but did you ever think of telling God that you are *willing* to die if that is what He wants?"

I thought over her question all the way home. When I got to my place I knelt down by my bed and said simply, "Lord, I'm willing to die if that's what You want." A great peace came into my heart. It was as though the Lord had been asking me, "May I not have the life that I have already bought?"

Most of the major decisions in my life have been made in the privacy of my own room, or as I was out alone somewhere with God, through the study of His Word. I don't remember ever making any major decision in a meeting. I don't say this to belittle such decisions, but rather to show that the Lord knows each of us and our individual temperaments. He knew that I was one of those people who respond best when dealt with individually and unemotionally. Many times the Lord has spoken to me during my own daily quiet times with Him. So it was again that, some days after I had expressed my willingness for Him to take my life, He impressed me with Psalm 27:14, "Wait for the Lord; be strong, and let your heart take courage; yes, wait for the Lord!" A few days later He spoke to me through Psalm 118:17, 18, seemingly hinting as to what He was planning to do: "I shall not die, but I shall live, and recount the deeds of the Lord. The Lord has chastened me sorely, but He has not given me over to death." I believed this was for me and I thanked Him for it. That same day I read the words from Isaiah 30:21, "Your ears shall hear a word behind you, saying, 'This is the way, walk in it,' when you turn to the right or when you turn to the left."

Committing my future to the Lord and counting on His promises, I went ahead with my studies as well as my medical treatment. Most preparation for my doctoral thesis and for my final examination and oral dissertation I did while in therapeutic baths. By having a special table made to fit over the tub, I was able to carry on quite well, though many of my books ended up being baptized by immersion!

As the Lord had promised, He led step by step, and I received my degree. He had not only picked up the loose ends of my life, but had revealed His faithfulness as I trusted Him, and had begun to mold for me a new life for His glory.

4

Stirred up

By the time World War II ended, I was in my third year
of teaching at Smith College in Northampton, Massachusetts. I had gone away for a vacation, and once
again out on the sand dunes of Cape Cod the Lord was
speaking to me. I got the distinct feeling that He was
about to stir up my nest.

Should I sign a new contract, committing myself
to stay at Smith for another five years? That was what
I was asking myself. But the Lord was saying, "What do
you want? Is this your goal — the sort of life you want
to lead? Do you just want to be a part of the 'rat-race'?
Are you thinking only of these things? What do you want
to do with your life?" Through this kind of heart-
questioning as I walked alone by the sea the Lord was
trying to show me how secondary concerns were getting
too much of a grip on me. Without my realizing it — in
fact, in a very insidious way — my whole life had now
come to revolve around science. I loved it. Science had
practically become my idol. I could almost say that I
had it for breakfast, dinner and supper. I reveled in the

opportunities it brought me to rub shoulders with some of the great people in my field and even to get my name on a paper or two with well-known men. Success had begun to go to my head.

That morning my Old Testament reading had been in the book of Jeremiah, chapter 45. "Behold, what I have built I am breaking down, and what I have planted I am plucking up ... And do you seek great things for yourself? Seek them not." Yes, I had been seeking great things for myself. Pride had come back. I didn't like what I saw in myself, and since it was too uncomfortable to continue reading in Jeremiah I turned to the *Daily Light* reading for the day. That wasn't any better. There the question was again, "Where have you placed your love?"

I wouldn't have been surprised if God had called me to the mission field right after I finished at the University of Pennsylvania. I had had such a keen interest then. But He didn't. Now I realized that lately I had been pushing anything that had to do with missions into the background. I had a legitimate reason, of course. After all, my parents were already up in their seventies. "Whom do you love?" God was asking me now. "He who loves father or mother more than Me is not worthy of Me ... and he who does not take his cross and follow Me is not worthy of Me. He who finds his life will lose it, and he who loses his life for My sake will find it." That was how Jesus had put it to His disciples two thousand years ago, and how He was putting it to me now.

For some time I was pommeled on every side by these verses. Then a letter arrived from a friend. She wrote, "When are you going to China?" I read the letter and laughed. *What on earth is she talking about?* I thought.

Why does she mention China? — I'm not going there. If there is one place on earth where I wouldn't go, now or ever, it is China! Why should she think that I might go to China? Though I laughed, it was hard to shake off the irritation this letter aroused in me.

About the same time the Lord brought to my attention a passage in Luke 14:33 — "Whoever of you does not renounce all that he has cannot be my disciple." All of my friends felt that I had it made with my Ph.D. and good position at Smith. They respected me. I had arrived. Was the Lord asking me to renounce all this?

Evening by evening as I walked on the familiar sand dunes, the salt air blowing my hair, the Lord kept putting His finger on the unwillingness of my heart to go with Him anywhere He led. Once I had prided myself on living by faith; now I saw how much I depended on my good salary, the lovely apartment I had at the college, and even my own private maid. I had not realized how love for these things and dependence on them had crept into my life. I had forgotten so easily the lessons of faith learned at university.

But I continued arguing with the Lord. This business about going to China, leaving everything to follow Him — I had all the answers for that. "You know I could never go to the mission field, Lord. I have such a bad medical record, what with my having had tuberculosis and that calcium condition, no mission board would ever pass me. Besides, I've already passed their age limit. They don't send people out over thirty ..."

"You are limiting Me," the Lord countered. "I am the God of the impossible. Mission boards are sending people out older now that the war is over. What are you waiting for?"

The war may have been over, but not the battle in my heart. I encountered more disturbing passages in my daily reading. One of them was Amos 7:15, "The Lord took me from following the flock, and the Lord said to me, Go." What did this mean in my circumstances? Did it mean that I should leave Smith, or was the Lord showing me that I had become a follower and no more a leader?

I got my answer two days later, through I Chronicles 16:24, "Declare His glory among the nations, His marvelous works among all the peoples." If God had written me a scientific equation His meaning couldn't have been clearer. So right there on the sand dunes of Cape Cod I responded, "All right, Lord, You have given me my degrees; I give them all back to You. If You want me just to leave everything, okay — I'm willing. It's up to You to show me the way I'm to go." As I spoke these words of commitment I didn't know at all what they would entail.

As I left the sand dunes that day, my path went by a lovely old cottage, and I was suddenly struck by the well-worn sign over the gate. It was made of a small bar of wood nailed over three inverted Vs and followed by an O all by itself.

What did it mean? Suddenly as I studied the sign, it flashed a message to me —

ANYWHERE — ANYTIME — ANYHOW bar NOTHING.

That is the meaning of obedience, I thought. *This is what He is wanting from me.*

In a few days I returned to Northampton and wrote my letter of resignation as the first step in obedience.

"You shouldn't resign until you have another position," remonstrated one of my colleagues on hearing of my decision. "Wait a while."

I couldn't explain. But I felt I had to burn my bridges behind me.

Not long after I handed in my resignation I had a visitor, a high official from China!

"I am here looking for teaching staff for Yenching University in Peking," he explained. "The university is in the process of returning to Peking from West China, and we need new personnel. My daughter told me how much you love the Chinese."

"Who, me? Love the Chinese?" I blurted in surprise.

When I was very little I was repeatedly reminded of the poor starving Chinese whenever I balked at eating what was on my plate. So often was this reproach rammed down my throat that I came to hate the Chinese, though I had never seen one. And that child-hood prejudice had stuck with me on into adulthood. Now here was someone telling me how much I loved the Chinese! I couldn't help but be amused.

He explained that his daughter was one who came to the open house I had on weekends especially for overseas students, and continued, "My daughter told us that you love the Chinese and that you have been kind to her and her fellow students. I know you are qualified for the teaching position at Yenching University, and that is why I've come to invite you. Will you consider this?"

What a bolt out of the blue! "I can't give you an answer today," I replied. "You see, I'm a Christian, and I must pray about this to be sure it is God's leading. If you will come back in say two or three weeks, I can give you my answer."

After my visitor had gone, it began to dawn on me how God had been slowly chipping away these past years to break down that old prejudice. I hadn't realized what He was doing. Now I recalled how in university, both in class and in the laboratory, the one next to me was always a Chinese fellow. When any one of these fellows had difficulty in understanding, or had any other problems, he would always turn to me. I got so I would say to myself, *Boy, this fellow is an awful pest!* and my usual reply to such pleas for help was, "Why don't you ask some of the fellows in class?"

"No! No!" would come the reply. "I want to talk to you."

Unknown to me, the Lord was trying to show me what a lovely people the Chinese were. I never guessed that God could be preparing me for the future by contact with these young people, nor did I realize then from what fine backgrounds many of them came.

In those days as I prayed about accepting this position, I discovered something new about prayer. If you really mean business with the Lord and want to be obedient, prayer can be a dangerous thing, because God doesn't always point us to what we want to see. This was my experience. Yes, the Lord was showing me that He wanted me in China all right. I understood that now. But He didn't want me there in the capacity of a college professor. As I prayed, He showed me that if I went on those terms it would once again be me seeking great things for myself — advancement, prestige. No, I realized that the Lord was asking me to go to China as a common, ordinary missionary, for Him.

I had to write now to my parents regarding the Lord's leading. I expected their reaction to be either that I had gone out of my mind, or else a complaint that they needed me now that they were old. But neither was the case. Instead, I had their blessing right from the start. I didn't find out why until after I arrived in China.

The next logical step seemed to be to send in an application to some mission board. The only mission I knew thus far was the China Inland Mission. Besides reading their books and being a donor, I had also become well acquainted with several of their missionaries while working at America's Keswick during the summer of 1945. What I knew about the C.I.M. made me conclude that their requirements for new workers were many and their standards very high. I felt sure I could not attain to such heights, but I decided to write anyway.

The only person I knew at the Philadelphia headquarters was the Home Director, the man on whose back I had slopped coffee! Though the coffee incident was hardly the best introduction, I decided to write to Mr. Griffin, telling him of my interest and how the Lord had been leading. I wrote very honestly about my health, age, training, and all the things I thought C.I.M. leaders were apt to want to know. After I mailed the letter, I wrote in my diary for that day, "Now it's all in God's hands."

About two weeks later I got the C.I.M.'s reply. It was not the answer I was looking for. The letter said that they at Philadelphia headquarters had carefully considered my application, but felt that it would be better for me to plan on staying home. If I were five years younger, they said, they might consider me. "You have a very poor medical record," the letter continued. "Perhaps the Lord could use you more as a donor and a prayer partner. After all, that is a ministry too." Next they pointed out that I had never been to a Bible school or seminary. Last of all, they told me that I had too much education and not the right kind. "You may not realize it," they explained, "but we do not do institutional work where such degrees are needed."

Well, that letter did something to me, for by the time I received it I was dead sure that God was leading me to China. So I did a thing I rarely do — I sat down and answered it immediately. My reply left little doubt of the steam inside me. As to the first point about being five years too old, I wrote, "Five years ago you would not even have considered me because I was sick and had one foot in the grave. I was not expected to live, and if I did live the doctors thought I would surely be a cripple. Besides, at that time there was a war on and you were not sending people to the field, but now you are. Also ... at that time, the Lord had not called, but now He has."

I went on to the second point, regarding my physical record. "This, I admit, is very poor. But I am willing to make the trip to Philadelphia at my own expense and to be examined by any doctors and specialists of your choice, also at my own expense, and I will take the doctors' decision as the Lord's guidance in the matter of physical ability to face life in China."

About not having been to Bible school or seminary, I wrote, "I admitted that in my letter of application. But you will remember that I told you I had studied practically the whole Bible on my own and made extensive notes. When I come to Philadelphia for the physical examination, I will bring the notes with me for you to look through and see whether I have had sufficient training or not. I am also willing to sit any examination you may choose to set for me."

On the C.I.M.'s last point regarding too much education, I really hit high C. I told them, "You people are really odd. You preach 'Give of your best to the Master,' but when someone wants to give something to the Lord, you don't want it. My thought in going to China is not to go in the capacity of a teacher in college or university." I reminded them that I had already turned down a very attractive offer to go to China in that role. I wanted them to understand that I was very clear about the fact that the Lord was asking me to put down my career and go out as a common, ordinary missionary.

I wrote that letter, reread it, sealed it and mailed it the same evening — giving it no chance to cool off until morning!

My letter obviously "got through" to the C.I.M. folk in Philadelphia. I received an almost immediate reply. They wanted me to travel to Philadelphia the very next week as a Dr. Paul Adolph of the C.I.M. was to be there giving physical exams to candidates, and I could be included in the group.

Never have I had a physical examination as thorough as that one, before or since. Speaking of fine-toothed combs — that's what Dr. Adolph used. During the examination he asked me if it would be possible to get the x-rays of the bones and joints involved in the calcium upset I had while doing graduate studies.

"Oh, I think so," I said. "It was in Philadelphia, and I think the doctor is still at the same location."

I made the trip to the doctor's office and asked for the x-rays of Pauline Hamilton. The secretary wrinkled her brow.

"She died."

"No, she didn't die. I am Pauline Hamilton."

"Oh, no. You can't be," continued the efficient young lady. "She died three or four years ago."

"Well," I huffed. "I don't care what you say — I am Pauline Hamilton!"

The doctor in his inner room had by now heard the discussion and came out to see what was going on.

"She's asking for the x-rays of Pauline Hamilton, and I told her she died. But she insists that she is Pauline Hamilton."

"Well, I am," I said, not a little annoyed.

"Well, you are!" the doctor blurted in recognition. "How does it happen that you didn't die?"

"I guess God still has a few things for me to do," I replied. "Could I borrow the x-rays for a few days? Another doctor would like to see them to compare them with some recent ones."

I went off triumphantly with the x-rays. After a careful comparison of the two sets of pictures, Dr. Adolph was obviously amazed and unable to do anything but give me a clear bill of health.

With medical clearance I now had the green light to proceed with my application for membership in C.I.M. And by the time I returned to Smith College everyone had heard that I had resigned. Now at least I didn't have to answer, "I don't know," when they asked me what I was going to do. I could tell them, "I am going to China."

My colleagues thought I had gone daft, especially when they learned I was going as a missionary. Since Smith College had a sister college in China, they thought that if one must go to China, teaching at Chin-ling Women's College would surely be a more respectable way to go!

"No," I replied to their suggestions, "God is leading this way, and this way I go."

One of these colleagues heard I was going to Boston one weekend, and she was so sure I needed help that she made an appointment for me with a well-known psychiatrist there. I'm afraid I never appeared for that appointment; I was convinced that I was more on the ball than the whole lot of them!

My father knew nothing of the China Inland Mission. As I told him about C.I.M.'s policies he became a bit concerned that it was a "faith mission". "You're going out there with no promise of anything? You'll probably starve to death!"

That's exactly what the Chinese official said when he came back to find out my decision about teaching at Yenching. When I told him that I was going to China, but as a missionary, he asked, "What board are you going with?"

"The China Inland Mission," I answered. (Of course, the C.I.M. didn't know it yet!)

"Oh, I know that mission," he nodded. "They have wonderful people — but do you know that they don't promise anything and you could starve to death? Why don't you try some other board that gives a good salary?" And he proceeded to name several boards.

To sum it up, everybody thought I had lost my

senses. Though gracious, my father was puzzled. "If you don't make any appeals for funds, how are you going to get your support?" he inquired.

"Well, I don't know," I replied, "but I'm sure that if God wants me to go, I can trust Him to work that out without my help."

Since my father was a businessman, it just didn't make any sense to him. "Well," he said, trying to provide me with a safety net, "anytime you are in need, let me know and I'll send you some money."

In all my years as a missionary I never had to take him up on his offer. My heavenly Father has always supplied my needs on time. Not only did I never come close to starving to death, but for many of my 32 years as a missionary I have had to diet because of being overweight!

After I finished my commitments at Smith College, I spent a few weeks at home and then hived off to take a four weeks' crash course at Biblical Seminary in New York. Into those four weeks I crowded classes on Isaiah, Hebrews, Old and New Testament Survey, and Paul's Epistles. As I wanted to get as much as I could out of the course, I really worked. But I'm afraid that was the sum total of my seminary training.

In the fall of 1946 I entered C.I.M.'s training home in Philadelphia, with four other candidates. Since we were so few, the C.I.M. home staff really got to know us. We had a wonderful time and a lot of fun. We were accepted as new China Inland Mission missionaries in November and immediately began to look forward to that great day when we would be sailing for China.

Once again the Lord had led all the way, confirming His call by clearing away every obstacle. But now I wonder, had we known all that lay ahead of us, would we have been quite so eager to be on our way?

5

China at last

Time fairly flew between being accepted into the China Inland Mission in November and sailing in January. There was so very much to do — getting an outfit together for life in China for the next seven years, seeing friends and attending farewell meetings.

One meeting I had was in Boston, at a church interested in taking on the support of a C.I.M. missionary. I spent the weekend there, first sharing my testimony at the Friday night prayer meeting. Over 150 attended. I was impressed.

Park Street Church is an old, well-known church on what is known as the Freedom Trail, an area rich in Revolutionary War history. The lovely brick colonial building, with its famous white spire, stands on Brimstone Corner, right off the Boston Common in downtown Boston. Amazingly, the church decided right after my weekend there that they wanted to take on my support. This was the beginning of a very close relationship that has lasted for 34 years and has been a rich blessing to me. They have stood behind me not only with financial support but, more important, with their prayers. The church's large praying force is divided into many area groups so that each person supported is prayed for by name.

On hearing about this development, my father was awed. Why in the world would this church — so far away and where his daughter was scarcely known — show interest and concern to the extent of promising to support her while she was in China? Father, the businessman, was beginning to see how wonderfully God works to supply our needs in answer to prayer. I'm sure he felt better about my going out to China with the China Inland Mission after this — maybe his daughter wouldn't be left to starve to death after all!

That year the first of the Inter-Varsity Christian Fellowship student missions conferences (now known as Urbana) was convened at Toronto. One of the main speakers happened to be Dr. Harold Ockenga, pastor of Park Street Church. I had been invited to attend and tell about God's leading in my life. What a thrill it was to stand before that great gathering of university students — there must have been nearly two thousand of them — all interested in foreign missions! It seemed a fabulous number in those days. Now, of course, almost ten times that number crowd into the domed pavilion at the Urbana campus of the University of Illinois for that great student missionary convention every two or three years during Christmas vacation.

I had just finished speaking when I was handed a telegram: "Return Philadelphia immediately. Prepare leave for China." This was it! Passages had been secured and it was time to go. I left for Philadelphia on the night train right after the evening meeting.

Among the people brave enough to come down to the Toronto railway station to see me off in the snowstorm that night was a middle-aged Indian man who had also spoken at the meeting earlier. In his testimony he had told of his long search for truth. He had tried all sorts of religions, then one day he heard a man preaching the Gospel, and his heart was touched. The next day, he said, when he went to see that preacher the man was too busy to see him. That night in the snow as he shook my hand in farewell he said something I have never forgotten. "Dr. Hamilton," he counseled, "always remember, 'Man before business', because *man is your business*." That advice has helped steer my course through the years.

After I got back to Philadelphia I divided my little remaining time between the C.I.M. office and my home not far away. What a scurry of packing and last-minute preparations! Kind people gave me all sorts of useful gifts for my outfit. One day as I returned to the mission home carrying on effusively over some extra gift the Lord had given, a retired missionary there said to me wisely, "Pauline, feast when you feast, and fast when you fast. There will be both feasting and fasting times." In later years these words, too, were to be a great help, and indeed they have proved true.

When I got ready to say goodbye to my family, I knew full well that it was unlikely I would see my parents again — with both of them already well into their seventies and with the C.I.M. terms of service then being seven or eight years long. Farewells were hard.

Our ship, the *Morning Light*, set sail from Gulfport, Mississippi, just two days before my 32nd birthday. My companion was Hazel Waller, another new missionary bound for China. Our route took us via the Panama Canal, up the coast of Mexico to California, with a brief stop at Los Angeles, then across to Yokohama, Japan, and finally to our destination, Shanghai.

What a thrill it was to see the line of muddy water from the Yangtze River meeting the clear salt water of the sea. China at last! It was now late afternoon and, characteristically of the Far East, the darkness fell very fast. Since it was so late we had to lie at anchor to wait our turn to go into Shanghai harbor the next day.

Shanghai, silhouetted on the horizon, had an air of mystery. As I stood on deck, I'm sure I wasn't the only passenger wondering about that big city and the country it represented. I tried to imagine what the years ahead held in store. Would I really be able to relate to the people? Could I eventually feel comfortable with their customs? Could I really learn to speak Chinese?

As day dawned, our surroundings came into sharp focus. The Shanghai skyline was really quite imposing. Shipping in port was a motley array. The multitudes of fleet sampans darting in and out without a mishap reminded me of busy ants. The junks came in all sizes, with large square or rectangular sails, these usually so patched that it was hard to figure out which cloth represented the original sail. These sturdily build junks looked much more clumsy close up than exotic paintings had led me to believe.

Now quite a variety of barges waited to unload our cargo. In the morning haze, too, we could see other freighters, from all over the world, as well as several big ocean liners that dwarfed our small vessel.

We lay at anchor most of that day waiting for the pilot who would take our ship up the Whangpoo River to the Shanghai docks. When our turn finally came, the trip upriver took us past an airport, the impressive University of Shanghai, and on past the Bund which is the thoroughfare along the waterfront and contains Shanghai's main business district. The *Morning Light* finally docked at about 4.30 p.m.

Though we had been informed that we would be met on arrival, no one was waiting for us when we reached the customs jetty. Without someone to help us, how would we manage the process of going through customs. Fellow-new-missionary Hazel and I both felt a bit panicky. But with little else we could do, we decided to go ahead with things ourselves, putting on our bravest front. Since the only Chinese words we knew were "I don't want it," and since the customs men didn't know much more English, we were just whisked through the formalities. Communication was too hopeless.

Eventually, however, the C.I.M. folk did arrive, and we were taken rather unceremoniously to mission headquarters sitting atop our trunks and other baggage in a big, open truck. Never mind the parade effect — we were actually seeing the sights of Shanghai first hand! What an experience it was — landing in this totally foreign land, but with a deep, overwhelming sense that this was exactly where God wanted us! We were in China at last.

Since we arrived at the mission home just as the staff and others there were finishing their prayer meeting, the whole crowd came out to welcome us. It was quite an end to the most eventful day in my life, and my head was whirling. Though I knew a few of the folks, most of the people I was meeting had been just names up until then. But as I made my way wearily upstairs to the room Hazel and I were to share with three others, I did not feel so much a stranger in a strange land as a welcome member of a big family.

As further evidence of that family spirit, in our sparsely furnished room I discovered several little welcome cards and notes, as well as gifts waiting for me. But naturally one of my first interests concerned mail from back home; it had been such a long time since we had had any letters! I was delighted to find quite a few for me, but the one from Mother was especially welcome. It turned out to be a very special letter indeed, because when I read it I discovered a secret she had kept from me all my life.

Her letter began, "The happiest day of my life was when I saw you leave for China." I was a bit shocked. I knew I'd been a pretty difficult child and had hurt my parents many times and caused them a lot of worries, but I didn't think I was that bad! I read on: "Now I can tell you something that I was never able to tell you before. You are the youngest of our five children and, as you always insisted, the 'odd one' in the family. You had two brothers and two sisters, and you always felt that you were not wanted. You also felt that we didn't care whether you were a girl or a boy and that that was why we had given you a 'hybrid' name. In part that might be true, but it is not entirely true. When I was expecting you I said to the Lord, 'If this child is a healthy child — I don't care whether it is a boy or a girl — I give this child to you for China."

I had to stop reading; tears were blurring the page. I could hardly believe what I had read. For these 32 years Mother had kept this secret stowed away in her heart. I had to get away somewhere and be alone, somewhere where no one could see the tears coursing down my cheeks and dripping from my chin. I stumbled out of my room and along the long, stark corridors until finally I found a little library just off the big entrance lobby of the mission home. I closed the door and sat with my back to it, so that if anyone opened the door they wouldn't see my face but would just notice someone devouring her home mail. My plan worked well. I sat there and read and re-read that letter. Now I began to understand the battle that had seemed to rage in me from the time of my birth.

"You never liked your name," Mother continued. She was right, I never did! "Hah!" I used to complain, "if I'd been a boy, you'd have called me Paul. But I was a girl, so you just added 'ine' on the end. Sounds like gasoline!' Mother now gave her explanation: "We called you Pauline because you were a girl. Had you been a boy, you would have been Paul, because I wanted a child to be named for the greatest missionary who ever lived. Long before you were born, I dedicated you to the Lord for China to do the work that should have been done by another. I despaired many times," she confessed, "because I thought maybe the Lord had not honored my prayer, made without the knowledge of your father. Then in those years when you were so far from the Lord, I shared with your father the covenant I had made concerning you, and together we renewed it. Today as you left us, I knew He had heard and accepted the offering. I wanted to share with you now what has been in my heart all these years." How my mother had held on in prayer!

I recalled how during my earlier rebellious years I had hated to see the door of my parents' bedroom closed to me. I knew in my heart that they were in there praying for me. It made me terribly angry! Now how thankful I was for Mother and for this letter! She had held on, and

I was in China. I went to bed that first night in Shanghai with a deep sense of awe.

I never saw my mother again. In a little over a year she suffered a heart attack, and the Lord took His servant to be with Him.

6
First impressions

Although Hazel and I were to be in Shanghai for only a few days of interviews and repacking, for me things started off with a bang. On my first morning I was taken out sightseeing by one of my former Smith College students. Young Hui-ling arrived to fetch me in her family's private pedicab, which I privately dubbed "a glorified tricycle". We sat in back, over the two wheels and under a canopy, while a man up front pedaled us along with firm strong strokes. Through Shanghai traffic we sped with nerve-shattering abandon (at least it seemed so to me!). With Hui-ling chattering happily beside me, showing me the sights, I stared in tense unbelief at the confusion all around us: rickshaws, pedicabs, bicycles, and speeding motorcycles all vying for the right of way. Trucks and automobiles drove primarily with their horns, creating a din that just added to the general chaos. People were everywhere, dashing precariously between the vehicles and packing buses and streetcars or clinging on the outsides. I really was frightened. "O Lord," I remember praying fervently, "I don't want to die in this mess on my first day in China!"

I got so dizzy with watching the traffic that now I can't remember a thing about where we went or what shops we visited. Finally, however, our pedicab turned off the busy thoroughfare into a small alley, which led into an even smaller lane. After some time we suddenly stopped at a gate, the pedicab driver rang his bell and immediately the gate swung open. Here was Hui-ling's home. Servants buzzed around us, ushering us into the large entrance hall where the walls were hung with beautiful scroll paintings from ceiling to floor. Now Hui-ling's mother came in, a lovely, gracious lady who fortunately spoke English very well. After some time we were called to dinner. Though this was to be my first Chinese feast, I did know enough Chinese etiquette not to make the mistake of plunking myself down anywhere at the table. I knew that the seat farthest from the door was considered the "high seat" and was reserved for the head of the clan or the most honored guest. This sensible custom had its origin in early days when enemy warlords or brigands might burst into the home, and the seat farthest from and facing the door was considered the safest. Hui-ling had told me that her grandfather would be there, and I knew that the high seat would be his.

Grandfather was a sweet old Chinese gentleman with white hair, a sparse beard and dark eyes that twinkled kindly. He was wearing a long dark gown covered by a short Chinese jacket. It was soon evident that he adored his granddaughter Hui-ling. While everyone was getting seated around the table according to their status in the family, I had opportunity to observe the lovely dining room. The furniture was beautifully carved teak. Here too the walls were adorned by lovely scrolls, and arranged around the room were exquisitely painted vases.

Now the feast began! First came platters of hors d'oevres, which included cold tongue sliced very thin, tripe, slices of cold liver, and blackened "hundred-year-old" eggs cut in wedges. Actually the eggs' unusual color and interesting texture are achieved by a special chemical process rather than by their age. They certainly looked most unappetizing to me, and I confess that that day it took a lot of courage to try one. However, it really tasted quite nice, and now I am very fond of them! Next some slimy sort of thing was served which I guessed was seaweed. I found this difficult to swallow, but I made it!

After the hors d'oevres the main dishes began coming in such profusion that I can't remember what followed what. There was the chicken — all of it, head, feet ... I even wondered whether its entrails were still intact. But I found that it had been stuffed with a delicious glutinous rice mixture. There were some sea slugs prepared in a rich brown sauce — I recognized these only because of my earlier studies in marine biology! Identifying them didn't make it any easier to eat them. They really looked anything but appetizing, and I knew how rubbery they were. But once I got over my inhibitions I found they were quite palatable.

But then, of all things, a big fish head was placed in the center of the table so that it was staring me in the face. It gave me a queer feeling to gaze at him as he stared at me in his bodiless state! I knew very well that this was a well-to-do family; so I couldn't understand why they were reduced to serving up fish heads! Later I learned that this dish is a "peculiar" delicacy in

Shanghai and that having the fish face me demonstrated the family's desire to wish me good fortune and blessing in my sojourn in China. I certainly had a lot to learn!

One thing I did know about cross-cultural living was to eat everything one is served. I soon learned that the second part of this lesson was to eat it slowly. At first when served something which made me feel a bit queasy, I determined to get it down as quickly as possible. But this method backfired. In their never-failing effort to honor their guest, my generous hosts would quickly pile on more of said delicacy which I so obviously enjoyed!

Despite everything, I really did enjoy the feast. My former student's family were extremely friendly and kind. They even took me back home in their car.

There was just one fly in the ointment of an other-wise delightful day, however. When I had set out early that day, those who knew my plans had forgotten to warn me of mission-home etiquette regarding leaving the compound. So late that evening, after waving goodbye happily to Hui-ling and her family, I pulled at the big compound gate only to find it soundly locked. I had no recourse but to ring for the gateman. When he finally appeared, he looked at me with bleary eyes which silently asked, "Who are you? Have I seen you before? Why are you coming in so late?" It seemed to take forever, but he finally did unlock the gate and let me in. I began to walk with dampened spirits across the dark compound. I noticed that both blocks were in gloomy darkness, but to my great relief I found the main door to the residential block unlocked. Once inside, I climbed the stairs to the third floor. When I arrived there and tried the door to the corridor leading into the residences — it was locked! My heart sank! Now what was I to do? I proceeded to climb to all five floors, carefully trying the door on each floor. Every door had been securely locked. What I didn't realize then was that I should have signed my name on the blackboard before leaving, so that people would know I would be returning late. Just one more new custom to get used to!

With no real hope I mechanically mounted all those stairs again, trying each door one more time. But with every step it became clearer that I was indeed very definitely locked out of the C.I.M. mission home at 11 p.m. on my second night in Shanghai.

I was ready to panic, when all of a sudden I saw a bell. I don't know how long I stood there debating about the propriety of ringing it at that hour. But I had no choice — I couldn't sleep in the stairwell all night in late winter!

Finally I pushed the little button. Before long, in answer to my ring, a little old lady with her hair in a single long braid down her back and wearing a faded bathrobe appeared. She was far from happy — I had obviously wakened her from a sound sleep. As she opened the door to me, I apologized profusely. She proceeded to tick me off just as profusely. *Boy*, I thought, *I'm off to a good start. Just my speed to do the wrong thing on my first day!*

Her scolding ringing in my ears, I started toward my room. But, alas, I now couldn't be sure of my room number! Quickly sending up an S.O.S. to the Lord, I continued my search. I turned up at the bathroom and briefly considered whether in the end I'd be sleeping in the bathtub! But from there I seemed to get my bearings and, taking a guess at my room number, made for that door with haste, turned the knob and gratefully stumbled inside. I hadn't been living there long enough to remember where everything was and in the dark I groped my way around trying to find the empty bed! I flopped down on it with most of my clothes still on. As I recall, four people besides me occupied that room. I found out later that, as I was fumbling my way around, at least two of them were awake, quite enjoying the performance. We've laughed about it many times since. What an impact I seemed to be making on the usual quiet routine and decorum of the mission home in Shanghai! I caught on fast, however. The next night when I was again out with friends, I returned at a decent hour, not forgetting to sign up on that jolly old blackboard, another adjustment having been made toward adapting to the lifestyle of the community.

Before long, interviews with mission directors were finished, repacking was completed and it was time to move on again. This trip Hazel and I would travel up the Yangtze River by steamer to C.I.M.'s language school at Anking in Anhwei Province. We were going second class and were supposed to have cabin space reserved for us. We discovered, however, when we arrived at the dock with all our stuff that our cabin was already filled — with men! So much for reservations! To top it off, we began to have serious doubts of even reaching our destination, as our eyes gave the ship the once-over. She had seen better days, Hazel and I concluded, and was definitely nothing to write home about; just a pre-war river steamer long in need of repairs. We did have the consolation of an escort, however. A German missionary lady was to travel with us and share the now appropriated cabin.

Just at this point the business manager from C.I.M. headquarters, Mr Wilhelm, came to our rescue. He got busy and, after much dickering with the men in our cabin, got them to move out. In their place, however, two Chinese women, each with a child, came to take up their abode with us. So we were five adults in the cabin, topped off with two crying babies.

The trip took four and half long days. The ship was greatly overcrowded, and sanitation was nil. Though built to carry 700 passengers, the steamer was jammed with probably three times that many. People were everywhere. Corridors were so full that it was nearly impossible to open our cabin door. In the cabin itself the cots were so close against one another that the only way to get onto them was to crawl up from the foot. There was hardly room enough to change our minds, let alone our clothes! Anyway, our escort strongly advised our keeping clothes on at night. After five days in the same clothes we felt pretty buggy when we arrived in Anking!

But to get back to our cruise. On the first night we were very tired and turned in early, aching for sleep. But with all the commotion from the passengers in the corridors, sleep was impossible. Later when they did calm down, it was the rats that bothered us. The first night they came into the cabin, quickly disappearing when the lights were turned on. The following night, though we kept the lights burning, they came in anyway, becoming more brazen as the days went by. They were no doubt after all the goodies on the cabin floor, dropped by the mothers who seemed always to be either eating, or feeding their babies.

Rats, however, were not our chief concern. One night I awoke suddenly. I don't think the others had been asleep. There was a terrific noise, with people shouting and crying in panic. To us, not knowing Chinese, the chaos seemed even worse. I couldn't imagine what was wrong. Our escort showed great concern and tried to open the door to investigate, but it wouldn't budge because of the mob outside. She was able to make out their screams, however. "The boat is sinking!" they were shouting at the top of their lungs. "The boat is sinking!" She quickly passed on the terrifying message to us. We all knew there wasn't anything we could do about our situation. Even if we could manage to squeeze open the door, there wasn't any safer place to go, and we would have been trampled by the mob. So we did the only sensible thing we could: we committed ourselves to the Lord and waited. Finally in exhaustion sleep came and, to our amazement, we were all still intact when morning's light filtered into the cabin. Our escort confessed that although she had been on many boat trips in China, this was the first time she had reached the point of really being alarmed.

We somehow continued lumbering along the Yangtze River. Each time we stopped at a port the passengers rushed to the side where folk were disembarking, tilting the ship dangerously.

Nighttimes were becoming unbearable. It seemed that more rats were getting on at every port. It's probably no exaggeration to say that their bodies, not including tails, were at least ten fat inches long.

Not only did Hazel and I live through these first vivid experiences, but they were a good initiation to inland travel in post-war China. However, you can imagine our relief when at long last we spotted the Anking Pagoda in the distance and knew we were almost at our destination. How good it would be to get off this ship, and be taken to the language school! We relaxed at the idea of spotting friendly C.I.M. faces among the crowds at the dock, ready and waiting to help us off.

But once again no one was there to meet us; our ship had arrived on Sunday right during church time! How desolate we began to feel as we pulled ourselves and our stuff together to disembark!

As there was too much silt in the river for our ship to put in by the dock, we had to get ashore in little barges and sampans. Over the side of the ship we went, bag and baggage, down a very narrow ramp which wobbled precariously. For the braver souls there were also some rope ladders. I left the ship first while Hazel remained on board to watch the baggage. Had it not been for a very kind German man who helped us with our baggage and the groceries we were bringing for the language school, we couldn't have managed. While Hazel guarded the stuff on the ship, our German friend and a couple of Chinese fellows began lugging our pieces down to me on the dock. As I stood there in the crowd, I kept scanning the area anxiously for someone who might be looking for us. There wasn't a white-faced, long-nosed westerner in sight. I stood my ground while coolies besieged me, poking their fingers in front of my face, yelling and waving their arms, obviously wanting to carry our stuff. I just kept saying all I knew how to say: *"Pu yao! Pu yao!"* ("Don't want! Don't want!") I guess the whole affair must have been extremely funny to them. It certainly was to us as we looked back on it.

After some time I became aware of one pock-marked coolie who was terribly persistent. Frantically he kept waving a piece of paper in my face. Finally it dawned on me that possibly he might have something to do with us. I took the piece of paper and read it. The note explained why no one was there to meet us. They would be down as soon as worship service was over; meanwhile we were just to let this Mr. Ma take care of everything. To me, he looked an absolute villain! But in fact, Mr. Ma turned out to be a lovely Christian man who helped around the language school. Quickly he took things in hand, much to my relief. I was fascinated to observe the performance as he haggled with the carriers good-naturedly, eventually driving a bargain to the satisfaction of all. As our things arrived from the ship, they were counted, then loaded onto the ends of bamboo poles and up onto the carriers' shoulders. Then off the laden carriers went, their straw-sandaled feet moving in a kind of gliding-shuffling gait.

Hazel, after much squeezing and maneuvering, was finally able to get off the ship. At about that time Miss McQueen from the language school arrived. She was a very sweet little Scottish lady dressed in a long Chinese gown, and her calm and serene manner in all that din was indeed impressive. What a help it was to have someone there who could communicate with these people — even though I seemed to detect that her Chinese had a bit of a Scottish accent!

Rickshaws were arranged for us, and soon we were off. Riding in one of these two-wheeled sulkies pulled by a coolie was a new and rather hair-raising experience. When I first took my seat, I felt as though I would fall out on my face; but when the runner stepped between the traces and picked them up I was suddenly flung backward and was just as sure I'd land on the back of my head! I need not have feared, though, for the runner soon skillfully had everything balanced and was moving along in his peculiar shuffling gait down the rough cobble-stoned street.

Children called to us and signalled "thumbs up" as we rode through the narrow streets. Hazel's rickshaw was surrounded and followed much as the Pied Piper of Hamlin must have been. Everyone was amazed at her bright red hair, shining beautifully in the brilliant sunlight. They had probably never seen anything like it before. Hazel was a good sport and took all the attention in her stride.

The trip through the city was as interesting as could be. There was not a car to be seen, and the streets would indeed have been too narrow for them. The slat-type coverings that protected the simple, unpainted shops at night were removed during daylight so that whole store fronts were open onto the street. There was no such thing as a show window. Neither was there anything resembling a department store; rather each shop seemed to specialize. There were cloth shops, pot-and-pan shops, a coffin shop, idol-worship-paraphernalia shops. There were food shops and stands of every sort. There did not seem to be a sidewalk, or if there was it was impossible to tell where the road began and the sidewalk ended. Business seemed to be carried on everywhere. The aromas drifting from the roadside food stalls were very tantalizing after the poor fare we had had on our trip, and I was suddenly very hungry.

When I was studying in New York City, I thought there were a lot of people milling around on the streets. But New York couldn't compare with Anking that Sunday morning. People were literally everywhere, with burdens on poles or babies on backs. Some bravely maneuvered bicycles, and some pushed large, clumsy wheelbarrows with tremendous loads piled on either side of the big center wheel. Lumbering ox carts and numbers of rickshaws added to the confusion.

Adeptly, however, our runner threaded our rickshaw through the traffic.

We knew we were nearing our destination when we were met by a welcoming committee composed of staff members and students from the language school. The prospect of joining the ranks and settling down in one place for a while now seemed attractive indeed. As we turned off the busy street and went through the gate into the quiet grounds of the China Inland Mission language school compound, I realized that this was the beginning of a new era in my life, a time of new tests and plenty of hard work.

7

Commitment tested

As I moved into my room in a building called EBENE-ZER, I had no idea how significant that name with its promise "Hitherto has the Lord helped us ..." would become as I began my study of the Chinese language. The rest of the compound included offices, staff living quarters and nearby the dining room and some of the classrooms. Everything seemed to be connected by gateways leading onto courtyards, and everywhere there were walls, walls, walls. I began to feel hemmed in.

School commenced the day after we arrived — nothing like getting on with the job! Moreover, we new ones were to go right in with those who had already been at it for six weeks. It was a humbling experience. My first day I just didn't know which end was up, either of myself or the Chinese primer! I already knew that I wasn't a linguist after earlier experiences studying French and German. But I discovered quickly that Chinese was totally different from anything I'd ever tackled before. According to my nature and training, I tried to go at it scientifically, and found Chinese absolutely unscientific!

My struggles were compounded by an attitude I detected in both classmates and teachers. "Why, Pauline," they would say with amazement, "We can't see why *you* are finding Chinese hard. You're a Ph.D.!" If I heard it once I heard it a hundred times. They forgot, of course, that my Ph.D. was in science. They just assumed that because of my degree I should be able to steam right ahead. I was steaming all right — inside — and what's more I felt like screaming at the whole lot of them. *Why couldn't they understand me?* I had to bottle up my feelings; I'd just have gotten sent home for psychiatric treatment if I'd screamed the way I felt like doing. Frantically I sent up S.O.S.'s to the Lord.

It wasn't a very agreeable situation, and day by day I felt increasingly inadequate, out of my depth in a way I had never experienced before. I hardly dared look at the progress others were making or compare myself with them lest I be tempted to give up. For example, Hazel Waller who had started out with me way back in Candidate School was now sailing along with flying colors. Chinese was a breeze to her. I kept praying for needed grace to plod on through my dark tunnel and to see this as one more opportunity to experience more of the grace of God.

But at the end of several weeks I could hardly pray any more. I was at the end of myself. The devil immediately took advantage of my feelings of turmoil and depression, and began bringing up all sorts of doubts. "Aren't you really a bit too old, Pauline, to be studying this difficult language? You never were a linguist! What are you doing here anyway?" *Maybe I did make a mistake,* I began to muse. *I probably should have just stayed at home and helped in other ways.*

How tempting it was to give in to such doubts! At last one night, in desperation, I spread all my doubts before the Lord. I began to claim His promises. First the promise of wisdom in James 1:5: "If any of you lacks wisdom, let him ask God, who gives to all men generously and without reproaching, and it will be given him ..." I turned next to Psalm 46:1: "God is our refuge and strength, a very present help in trouble." Then I recalled 1 Peter 5:7: "Cast all your cares (or anxieties, or language lessons!) on Him, for He cares about you." What encouragement these Scriptures brought to my heart in that hour!

Yet as I hadn't been expecting such a test, those were some very rough days. Imagine what a put-down it was for me, just fresh from being a college professor, to have the language teacher make me rewrite incorrect sentences ten times correctly, like a little grammar school child! Oh how that hurt my pride! Then, to make it worse, she would say, "What would your Smith College students think of you now, sitting here writing your sentences!"

I probably needed the humbling, for once I could face all these unpleasant trials from a spiritual perspective I began to make progress. After all, the Lord promised to give us the land to possess it for Him. China was part of the land and language a most important instrument or weapon to wrench the land from Satan's grasp.

After a while classes were divided. Hazel and some of my other friends skipped up to the highest level while I stayed on in the original class. It was some comfort that I wasn't put down to the dumb or dumbest class. Now, in preparation for the school's move to the mountains for the summer, it was decided to choose some students to take on extra study so they might complete the first big language examination before going to new assignments at the end of the summer. You could have knocked me over with a feather when I was chosen from our class to work towards that goal. A friend of mine who had also been chosen echoed my sentiments exactly: "I know the Lord's able to do anything, but look what he's got to work with!" However, the Lord proved again His faithfulness in my need, and I passed without difficulty.

Lest you get the impression that life in the language school was all study, I had better explain that a fair bit of our time was taken up with just the business of living. We were learning to do chores the way our grandmothers had done them, like scrubbing floors on our knees. Not only did we not have floormops, but the broom was a shocker and a back-breaker — like nothing I'd ever seen before — just a crude bundle of grasses with a handle only about a foot long, forcing the user to stoop way over to sweep with it. Maybe the idea was to get your eyes closer to the dirt or something!

We had been told we would have electricity at the language school. That was a bit of an overstatement. *If* the electricity came on, it did so only in the evening around six o'clock, and then it was so weak it lit the filament of the light bulb to just a thin red thread. To read we had to use oil lamps. As for water — the only thing running about it were the men who carried it in from outside. Each of us had to make do with only a basin of hot water in the evening. That was hard. These things made Anking seem very remote from Philadelphia!

Saturdays, besides being house-cleaning days, were also when we learned more about Chinese culture. On

a dull boy" and so recreation had its place in our daily program. At 4 p.m. there was a choice between volley ball or going for walks. There was more to be gained from walking than just the exercise. Often we walked on the city wall, and from this vantage point we got some good glimpses of local life at close range. From the wall we could see the farmhouses outside the city — low, thatch-roofed buildings of sun-dried mud brick, housing several generations. As each son got married he brought home his bride, and a new room was built on to the house. Children were all over the place, of course, and they eyed us curiously and somewhat fearfully.

One of our favorite places to walk was the cemetery outside the city wall. We loved the bright flowers we found growing wild there, for there were few flower gardens as such anywhere else. Not at all like the cemeteries I was accustomed to seeing in the West, these had really huge burial mounds with name tablets instead of gravestones. Some of the graves of recent origin still had food offerings and joss sticks placed before the name tablet. Quite a few coffins, covered first with loose straw and then a straw mat to protect them from the weather, awaited burial. The families of the deceased, I learned, were waiting for a lucky or auspicious day for the burial, trying to avert trouble from evil spirits.

With the coming of warmer weather we began to get acquainted with some other native inhabitants — little creatures of strange form and untrustworthy behavior. They were not really welcomed by us ladies! Take for example the big, red-headed centipedes. As a scientist I wasn't a stranger to little creatures, but I had never seen such big centipedes in my life! It was bad enough that they were big, and red on top of that; but what was worse was that they could travel so fast you never knew where they were going or where you'd meet them next!

One evening while I was writing letters in my room, one of the other girls burst in, exclaiming that she had two creatures in her room and didn't know what they were, and would I hurry and come, please? When I got there I saw why she was so excited — her room had been invaded by two big, ugly scorpions. Fortunately I had a D.D.T. bomb in my room, and it wasn't long before the scorpions came scuttling out by the score from everywhere. We learned to shake out our shoes before putting them on, or to undo our beds at night and shake out the bedding lest there be a scorpion having a siesta there. We slept under mosquito nets not only for protection from mosquitoes and the disease they carried, but even more for defence against these other creatures. In time, to add to my other honors, I earned the status of official bug exterminator for the girls' dormitory!

When summer heat really hit us on the plains, the whole language school moved up to the mountains of central China. The trip up the Yangtze River to the city of Chiuchiang in the neighboring province of Kiangsi took 14½ hours. There were about fifty of us all together taking the trip, and in my particular group we were thirty travelers. We took off early one morning with no less than two hundred pieces of baggage! The launch we were to travel on was quite small and, though one end had been reserved for our party, we had to get there early to claim our places. Sure enough, before the scheduled 6:30 a.m. departure time the boat was already so loaded that no more people could get on, and off we sailed. After arranging all our stuff in the stern end, we just settled ourselves down to enjoy the

landscape artists were impressionistic in their portrayal of mountains; now I realized that their paintings were on the contrary very realistic indeed — the mountains of Central China *were* jagged and craggy and mist-covered. The views as we went up were absolutely awe-inspiring. It was a trip to be remembered, and we even got to the point of enjoying the rhythmic swaying ride. At one point in our climb we came to a spot with one thousand steps going straight up, but they were artistically interspersed with little alcoves for resting, where we would stop and have a snack, making it all rather like a picnic.

Then, all too soon, we were at the top, jolted out of the fairy-tale-like adventure and back to reality as we caught a glimpse of our new language school and home. It was a pleasant surprise to find that home such a lovely place — a large, rambling stone building with huge porches on the front, stretching the whole length on both the first and second floors. The window to my room opened right onto this porch, and I had such a view! Just near the building were several stately pine trees and beyond them an inviting foot path. A little way past the path was a stream — not a large one, but a lively rushing one, bubbling its way down over the well-worn rocks, with here and there a little waterfall. On the other side of the stream was the beautiful home of Generalissimo and Madame Chiang Kai-shek. It was one of their summer retreat places, and we heard that they would soon be coming up to enjoy the cool, fresh mountain air.

How thankful we all were for the envigorating environment at Kuling after months on the dry, brown plains of Anking! Here we were living in the clouds at an elevation of some five thousand or more feet. Every once in a while a cloud would decide to join us in the living room, and we could actually watch it float right in. Then in a few minutes the sun would shine again and the cloud would be gone.

There was no question that studying was easier now. There were better opportunities to practice Chinese. The very friendly people holidaying up here from various other parts of the country all spoke the Mandarin dialect, the one we were learning. I began to feel that finally the testings were over. I was going to make it. Little did I know!

During recreation time here in Kuling there were absolutely wonderful walks to take and perfect places to go to meditate or to relax together after hours of study. One favorite spot was called the Emerald Grotto. There a stream came dashing down over the high cliff, forming horse-tail falls and splashing into the lovely emerald green pool. It must have been the beautiful mosses and ferns lining the banks of the pool, with the dense shade overhead, which gave it its name. Ten minutes' walk from there down some steps took one to the Dragon Pool, where we would go swimming and sometimes shampoo our hair.

If we really wanted an outing we went to the lookout over the West Valley and the Poyang Lake, a place which was to take on special significance to me in days to come. After a beautiful walk all the way there, one was rewarded by a marvelous view of this lake 120 miles long and 70 miles wide. The view was specially lovely at sunset. The fields around the lake were a show of symmetrically-planted gardens, with their lush green hues and impeccable neatness. Many of our vegetables at the school were brought from this productive area.

and were going off on their way, and there was still no news about me, the language school directors wired to Shanghai to discover if there had been some oversight. The answer that came back was more mystifying than ever: "Hamilton proceed to Shanghai about alternative designation." This was Saturday evening, and I was told that I should travel the next day with the group going to Shanghai. It was one mad scramble, to put it mildly, to get myself organized. I had already started to unpack since there hadn't seemed to be any hurry to get me out of there until now. Some of my trunks had already started up to Honan. One of those trunks did come back eventually, but another never did. And so I learned early the lesson of taking the spoiling of my goods in stride. I have lived without the trunk. I hope that someone else was able to enjoy its contents —I haven't the vaguest idea anymore what they were!

The river boat trip down to Shanghai was lovely, the boat being as nice in every way as the one up to Anking had not been! To top it off, for some unknown reason I was told that I was to travel first class! You can imagine how this affected me — everyone else in the group down in second class and me getting the red-carpet treatment! I knew there was plenty of room below where they were because, of course, I went to see my friends. Something was queer, but I decided that since I had been put in first class, I might as well enjoy it! I rested well, ate well and was feeling pretty well, all things considered, when we got to Shanghai late Wednesday evening.

I was called the first thing Thursday morning for my interview with Bishop Houghton. It was a relief to be summoned early as I don't think I could have stood the suspense much longer. However, I was far from prepared for what I was to hear.

As I walked into his office Bishop Houghton rose to his feet, quite a tall slim gentleman, and greeted me warmly. "Well, Pauline," he said, "today I'm going to throw a bombshell!" I didn't have the vaguest idea what he meant — it was too early to think I might be getting kicked out of the Mission. As my imagination continued wildly churning out possibilities, I heard Bishop Houghton say that because of the nature of what he had to tell me he had felt it best to talk to me face to face. As my heart pounded, he talked on a bit about Honan and why it had been felt unwise for us to go there.

Then suddenly he said, "Now for the bomb!" I listened in unbelief. He was asking me to consider going to teach at the C.I.M.'s school for missionary children, called Chefoo. They desperately needed someone in the science department.

I nearly keeled over! He was watching my reactions closely and then, so wisely, did what I was afraid he would do. He gave me a choice. It would have been so much easier if he had just said, "I'm appointing you to Chefoo School." But instead he began to explain without mincing any words what it would cost me should I agree to go to Chefoo. There would be a delay in language study, for one thing. Then in a very open and honest manner which I appreciated, he laid before me two other opportunities. He did not try to pressure me or make up my mind for me. Then as the interview came to a close he said "Take the day for prayer, fast if you feel the need of it, and come with your answer at five o'clock this afternoon."

being run on the British system. For example, they kept talking about a form. I couldn't make any sense out of this since I thought a form was something you fit a dress on, or else what you filled in when applying for a job or for entering college! They also talked about a sweet cupboard and a torch, and I was really mystified. After the meeting I solved some of the puzzles — a form was a class of students, and the sweet cupboard turned out to be the place where the children's candies (or sweets) were kept. A torch, I discovered, was a flashlight. And so began my education at Chefoo!

Time was running out, with school beginning Monday morning, and the next thing on my mind was getting together my teaching materials. I sought out the headmaster for assistance.

"Where will I find my textbooks?" I asked him. "I really need to do some preparation for Monday's classes, and I should look over the books."

His answer was most distressing: "There are no textbooks, I'm afraid," he said. "The person we were expecting to come for this position was to have brought the textbooks. I'm very sorry to say that since the teacher hasn't come, neither have the books."

My heart sank, and I could have cried. How on earth was I supposed to teach all the sciences to seven different classes without textbooks? I almost had no voice to ask my next question. "What about the laboratory equipment?"

"There *is* no equipment. There is no laboratory. We have nothing!" he answered with much feeling. "Everything we had was destroyed by the Japanese during the war. The books were burned along with the school buildings. We have nothing ...."

What could I say! The interview seemed to have come to a hopeless dead end. And so I walked out of his office feeling at a very low ebb indeed. I went back to my room and breathed up a desperate S.O.S. to the Lord. "What am I to do now, Lord? How can I possibly teach science to an age group like this, with no equipment of any kind, and, to top it all off, in this school system that is absolutely foreign to me!" I felt as if I was up against an impossible obstacle, since it was not just classroom entertainment these children needed; they were supposed to be preparing for the Oxford and Cambridge examinations. I continued to cry out to the Lord. "What have you got me into this time?" I complained. "I didn't come to China for this!" As you might guess, I came very near to going back to Bishop Houghton and telling him, "I'm sorry, I can't do it." But something within me made me feel that that would not be right either. It was as though my heart was saying, "Here's a challenge — give it a try!"

As calmly as I could I began to reassess the situation. The only piece of scientific equipment I had was a microscope. It was my own research microscope which I'd decided to bring out to China rather than to sell at home. Now how thankful I was that I had been led to bring it! But how was I to manage teaching things like chemistry and physics? It just seemed impossible.

We were very crowded on the C.I.M. compound in Shanghai in those days. Big as the compound was, it just wasn't big enough. The school was there, including dormitories for all the children; the offices were there; and in addition the post-war stream of missionaries returning to the field passed through Shanghai. We were just all on top of each other, with

compose myself a little. I walked in. The monks and priests, all in their saffron robes, looked at me very strangely and asked what I'd come for. Embarrassed to death, I managed to get out my request for a frog. Naturally they asked me what I wanted a frog for, and I explained the best I could. What a reaction this produced! They were appalled, and I knew it wasn't just my bad Chinese. Then I learned something new about Buddhism. The priests informed me sternly that those frogs — those mocking, croaking frogs that would have made such a good science demonstration — were holy. Once people, they had been reincarnated as frogs, and so science and religion came to an impasse. I certainly wasn't going to get any of those frogs for a science demonstration! I don't remember ever having been shown out of any place as fast as I was ushered out of the temple that day.

I had a pretty good laugh at myself as I went back to the compound, but I didn't dare share any of the details of my escapade as I probably would have gotten a good scolding. After all, I might have caused some real trouble in my ignorance. But there I was, still without my frog. I'd finished my preparation for my other classes, but had nothing for the physiology class. As I prayed that night, I quite simply said, "Lord, I'm so tired. You'll have to provide something — I just don't know what to do."

Next day, because I was on morning duty with the children, I was late getting to breakfast. As I walked in, a fellow worker seated at the far end of the large dining room started calling my name, "Pauline! Pauline! Good news! Could you use a rat?"

Forgetting myself, I yelled back in an excited voice, "Do you have a rat? Why, that's an answer to prayer!"

Well, that just brought the house down, and with the sound of two hundred diners laughing at the "mad scientist", I ran out to collect my rat. Since it had been banged over the head, the rat was just stunned. I proceeded to destroy the brain, allowing the animal's bodily functions to continue. This a very humane way of working on animals.

Fortunately the physiology class was the first period of the day, and the rat's heart was still beating regularly, though it was feeling nothing. When the children arrived in the classroom, I cut the rat open for them and showed them the circulation system. Everybody was very excited and became so enthusiastic about what they had seen that they talked and talked about it. "This is real science," some of them told their parents. "Now we're really getting to see things happen." Unfortunately some parents did not like this sort of presentation, and they came to tell me they did not approve of their children being shown such things! After all my pains, my "wild goose chases," this reproof was the straw that broke this camel's back and so, feeling very frustrated indeed, I sought out out Bishop Houghton.

"Bishop Houghton, you asked me to teach in this school," I began. "I need to know one thing, please. Am I here to teach science as I think it should be taught, or must I listen to all these parents!"

"Now, now, let's have the whole story," he said patiently. I told him what was bothering me, and after listening sympathetically he replied, "Well, Pauline, you do it the way you feel it should be done. I'm sure it did the children no harm."

I left his office quite elated and reassured. I had my orders now, from the highest authority, and after that I paid no more attention to complaints. In fact,

And now my relationship with those praying for me at home was breaking down. Letters kept on coming with advice. Some said, "Well, if you want to teach out there, you should teach in a college. That's what you're trained to do." Former fellow workers added to my sense of dissatisfaction by reminding me of the college teaching position at Yenching University which I had turned down. "It's probably still open, you know," they advised. As I look back, I can see how God was putting my commitment to the test once again. I figured that no matter how unsettled I was feeling, I would just have to keep my promise to the school until the three months was over.

Just about now the school was planning a move to Kuling, in Kiangsi province, the place where I had spent such a great summer in language school. This move was to take place during the winter holidays, while the children were visiting their parents. I should be on my way to my new appointment by then, I reckoned with relief. The holidays were going to be a bit longer this year because of the move. In one of my letters home I mentioned this long holiday, and Mother's reply was, "It's wonderful you have such a long holiday coming up; you could fly home for a vacation and still get back in time for the new term. I'll send you the money for a round trip ticket!" In my frame of mind this letter prompted a really desperate reaction. *Round trip ticket, my hat! I don't need a round trip — all I need is a one-way!* Tearfully I started packing my bags.

While still grappling with this very real temptation to go home, I had an unexpected visit from a fellow staff member, Miss Broomhall. An English lady who had been teaching in the school for many years and who had even been a pupil there as a child, she came to have a little talk with me. I had no idea what to expect as I asked her to sit down. This lady loved Chefoo, and she just couldn't understand someone like me who didn't. I didn't have to wait long to find out what was on her mind. In a stern businesslike manner she began, without any preliminaries, to reveal to me many unpleasant things she had observed in me and in my attitudes. As she shared these impressions, she really did portray a very unlovely Pauline. "We heard what a wonderful person you were," she continued, "but I fail to see it." She didn't mince her words, but just enumerated my failings one after another until I began to feel more and more like some dirty old rag used to wipe up the floor. As she concluded, she said with much feeling, "I know you don't want to go to Kuling with the school; you don't want to go up there with us, and you don't want to teach the children."

I shall never forget her finishing stroke as she looked me straight in the eye and said, "We wouldn't even mind some of your American lip." That really ignited the embers that by now were smoldering inside me. My thoughts raced madly, *I'm an American all right; you don't need to rub it in. We're an international mission, and we should appreciate each other.* Rather rudely I flung back, "Well, you'll probably get some of my American lip some time." Graciously ignoring this remark, she asked me if I had anything I wanted to say. *Did I!* I had volumes I was aching to tell somebody.

"Do you realize I have been in this school for four months, and no one yet has taken the time to help me understand the school system? No one has explained to me what these Oxford and Cambridge examinations are all about!" I could tell by her expression that she

she called, "you're looking awfully tired and strained. Can't you come to my place for the weekend?" It was in a lovely spot out in the country, and I always thoroughly enjoyed my visits there.

"No, I'm afraid I can't," I replied gloomily. "I'm on duty with the children."

"Can't you change your duty with someone?" she asked, knowing nothing of the strain I was under, nothing about the talk I had had with my fellow-worker or about Mother's letter. "I think a few days' rest would do you a world of good, Pauline."

There was no doubt in my mind that the change would do me good — but more than that, I also began plotting that if I went out to her place, I would have a chance to sit down and write Mother everything and tell her I was coming home for good. I quickly approached a couple of teachers to see if they would change duty for me, and soon it was all arranged.

Out there in the country folk really spoiled me — breakfasts in bed, plenty of opportunity to relax, to listen to good music, to rest and enjoy myself with no duties of any kind. What a heavenly treat! No children anywhere! The time just flew. Sunday dawned a beautiful day, and I went out for a walk on the little dikes between the rice paddies.

Suddenly I stopped short. *I'd better turn around and go back to write that letter to Mother*, I thought. As I turned I caught a glimpse of a man plowing his field, and all at once the Lord's words spoke to my heart, "No man having put his hand to the plow and turning back is worthy of Me." It was as if a bolt of lightning had struck me. I felt a shock all through me and quickly ran back to the house. Grabbing paper and pen, I wrote to Mother explaining that I would not come home for the holiday. I confessed that if I were to go, I would want only a one-way ticket; but that the Lord had met me just now, out in the fields, and reminded me to keep my hand to the plow. When Mother replied to my letter, it was clear that she had had no idea of all the turmoil I had been going through. She apologized for suggesting a trip home since it had put temptation in my way.

It had been a very close call, but the Lord had helped me to resist this temptation and stay at His bidding in China, no matter what happened. As I continued to rest there at the seminary, He reminded me once again of my initial commitment to Him while walking on the sand dunes of Cape Cod; I was strongly reassured of His presence with me and His promise never to leave me but to guide step by step. I knew there could be no turning back.

The days which followed didn't get much easier as far as work and responsibilities were concerned, but at least there was now understanding. Miss Broomhall became a very close friend and confidante. I admired her so much for daring to confront me, for being brave enough and faithful enough to come and tell me the things she saw in me that were not right. I can honestly say that if I have a real friend in the world, she's the one. Years later when I became very sick in Hong Kong, it was she who cared for me, being like family to me those several months in hospital.

Gradually the general atmosphere at the school began to improve and personal differences were disappearing as we made every effort to air them and iron them out before misunderstandings occurred. I had always thought of myself as such a broad-minded person until that time, but all at once I realized how very narrow-minded I was. I didn't naturally under-

Oh no! I thought. Here I'd been living for the day when I'd be told of my new assignment, and instead I was being asked to endure three or four more months of biting the bullet. After a few minutes of trying to pull myself together again, I very reluctantly said I would stay. There wasn't anything else I could do — I couldn't start something and then walk out in the middle of it, even if I was making a mess of it. I wasn't brought up that way. As children we had been taught that we should finish what we started. Once again temptation to get out of the Lord's will had been just within my reach, but He faithfully kept me to my promise to follow His way for me step by step.

By this time some of the school staff had gone on ahead to prepare things at the new school in Kuling. The rest of us remained behind to finish clearing out, and we would escort a group of about thirty children from Shanghai up to the school. Things were really humming now; packing boxes lined the school hallways, and the last-minute chores seemed endless. When the day arrived for the actual departure, the children were so excited I knew it was going to be quite an expedition! We even looked as though we were part of some arctic expedition by the time we were all bundled into our layers and layers of warmest winter clothes. The main leg of the trip would be by airplane, without heat, and what's more we would be flying at high altitudes because of the mountainous terrain.

At about 4.30 a.m. we climbed onto the mission truck, scarves flying, bright hats bobbing, mittened hands waving to the band of farewellers who had loyally come down to see us off in true C.I.M. fashion. Spirits were high despite the early hour, and one of the directors couldn't resist the opportunity for a hilarious last word to me. "Pauline," he shouted, "if you should happen to fall out of the plane, it looks as if you'll bounce right back!" *Well*, I consoled myself as everyone laughed, *the rest of our group looks just as funny, bundled up like Eskimos.* It was a good feeling to be part of such a tightly-knit family, and humor helped at times like these. It was good as well to know that their prayers went with us as we set off.

There was really nothing to worry about; the staff at Kuling had been wired about our arrival time and all details of our landing — by special permission we were to touch down on President Chiang's private airstrip in Chiuchiang. Personally, I had some slight misgivings, since I'd never been up in an airplane before, and when I got a look at the plane I wasn't so sure I wanted to break my record. The *St. Paul*, as she was aptly named, belonged to the Lutheran mission, and she was an old prop plane. Even the barest comforts had been removed in order to accommodate the thirty children and three teachers, and that meant no buckets seats — we sat on boxes. The cabin was not pressurized either, as we were to experience before too long.

The air trip was very rough. To add to the excitement of flying over the mountains, we ran into clouds and poor visibility, so had to climb even higher. The children began to complain tearfully of the pressure in their ears. Mine too were popping as though they would burst, but we three staff members were too busy trying to keep the children happy to take much notice of ourselves. Suddenly the pilot spied the airport through a break in the clouds and skillfully maneuvering the plane, banking and turning, zoomed down between the mountains to the small airfield below. The children cried with pain as their ears popped; and though I really felt like screaming myself I didn't dare. What a relief to feel the wheels *bumb ..bump ... bump* along the runway and know that soon we could all get out of the cramped cabin, safe and sound! Soon we would be on our way, climbing up the mountain just as I had done the previous summer. We even optimistically pictured ourselves making it in time for lunch. The children were all happy again, and we cheerfully tumbled out onto the airstrip loaded down with baggage, straw hats and teddy bears.

Waving goodbye to the *St. Paul*, which was bound for another city in West China, we began to look about for the welcoming committee. But there was no one there. We could do nothing now but wait. We arranged all our boxes so we could at least sit down, there not being any waiting room or any other sort of shelter. Fortunately it was a clear day. The youngsters were getting more and more excited now that we were so close to our destination. As they had never been up the mountain, I told them, to their delight, all about the trip by sedan chair, especially the part about the thousand steps climbing straight up. Next we played some games — but still no one showed up to meet us and to escort us to the next part of our journey. Since the airfield was fairly near Chiuchiang City, we decided two teachers should go in to see if they could contact our people at Kuling. I stayed on the airstrip with the children.

Time dragged by, and I began to wonder where the other teachers were. They had had time to come back from the city by now ... what could have happened to them? Finally they did return, but didn't seem to have much to report. We tried to get the children to take a little rest, but it was impossible. They were hungry, and could only think of getting going. We couldn't calm them down.

At dusk, when we were really getting a bit panicky, Mr. Mayer from the school staff arrived! What a welcome he got! The questions fairly flew. What had happened? It appeared that although Shanghai's wire had been delivered to the school, Mr. Mayer wasn't there to receive it. He had come down the mountain on other business, and since he wasn't aware that we were already in Chiuchiang waiting on the airstrip, he had gone back up again. What did he find upon arriving? The telegram from Shanghai! Of course, he immediately came down the mountain again (he must have felt a bit like a yo-yo that day), and now here he was at 5 o'clock in the afternoon, the pale winter sun sinking and cold and darkness settling on our weary little party.

Now we had the mountain climb to negotiate, and since it was winter there weren't many sedan chairs available. It was decided that some would have to walk up the mountains. The younger ones were stuffed in twos and threes in the chairs, escorted by their teachers. They went off first, and I followed with the older ones. It was quite dark by now. I kept thinking about the narrowness of the path, the many cliffs along the way, and the sheer drop over the sides. There could easily be little icy patches on the path, too. And then I remembered, with cold shivers up my spine, how the previous summer when I was in Kuling doing language study, a number of dogs had been lost. Some footprints turned up subsequently which were identified as tiger tracks! A tiger hunt was organized as folk were afraid it would be their children who would be missing next. Then one day we heard that a tiger had been killed, and some of us went to the village to see it, strung up; what a sight!

Now as I climbed the mountain in the pitch darkness with those children, I wasn't so sure that something quiet and alert in the bushes wasn't watching or smelling us.

We climbed for a while and rested for a while, not making very fast progress, tired and hungry as we were already from the long day. When we finally got to the little resting place just at the top of the thousand steps, there were some of the school staff to meet us with hot chocolate, sandwiches and chocolate bars. I don't know when I have ever been so glad to see anyone in my life!

At the beginning of the climb I had thought of how Moses led the children of Israel out of Egypt. The Bible says that God led them in the right way, and goes on, "He led them softly because of the young ones." And he had. Everyone arrived safely; every child was in one piece — no one had slipped or fallen or gone over the precipice; we hadn't encountered tigers — all the way from Shanghai to Kuling the Lord had indeed led us.

I really began to get into the groove of teaching in Kuling. In the woodsy mountain environment it was much easier to find materials for teaching sciences. Botany was no problem — this was a happy hunting ground for plant specimens; teaching biology was now a joy since here I could find all sorts of little creatures without going to temples to beg for them! I finally had to make a rule against bringing snakes into class as some of the children in their zeal were bringing in poisonous ones. As Teacher, I was supposed to act as though I wasn't the least bit afraid of them, but I loathe snakes! Anyway, things were going much easier now. If I had to teach, at least I wasn't having to cope with the tensions of not getting on with people.

But I was still keeping my eye on the calender, just itching to finish off this additional teaching stint. Easter came, and Easter went — but nothing was mentioned about my leaving Chefoo. As I dejectedly wondered whatever could be going on down at headquarters, a letter arrived telling me to get my things packed. Mission Director Sinton would be coming up from Shanghai soon, and I would be traveling down from Kuling with him. At last!

Mr. Sinton arrived just before supper. I was terribly surprised when someone came saying that he wanted to see me immediately. *Why*, I thought, *the poor man hasn't even had a chance to wash his face! Why should he want to see me even before supper? Something smells fishy here!* My heartbeat had speeded up, and I could feel my face getting flushed as I walked over to the head-master's office.

Mr. Sinton, sitting there with his full head of white hair and ruddy complexion, reminded me very much of my own father, not too tall and about the same build. Mr. and Mrs. Sinton had been very kind to me in Shanghai. Now as soon as our eyes met, he said very soberly, "Pauline, I'm afraid I've got a hard thing to ask you." I knew at once what was coming. "I know we promised you that you could leave Chefoo about now," he said very gently, "but there's absolutely no one in sight who can come for this position. Could you possibly stay — finish the school year?"

Somehow I managed to say a feeble "Yes," after swallowing hard. But I immediately blurted out my pent-up feeling about not really doing a good job; how I felt the children weren't getting what they really should, and that I was learning more lessons than they were!

Mr. Sinton replied very kindly, "Now Pauline, I understand all that. If you want to have a good cry, here's my shoulder." I accepted the invitation and wept my old heart out on his shoulder.

That evening someone had the thoughtfulness to send my meal over to my room, sensing that I wouldn't want to face people after yet another disappointment.

Now mechanically I began to unpack, all the time pondering, *How long is this going to keep up? What will I say now to my prayer partners?* I'd answered enough queries about having become a children's schoolteacher already. But I knew it was my duty to stay. I couldn't just walk out on the school.

Shortly after Mr. Sinton's visit, I had to face a far greater trial than anything before. One day while at lunch in the dining room I noticed someone hand a wire to Mr. Houghton, the headmaster. This was a fairly common occurrence, and I promptly dismissed it. But after we had finished eating, Miss Broomhall came to my table and started walking back toward our living quarters with me. When we got there, she insisted on coming into my room. *This is strange,* I thought. *She doesn't do this sort of thing. I wonder what's on her mind.* As she closed the door of my room, she said, "A cable has just come."

In a flash I replied, "It's my mother, isn't it? She died, did she?"

Miss Broomhall seemed stunned. "How did you know?" she asked. "Was she sick?"

"No," I answered quietly.

"Well, then, how did you know she had died?"

I explained to her the special means the Lord had used to suggest what was about to take place in my life. My daily custom was to pray for my family every morning after the school children were off to breakfast. That would be about 7.30 a.m. in central China, 7.30 the previous night in Pennsylvania. For the past three days I had been unable to pray for my mother, and it had really bothered me. I even mentioned it to a fellow teacher. Now, here in my room when I heard the word "cable," I was sure it was about Mother. As the cable had been more than three days coming, it seemed that when I had first felt unable to pray for Mother, she had already gone to be with her Lord. The Lord had lovingly prepared me, ever so slightly, for what He knew would be a tremendous shock.

I was encouraged to take a week or so away from classes and duties, and that very afternoon I went to one of my favorite places looking out over the Poyang Lake. It was early May — a beautiful time of year back in Pennsylvania. Here I was way out in Central China. I stood there a long time thinking things over — Mother had been almost, if not totally, blind by the time she died. She had had diabetes for many years and had died of a heart attack. Graciously the Lord brought the very comforting thought to my mind: *There's no blindness in Heaven. Now she can see. How wonderful for her to have sight restored, and her first sight of the Lord!*

I began to let the tears flow now, and I cried and cried. But in the midst of my sobbing the Lord seemed to rebuke me since these tears were for myself, not for her. He had taken her the way she had always wished to go, quickly, without being a burden to anyone. God had given her her desire, and spared her all the suffering so many diabetics have at the end. There was a glorious sunset as evening came on, and it was as though the Lord was reminding me of the glory of Heaven, greater than any sunset, and Mother's being Home with Him there.

Back at school, everyone was very kind and helpful, and how I thanked the Lord for this! I overheard one of the older children say to her little sister, "Now don't forget to pray for Dr. Hamilton and her family." These little ones didn't know that I was nearby nor how this word impressed me afresh with the close-knit family relationship we have in our Fellowship. This knowledge was reinforced by the many letters and notes stuck in the door to my room, or flowers put on my table picked by some child who cared. One poem especially touched me:

"Here there is naught but triumph; naught for tears,
When God's great trumpet sounds for one
　　　Whose task is done
　　　Whose course is run;
Now for the crowning glory of the years
The great "Well done," the simple "Enter In"
And the whole Heaven of heavens is bright,
　　　As God's Own Light
　　　Breaks on the sight
Of God's own child released from flesh and sin."

I didn't take any more time away from my classes as I knew I would only be tempted to give way to self-pity. In sympathy the children were especially well-behaved, and more than one came up to me, squeezed my hand in an understanding way, and ran away. One night as I was putting the little girls to bed, one called me over to tuck her in, and as I bent over her she pulled me down, kissing me and whispering in my ear, "Dr. Hammie, we're really twins now. We're both short and fat, and we both have mommies in Heaven."

The next weeks weren't easy. I had a real problem with sleeplessness as quite naturally I kept thinking of home. The devil is not one to stand back when such an opportunity presents itself, and as I lay there thinking, he tempted me to doubt. "Now, don't you wish you had taken your mother up on that offer to go home? You could have seen her one last time!" I clung to the Lord, and I was able to say in my heart, *Yes, I could have seen her again, but it wouldn't have been to God's glory if I had run home to Mama when I was so depressed. I might have had the desire of my heart, but I would have had leanness in my soul.* I remembered again the commitment Mother had made to the Lord before I was born, dedicating me to God for China. Here I was going through yet another test of my own commitment, allowed at a time when things weren't going my way. Yet even through this trial, in His mercy I was tasting His comfort in a new way. Often since then He has used my experience to help others, as it is only as we have gone through things ourselves that He can really use us to help others.

As the school year drew to a close, the headmaster called for me. He wanted to know if the Lord had possibly spoken to me about staying at school permanently — would I really pray about it? Well, I did as he suggested; I prayed, and apparently a number of the staff were also praying that I would stay. When the day came, I was very clear what I should say.

"Mr. Houghton, I have no indication from the Lord that Chefoo is His place for me. I just cannot stay on permanently. The Lord has very clearly called me to the Chinese."

"Well," he replied thoughtfully, after listening to my additional reasoning that I wasn't even properly trained for Chefoo, "if that is how the Lord has been leading you, I fully understand." And he went on to say I would free to go at the end of the school's summer holidays.

The senior students of the school had a farewell for me, putting on a skit portraying scene after scene way back from when I first started at Chefoo. They had me down to a T, my teaching methods, gestures, and the way I lectured on subjects way over their heads. I laughed so hard my sides ached. The staff too gave me a surprise tea.

After leaving the school, I was able to get a good rest at the newly acquired vacation home, Fairy Glen, right there in lovely Kuling. Towards the end of my resting time I had to undergo a language assessment to see what, if any, Chinese I still retained. Much to my astonishment, I was reassured that I really hadn't lost very much fluency by being out of school and that after a good review I could go on rather than starting all over again.

Then the Lord confirmed that His timing is always perfect, for less than two weeks after I left the school the long-awaited textbooks, ordered when I first started teaching in Shanghai, arrived! Simultaneously three people came forward offering to go into the school. One of them explained to me, "I've always felt that God wanted me at Chefoo, but I thought it was where *you* wanted to be." How interesting that all the while I was itching to get out! (Of course, while I like to say that it took three people to take my place, I know that's not entirely true — they had other things to do besides teach science!) The Lord kept me there until I had learned the lessons He wanted me to learn; lessons about myself, about other people, about how important it is to keep lines of communication open and to appreciate each other. As I look back on the experience, I think teaching at Chefoo was the making of me as a missionary. No wasted lessons in the Lord's school! And I realized there was even a little fruit which remained when a few years ago I got a letter from a former Chefoosian who said she heard the Lord's call to the mission field through something I said one night while scrubbing her back. I surely hated scrubbing backs, but if the Lord could use it, that's okay with me!

11
Reward of obedience

The rainy day fit my mood well. I had very mixed feelings now that I was finally leaving Chefoo, facing the unknown in Nanking. There were some strong tugs at my heart for those I was leaving behind. But I knew that these good friends would stand behind me in prayer.

Friends thought that I should take a sedan chair down the mountains as the weather was so very bad, but I love walking in the rain. As the men carrying the chair with Mrs. Adeney and her son Michael went fast, and Mr. Adeney easily kept up with them, I was by myself for the nearly three hours it took to get to the bottom. As I walked I thought about how the Lord had enabled me to endure the unexpected delays, and how many lessons He had taught me in that year or more in the school, priceless lessons of trust in Him, about my own weakness and about understanding the needs of others. Now the reward of my obedience was before me — I was on my way to Nanking at last! What surprises would await me there? And what new lessons ...? Well, at least I knew where I would be living — with the

Adeneys, Ruth an American and David from Britain, both already active in student work in that city.

As I reached the bottom of the mountain, the bus which would take us to the docks was waiting. Although the trip down the Yangtze River to Nanking usually took three days, we actually made it in about eighteen hours because of the flooded condition of the river. The havoc which the flood had caused was visible on all sides, and as we floated along on our way we couldn't help but be very sobered by the sight of fields now under water, the crops destroyed, cottages with only the rooftops visible above the water and in some places only the tops of trees. What would this mean to the people in winter months — definitely food shortages, possibly famine, and soaring prices.

What a contrast Nanking was to the mountain settlement of Kuling we had just left! In trishaws we entered the still war-scarred city through huge heavily-guarded gates in massive city walls. At that time the capital of China and a manufacturing center for fine satin and cotton materials, paper flowers, pottery, paper and ink, Nanking was no place for the claustro-phobic. Not only was its population of over a million being swelled daily by refugees fleeing communist insurgents in the countryside, but the city was a maze of walls — often walls within walls — brick, adobe, stone, or wood walls that hemmed you in and shut you out. As we wove our way through constricted streets and narrow lanes crowded with military trucks, ox-carts, trishaws, bicycles, people, and animals, everything seemed a jumble. Modern buildings con-trasted with weather-blackened store-front homes often decades past their prime. And the beautiful homes of the rich stood out in irritating contrast to the make-do shelters of the poor. On a hilltop outside the tall city walls stood the impressive mausoleum where the famous revolutionary Sun Yat-Sen was buried. It was because Nanking was also a university city that the China Inland Mission had built a new center for student work in the populous capital.

As soon as we could we went around to see our new two-story, seven-bedroom house and to lay plans for moving in, though we expected it to take some time before it was fully furnished (it never was!). In the area of our new home was a long-established Presbyterian hospital, and also an ancient temple drum tower which was at that time a refuge for beggars.

The very next day Mrs. Adeney and I took the train to Shanghai, 150 miles to the southeast, where she was to await the birth of their fourth child and I was to do some special shopping. I had been commissioned to buy new equipment for the science department of Chefoo School — now at last they were going to be able to set up a real laboratory. It took me several days to make my purchases as I had to haggle over prices with my rather inadequate Chinese. But it was fun, for all the while I was imagining what joy there would be at the school when this precious equipment was at last unpacked and put into use. It was like a last fond act for the school I had learned to love.

I returned alone from Shanghai to help with moving, which was now well under way. It was quite an experience for me settling into a household instead of an institution, and it seemed that this household was particularly full of surprises. We never knew who might be coming to stay, and from the very beginning we seemed to have a full house most of the time. To top it off, we had not a woman, but a *man* to do the cooking.

He couldn't cook, I couldn't speak much Chinese, and Mr. Adeney knew less than nothing about cooking! We had some hilarious times.

I remember particularly the visit of three of our C.I.M. men who were on their way to Kaifeng, Honan, to determine if the situation in Honan was as bad as reported. As they were delayed a few days in Nanking, they gladly pitched into the chores, scrubbing the floors and washing windows. One man helpfully went out and procured some boys, from goodness knows where, to come in and do some washing and ironing. These boys weren't any good at all at the ironing. I really doubt that they had ever done anything like it before.

A few days after my arrival in Nanking a lovely Chinese Christian was introduced to me to be my teacher. Mrs. Yu was from Peking, which meant that I would not have to change my dialect. She attended the same church that I did and was both a lovely person and a real teacher. As God is no man's debtor, I have found that He always makes up to us for all we ever give Him. Under her excellent tutelage we quickly covered all of the first-section material and were very soon ready to sail on into the second-section work. I was just amazed, and so very encouraged to see how much I did remember after being away from language study so long.

By and by the stream of guests to our house seemed to dry up, and then Mr. Adeney was off to Shanghai, leaving me alone. When everyone else left, the cook left also, which was actually a relief. So there I was in an empty house in the middle of Nanking, not able to speak very much Chinese, knowing only a handful of people and not really sure where in the big, sprawling city they lived. Rumors about unrest were now beginning to run wild; the sound of gunshots often echoed from outside the city and the situation out in the countryside was such that no fresh produce was coming into the city. I understood only enough Chinese to get a little inkling of what was being said about these things, and I read into what I heard the worst possible connotation.

My bedroom in this big house was the last one down what seemed to me a very long corridor. I must admit it was a bit eerie in that empty house, especially at night. I was very glad to see my teacher coming each day, though she had no idea how scared I was.

Then, late one night, I was roused suddenly out of a sound sleep by a blood-curdling noise from the other side of our garden wall. It sounded for all the world as though people were being beaten. I have never heard such yelling, howling, and crying in my life. *Maybe children are being beaten,* I thought with horror. A chill went up my spine as I remembered some of the things I had been hearing from the students about what was going on out in the country. Now the dreadful activity seemed to be right at my own door! What should I do? I wanted desperately to look out and see what was going on, at the same time really afraid to find out. I stood there for a long time in the darkness, petrified, not able to bring myself to look down into the courtyard. Finally I mustered up my courage and carefully crossed over to the window. When I looked down, I burst out laughing with sheer relief. The blood-curdling screams were not coming from tortured children but from donkeys! Yes, that's right, donkeys. Men were trying to load about ten of the beasts, and all the while the donkeys in characteristic manner were rebelling strongly. How silly of me to be so frightened! Yet, I'm not sure it was so silly. Many dangerous things really were happening around me. My situation alone in the midst of them threw me afresh onto the Lord, who graciously comforted and strengthened me through His Word.

I hadn't expected to be left alone very long, but the Adeneys were away somewhat longer than planned. Now down to the last of my money, I had to send to Shanghai for more. Notice of the money's arrival came several days later in the afternoon mail, but the bank was closed by the time I got the letter. Though I rushed down to the bank first thing next morning, by the time I actually had my hands on my money its value had dwindled to practically nothing because of inflation. In principle I was a millionaire, for at that time one U.S. dollar exchanged for seven *million* Chinese ones. But I couldn't even afford to buy a loaf of bread, which now sold for something like 45 million dollars, or $6.50 in American currency. What's more, no one would have taken my money, since no one wanted to accept the worthless local currency.

I had run out of flour about this time and had no rice or other staples either, except for a little sugar, some salt and a tiny bit of oil. *If I only had some flour, maybe I could get by making myself some pancakes or biscuits,* I thought hopefully, and so one morning I got on my bicycle and rode off into town to see if I could find any. Every place I stopped I was told they had no flour. It was discouraging, especially since I was new to the city and really didn't know where to go to find it. Finally I went into a tiny shop, just a little hole in the wall, and asked wearily if they had flour to sell. I could hardly bear to hear the answer, but once again it came, "No flour." This time I couldn't take it. I had a hunch something wasn't right.

"You do have flour," I argued. "You just don't want to sell it to me."

"Yes," he agreed slowly, "I do have some, but you wouldn't want it."

"Let me see it," I demanded impatiently.

He brought the flour out and placed it in front of me. I was full of disgust as I looked at it; it was simply crawling with little black weevils.

Once I got over shuddering I asked him the price, and then eventually bargained it down so that I could afford it.

"I'll take it," I exclaimed triumphantly. The shopkeeper was amazed.

"But you foreigners don't eat flour like this," he stammered. I insisted, and so he finally gave in, loading the sack of flour onto the back of my bicycle.

At home I began to work on my precious flour, putting it through a sieve. That turned out to be a tedious and seemingly endless job. I was sure I'd never get all the weevils out that way so finally I knelt down wearily before the bag of flour and prayed. "Lord, it's been raining for days; please give me just three days of sunshine to get the weevils out of this flour." I don't know if I really believed that it would happen, but the next day the sun was shining as brightly as I can ever remember. Hastily I prepared newspapers, bed sheets and anything else I could find on which to spread the flour. I couldn't help laughing as I looked at the flour spread out all over the garden, thinking what a crazy sight it would be to any visitor who might appear. Again I prayed, asking the Lord to keep people away! As my teacher had gone to Shanghai to visit her daughter, I knew she wouldn't come; but no one else came along either, and as the sun shone its brightest, the weevils started crawling out of my flour. That evening I sifted the flour again, removing lots more bugs. Rain teemed all night, seemingly to make up for what it had missed in the day. But again the next day the sun came out, and so did the weevils! By the end of the third sunny day I had beautifully clean flour. Now I could even feel a bit sorry that there was no way I could use the weevils — all that good meat! But I really couldn't bring myself to do anything with them. When it poured rain the next day, I realized how very wonderfully God had heard my prayers and how he had answered so specifically, meeting my real need as only He could. It was a very precious lesson to me.

Before long, however, I faced another very difficult financial crisis. Mrs Yü was coming back from her visit to Shanghai, and her salary was due. I felt it wouldn't be right to pay her with local currency since it was worth next to nothing. Whatever could I do? I had already received all I could expect from Shanghai and had lost most of it through devaluation. At last I decided to rummage through some things I'd stored in the box room to see if there was something I could sell. As I opened one of my trunks, there on top was a beautiful piece of cloth, just the color the Chinese love. It seemed to be a very good piece, double width and a good length. I couldn't even recall where it had come from, but I quickly pulled it out and folded it again carefully with the prayer that Mrs Yü might accept it as part payment for a month's salary.

"Mrs Yü," I said to her when she arrived for my lesson the next day. "I don't have any money because of inflation. I can't pay you the way I should, but I wonder whether you would possibly accept this piece of cloth as part payment for this month's teaching?"

She took the piece of cloth and examined it carefully. She felt it between her fingers and thumb and ran her hand over it, while I watched worriedly. She opened the cloth up and looked at the width, then measured the length from the tip of her nose to the tips of her fingers, yard by yard, not saying anything. Finally she turned to me and said, "No, I won't take it for part of a month's salary." My heart sank to the floor. *Oh no!* I thought. *Have I done the wrong thing?*

She continued, "No, I can't take this for part of a month's salary, but I will take it for two months'. I can get several dresses made out of this beautiful piece."

I was thrilled, and she was too, for she had something better than money, something negotiable which she could sell for a good price if need be. And so the Lord continued to look after me while everyone was away.

I had my several English Bible classes to teach and students coming in occasionally to visit me, and in spite of trials I was feeling like a real missionary at last! Then after about three weeks the Adeneys returned with their new baby, along with two other missionary couples who moved in with us as well. Far from being alone, now I found myself living with three couples and two little children!

Strangely, it was lonelier for me now than when I was alone. As I didn't have household responsibilities, I could be free to get on with my Chinese studies. But leisure time was my problem. They had each other; I was alone. I could hear them chatting and laughing, but I had no one with whom to chat or laugh, and I do enjoy both!

If I had been introspective, this situation could have quickly gotten me down, but instead the Lord helped me to see it as an opportunity to spend more of my time with the Chinese students. The girls came to visit me after classes. We went boating on the lake, or shopping, or rode bikes to the park nearby. In the beginning our conversations were a jumbled mixture of English and Chinese, and we laughed at each others' mistakes and learned a lot about our language and each other. Things had calmed down now around the city, and there were marvelous opportunities for student work; Chinese fellow workers were friendly and a joy to work with, and so I began to get into the swing of things, enjoying every bit of it.

Living with three experienced couples, I sometimes felt I had rather an overabundance of seniors. Take for example their favorite trick of inviting over a Chinese guest who knew very little English and then one by one excusing themselves, leaving me alone with the guest. With no ready excuse for leaving, I was stuck with the entertaining. Then followed those long and embarrassing periods of silence while each of us tried to think of what to say, and worse, how to say it! As it was a matter of sink or swim for me, I realize now that it was excellent practice for my Chinese. But at the time it was most painful.

One day my seniors were all going out. "Pauline," they remarked casually, "you'll have to take prayers this morning."

"Oh, no!" I squealed. "You know I can't pray in Chinese yet!"

Their response was quick and to the point. "What kind of missionary are you if you can't pray?" Then off they went, having a good chuckle at my dilemma.

With that rebuke ringing in my ears, I just stood there in the middle of the dining room, casting about in my mind for ideas. After some time and an S.O.S. to the Lord, I called the boy who served us to come to prayers. He looked positively bewildered but came in obediently. I started off by reading a portion of Scripture from my language lesson a few days earlier. Then, so thankful that I had had to memorize it, I recited the Lord's Prayer. The servant boy appeared more amazed than amused with my performance, especially since he wasn't even a believer. But for me it was another real step of progress.

Through an entirely different sort of experience while living with these senior missionaries, I discovered something interesting but a bit alarming about myself. As I went out regularly to my meetings, I always took the same route past a shop which sold foreign goodies. Sometimes I stopped just to see what they had. One day I spotted in the window something which really made my eyes pop out — a jar of olives! I am very fond of olives! As I looked, my mouth began to water. But even though the exchange rate had stabilized a bit now, I knew I couldn't possibly afford olives. Day after day as I came to that shop I would slow down, get off my bike and push it along as I looked to see if my olives were still there. The next month when my money arrived, I couldn't bear looking at the olives any longer; so I went into the shop just to price them. They were an exorbitant price, but before I knew it the temptation to have them had overcome me, and they were mine.

I didn't have the pleasure of telling anyone about my delicious purchase because I was sure they would scold me or, worse, laugh at me. I decided just to put my precious jar away in the cupboard. Then, with a smile, I thought to myself, *I'll just have one now and save the rest for later since they are so expensive.* Then I tried to turn the jar lid but it didn't want to open. (Goodness knows how old the jar may have been!) I gave it all my strength, but the lid wouldn't budge. Oh dear! I had my olives, but I didn't have them. I put the jar away dejectedly. I don't know which was worse — the olives in the shop or the olives in my cupboard. Day after day, try as I would, I couldn't get that lid off! I banged the lid; I pried the lid. Slyly, I took the jar to the kitchen and soaked the lid. Nothing worked. Days turned into weeks, and I tried everything one could try to get a jar open, but this one just would not give. I determined not to go and ask help of any of the men — I might have to tell him where I got the jar, and he'd be horrified at my extravagance. Or I might even have to share some of my precious olives with all of them! I didn't want to do that either!

Up until the time I had to leave Nanking, I struggled with the jar of olives. I drooled over them practically every day. I hadn't had any for nearly three years, and the more I thought of olives the more I yearned for them. Silly, isn't it. I never did get that jar open. When I left Nanking that precious jar of olives was left behind! I still do love olives, believe it or not. But now I'm willing to share them!

12
Gathering darkness

Communist activities and student unrest were worsening around Nanking in those days of late 1948. Still, opportunities for work with students abounded. Many of the students had communist literature, but no one seemed to know where it came from. Confused and worried, the students were asking us all sorts of questions, and we tried our best to help them understand the situation.

And then one day word came from the United States Embassy that all Americans had to leave Nanking! First the women with children were to go, so happily I was not included yet. The Embassy had moved to Shanghai and informed us that they could not bear any responsibility for us if we stayed on in Nanking. We heard the U.S. Navy was sending in two landing crafts to take people out; but since it was not yet considered emergency evacuation, I was allowed to stay on with Henry and Mary Guinness, a British C.I.M. couple, while Mrs. Adeney and her children and another couple expecting a baby would leave.

However, Saturday morning brought several more messengers while we were hastily packing things for the others, and this time the word was most insistent that we *all* leave. It had become an emergency situation now that a British ship had been sunk in the Yangtze River, and there was increased fighting throughout the whole area. The picture had completely changed within just a few hours.

I didn't want to go. The Guinnesses felt it would be unwise for me to stay, however, and in the end I gave in reluctantly to their advice. I didn't want to cause trouble for anyone because I was an American, and I had to admit, too, that I was not indispensable to the work there. I began to pack and to prepare myself for another uncertain future, all the time praying that if it was not the Lord's will for me to go, He would stop me. I didn't pack everything; we all felt sure that in a few days things would improve and I'd be back.

We traveled downriver to Shanghai on a troop landing barge. We were a motley array of westerners, as people of other nationalities were taking advantage of the opportunity to leave too. With about fifty bunks in a cabin, we had all the privacy of a goldfish bowl!

On the trip to Shanghai my mind was full of questions. *Is this the end of everything?* Was this goodbye to China, just as I was beginning to get my teeth into missionary work at last, beginning to feel at home with students, getting to know them and their problems a bit? I'd been working with some of the most wonderful people I'd ever known, and now it seemed to be all over, and I was going back to headquarters in Shanghai for what seemed the umpteenth reappointment! Disappointment was what I felt, but I knew God was expecting obedience from me, obedience to those over me in the Lord.

Actually Shanghai seemed the same as ever. Except for the tremendous influx of people from all over China, the city seemed amazingly unaware of the troubles up-country. And before long letters from Nanking were arriving informing me that things were back to normal again and that there were unprecedented opportunities. How I longed to get back to that work! Shortly, in fact, I was called in by Mr. Sinton, on whose shoulder I had once wept, and as I entered his office he said, "Well, Pauline, it seems as though we're always designating you. How would you like to go back to Nanking?"

"Are you serious?" I responded with surprise. "You know I'd like nothing better than that!"

"I am very serious. The situation seems to have stabilized; so we're letting you go back to work with the Guinnesses."

"When do I leave?", was my exultant response.

"Can you be ready in two days?" Could I! I could have been ready that day if he had asked me. I went flying over to the residence block and announced to everyone I saw that I was going back to Nanking! Two days later, packed, ticket in hand and already on the truck to go to the dock, I was told that the boat was not sailing after all because of renewed trouble up-country. Dejectedly I retraced my steps back inside the mission home, just in time for that practically changeless institution, afternoon tea!

One week later I was called to see Mr. Sinton again.

"Designating you is becoming a habit, isn't it?" he chuckled as I walked into his office. "We are still thinking you should go back to Nanking. Things seem to be much better now, and the opportunities are really great. When can you be ready?"

I had not unpacked much since that last false alarm. "I could be ready by tomorrow." I told him.

With the decision made that I should leave by train the next day, my ticket was bought and once again I was all set to depart. Some bright soul, however, thinking it the better part of judgment to telephone first to find out if the train would leave on schedule, was informed that it could not leave at all. A bridge had been blown up during the night! It looked as though I was being stopped at every turn. My superiors also thought that perhaps this was the Lord's indication that I was not to return to Nanking after all. To clinch their decision, I fell on the mission compound and broke my right arm!

It was then decided that I should stay in Shanghai to work among students. Though really disappointed and feeling quite frustrated, I had to believe, since we had all been praying about these moves, that God knew what He was doing. As He had obviously guided, I knew I should rest in Him and His perfect will for my life. As time went on and the situation continued to worsen, we all saw the rightness of my being prevented from going back to Nanking. Opportunities soon began to open up in Shanghai, where students filled over thirty colleges and universities, and before long I had four Bible classes.

The students mostly came onto our compound, meetings being prohibited in many colleges because of the fear of subversive activity. I did have two classes outside, however — one at a medical school and another at a training institute for kindergarten teachers.

One evening when I was to go to the training institute, some of my fellow-missionaries expressed concern about my going out alone. I felt I ought to go, however, as they were expecting me. I had to walk, for so many people were crowding the streets that I couldn't ride my bicycle. Anyway, the school was not that far from the headquarters. As I pushed my way through the throngs that included many people dressed in the different national costumes of other parts of China, speaking strange dialects I could not understand, I had a deep sense of the Lord's presence with me; I wasn't alone. Walking along, elbowing my way through the mobs, I couldn't help being moved by the changed aspect of the city these days. Such a beautiful city, Shanghai was now swollen with humanity. Daily floods of people were pouring in from more remote areas, fleeing before the communist army. These refugees had no recourse but to live in makeshift houses made of straw matting or sheets of tin, anything they could get their hands on. They had no privacy — their life was lived on the streets, and children were everywhere.

I was somewhat relieved to arrive at the school at last, and as a friend was helping me off with my coat he suddenly said with alarm, "What's this? Who put this on your back?"

"What is it?" I asked. "I didn't know there was anything on my back."

By now several others had gathered, and I could tell that they were all frightened. "Who touched you?" they persisted, their voices now quite excited.

Laughing and trying to make light of the matter, I said, "My goodness, there were so many people on the street, and I was being jostled all about, how can I possibly know who touched me? You haven't been on the street, that's for sure; there are people everywhere, and I had to push myself through the crowds." And with that I closed the subject, and they calmed down. We had a particularly good meeting together that night, not many in number but with a wonderful spirit as we discussed the Word and prayed, very aware of the Lord Himself standing in our midst as He has promised. At the end they once again became concerned about my returning alone. It ended up with a large group of them accompanying me to our gate, making me promise never to come and go by the same route.

Once safely home, I did wonder plenty about how that paper got on my back. But it was ten years before I got more light on the incident. In Hong Kong for medical treatment, I met a girl just out of China who had been a member of that very group at the training institute. Now safely in freedom, she was able to talk about that night a decade before and verify what I had supposed. That mark was special identification; I was probably supposed to be waylaid. But why me? I don't know — maybe it was a mistake; maybe it was the work of an anti-foreign reactionary. In those days it could have been almost anything, but the Lord had guarded me; He had walked with me that night.

Before very long there began one of the hardest times I had faced yet. A change of government was imminent, and I felt I must tell the students and my other Chinese friends that if a change did take place, I was going to act as though I did not know them when we met on the street.

"Oh!" they replied politely, "that won't matter."

"Yes, it will," I insisted. "There won't even be a twinkle in my eye to let others know that I know you. I don't want to make things difficult for you." As time went on, they knew that I was right.

The change of government actually took place in Shanghai on May 25th, 1949. No one knew how it would happen or what to expect. There was some fighting, but it was not heavy in our section of the city. I slept soundly right through it, as a matter of fact, and awoke the next morning under a new regime!

Immediately a new type of currency was issued, and new residence certificates. The streets were well policed by the new army.

In the beginning things were very calm, almost an eerie kind of calmness. It was great to see the peace the students were experiencing in their lives, God keeping them steady and giving them wisdom to replace the panic and anxiety which they had shown right before the takeover.

I continued to go to meetings at the student center, but we were never sure who might be in the meeting or what they might be writing down. When questions were asked, one could never be sure which side the questioner was on. That was one of the greatest strains for me. I wanted to believe the students were sincere, and yet how could I be sure? How could anyone be sure that things he said now might not be used against him some later day?

There was much a person could worry about in those days. My personal sense of calm came from the Lord's speaking to me through a plaque I had on my wall at that time. Written in beautiful Old English script by one of the C.I.M. missionaries, it consisted of three words from Psalm 37: "TRUST — COMMIT — REST." Those three words spoke volumes to me many times as I entrusted myself to Him in the midst of all the events around me and experienced rest in the center of His will.

Over the next few months the numbers of students coming for meetings gradually diminished as political meetings in schools and colleges increased. As the students were compelled to attend those meetings and processions also, they had less and less time for Christian activities or Bible study. Soon a full-scale indoctrination program was launched, and the students' days were filled from early morning to late at night. Other classes now stopped in an all-out effort to indoctrinate students with the principles of the new regime. There were political dances, which seemed very strange to some of us who had never seen Chinese dance before, dances portraying industries, or farming, or capitalism. During processions there was much shouting of slogans and singing of political songs. On and on every day and into the night the indoctrination dragged on. After about six months things really began to tighten up, with self-examination meetings initiated. Students were required to write their life history and thoroughly examine their actions and thought-life. Some frequently sneaked over to our compound to share with me the things they were having to participate in. They longed to get on with their university careers, but could not.

One day a student came in very upset because her father was missing. Several days previously he had gone to work but had never come home. I don't know that he ever did return. Things were tightening up more and more like a vise closing on the people. After about eight months my outside classes were practically non-existent.

As normal life became more and more just a memory, the number of missionaries who were leaving on their own increased. Though we hoped that things would change for the better, rumors were rife and it soon became clear that it was neither feasible nor advisable for the mission to stay. There were still opportunities; we could still go out to some meetings. But pressures were increasing on the people we loved, and we didn't want to cause them trouble in any way or be an embarrassment to them.

So as a mission we were much in prayer about the future. Perhaps the greatest advantage of our being there just at that time was that we were learning the needs of our Chinese friends and how to pray for them as they began to go through deep water. Prayer was something real and vital that we could do for them in those dark hours.

C.I.M.'s official withdrawal from China was announced on December 13, 1950. We all knew it was coming, but it was still a shock. I had been in China a little more than four years. Though I knew leaving was for the good of the Christians, I was not to be one of the first to leave; I would have to wait for official permission to go, the precious exit permit. So I made plans to try to finish several projects, one of which was writing Bible study notes for students' daily devotions. I had started doing this in Nanking with a very fine young Christian. Now a certain portion of my day was blocked out for writing the notes.

But each time I got down to this work, I felt the devil's opposition. I am not a person given to depression. However, on several occasions lately I had gotten up bright and cheerful but, after breakfast when settling down to work on the notes, had felt a dark cloud settle down over me. This was a completely new experience and something I couldn't seem to get out from under. I couldn't think, I couldn't pray, and I couldn't write. Nothing seemed to matter.

One day when I was in this condition, a friend came into my room and asked me what was the trouble. When I tried to explain, I couldn't seem to describe it, but it was evident to her that something was drastically wrong. "Come on! You've got to pray!" she exclaimed.

"I can't!"

"You've got to," she insisted. "Now you get down on your knees!"

"It's useless," I moaned. As far as I was concerned, God did not seem to exist. I couldn't get in touch with Him and could almost go so far as to say I didn't want to. It was a horrible state. But my friend kept at me.

"Now pray," she commanded.

"I can't!" I kept repeating. Nothing would come — the words seemed empty and useless, senseless. But my friend didn't give up. She pounded me on the back, shook me and did everything she could think of to get me to pray.

Finally in desperation she said, "If you can't pray, Pauline, just call on the name of Jesus!" That seemed more senseless than anything.

Now you ask, "How can a missionary get into a state like that?" I can only answer that the darkness of that cloud of depression was just as though the devil was fighting me in every realm of my existence. I don't recall how long the struggle went on that day; I'm sure it was more than half an hour. Finally, however, I was able to call out Jesus' name and the cloud began dispersing immediately.

The work I was engaged in was something we hoped would help the students after we had gone. I was producing materials to promote study of the Word of God, and the devil didn't like it and was out to fight it. I had the same experience several times after that and only when I cried in desperation to the Lord Jesus, pleading His blood to cover and keep and bring me through, was I able to have victory.

The words of the plaque, "TRUST — COMMIT — REST," took on new meaning. I realized that if I committed a thing to the Lord I should have the rest that He promised; if I didn't have the rest, then I hadn't really committed it to Him, and wasn't trusting Him, and that was *sin*. So once I had laid this whole matter before the Lord, I never again experienced the bouts of depression; the Lord was in complete control, and the work got finished before I had to leave. Over thirty years later I heard that some of these Bible study notes were pasted on to bottoms of drawers and memorized from there as a basis for Bible teaching.

Ironically, I got word to apply for my exit visa on my 36th birthday! Some birthday gift! Was this how my missionary career was to end? Four years earlier I had been sure that mine was a lifetime commitment, but now? And as I faced an uncertain future once again, the devil took advantage of the circumstances to tempt me to doubt and question. When I got home, how people would laugh at me for having left a fine teaching career to go out to China! But God reminded me that He was sovereign and in control. He who had led me safely over many rough paths those years in China, couldn't He be trusted for the future? He knew, and the next step He had for me was one of preparing to *leave* China.

It was about four months before I actually left. My Chinese friends, always so good at showing appreciation and love for help received and fellowship enjoyed, somehow found out that I was leaving and came with presents. One of the most touching gifts was a bundle of eggs brought to me by a dear old woman from the interior who had fled to Shanghai as a refugee. Thirty fresh eggs she brought, because she thought we didn't have them in America! At that time eggs were terribly expensive, and she had sacrificed much to buy them and risked more to bring them to me. However, the precious eggs became a bit of a problem for me, leaving on a trip that would take me halfway round the world! I didn't want to give them away — I felt like David when he received the water from the well of Bethlehem. In the end I decided to hard-boil them since on the last stage of our journey out, from Canton to the border, there would be no dining car on the train. The fifteen of us who would be traveling together would at least have two eggs each!

We set off for the station in a big truck, but as there were some "bigwigs" traveling on the same train our truck was stopped quite a distance from the station and we had to walk the rest of the way, carrying our baggage and looking for all the world like homeless wanderers. We were all feeling sad, to be sure, but perhaps as well as sadness we were beginning to feel some trepidation. There would be examinations en route. Would we run into any snags?

The first examination came in Shanghai itself; then there were three in Canton, and a final one at the Hong Kong border. At every examination Americans were asked to identify themselves, and my hand was always the only conspicuous one raised. Each time my baggage was inspected I was asked about those eggs! The question was always the same, "Are those eggs hard-boiled?" Each time I assured the examiner that they were. In each of the three examinations in Canton I was asked the same question by the same examiner;

perhaps his design was to annoy me, but I was too close to the border to get annoyed.

The final act in the egg episode starred this same examiner. After being assured a third time that the eggs were hard-boiled, he picked one up, cracked it, peeled it and then carefully proceeded to dissect it. Of course he found nothing, but he continued cracking and examining all the remaining 29. I began to find this funny! He was such a young fellow; he might have been 16 or 17 years old though he looked much younger, bristling with authority in a uniform several sizes too big for him.

The eggs finally attended to, he turned to me and said, "You have American dollars in your hair!" I quickly assured him that indeed I didn't; but ignoring my reply he was on me in a minute, disarranging my long thick hair which was twisted into a tight roll around my head, as I've worn it for years. I suppose I was expected to lose face by this treatment, for in China if a man takes down a woman's hair in public it is a shameful act. I had the presence of mind to think to myself as he gave my hair a good going over, *I'm a westerner; this really doesn't make any difference to me.* He found nothing, of course, except a lot of hairpins!

Thus far stumped in his efforts to find me guilty of some misdemeanor, my youthful examiner decided to give me a body search and immediately felt the special corset, with its heavy steel staves at the back, which I wear because of a past injury. "Aha, what's this!" he demanded, bristling more than ever. I tried to explain to him, but he waved my words aside, ordering, "Take it off. Take it off!"

As I saw no appropriate place to comply with his request, I just stood stock still. Seeing my hesitation, he sternly repeated his order. I was praying earnestly that the Lord would intervene in some way, but there didn't seem any possible escape; my fellow travelers were all busy with their own examinations and not at all aware of my awful predicament.

Just then a young woman examiner came over to us. "You're going too far," she murmured to the young examiner, and thereupon she ushered me kindly into an inner room. I disrobed and removed the source of suspicion, handing my corset to the young lady. She took it out to the inspector, and he pulled it and ripped it to pieces until he was content that it was not some sort of secret weapon, or a cache for treasures. Quietly, but with a heart full of rejoicing, I thanked the Lord for His timely help in this situation when I might have been terribly humiliated or, worse still, might have exploded in a fit of anger at the zealous young officer.

Now at last done with this irksome fellow, I faced the last examination, the one at the Hong Kong border. It was very different. My examiner was an older man and he asked, not unkindly, "Why are you leaving China? You write our words, you speak our language and you eat our food — why are you leaving?"

I suppose I was expected to say, "Well, you won't let us stay any longer, and if we did we wouldn't be allowed to do anything." But somehow I knew enough not to put my foot in my mouth like that and possibly get sent back to Shanghai. Instead I answered simply, "Well, I've been in China for almost five years now, and it is time to go home. My father will have his eightieth birthday in July, and if I leave now I'll be home in time for his birthday celebration."

The eightieth birthday is a very big celebration indeed in China; so my examiner replied, "Oh yes!

You should certainly go home for your father's birthday. Give him my regards, and do hurry back!"

Much relieved, I replied, "Yes, I'll be happy to give him your regards, and I hope to be back soon." Even as I spoke I thought, *I wonder where God will send me for further work with the Chinese?* And a more sobering question surfaced too. Would I indeed be able to help Father celebrate his eightieth birthday? Back in Shanghai I had received word that he was seriously ill with a very bad heart condition. Because then he was expected to have just three months to live, I had no idea now if he was living or not. At times like these God Himself is our only resting place.

As we crossed at last into freedom, we really began to experience the sharp pangs of fear for those we had left behind. I was especially remembering the students from my Bible study in Shanghai. At our last study, knowing we were about to part, I had asked them, "What message do you want me to take to the praying people in America?"

One girl replied immediately, "Tell them to pray that we will know we are overcomers; that He that is in us is greater than he that is in the world." And then another girl started the chorus, "Thou wilt keep him in perfect peace whose mind is stayed on Thee." After that we sang, "He will hold me fast," and finished with the doxology, "Praise God from whom all blessings flow." That is the spirit in which they were facing the future!

And so, although we were leaving them physically, it was clear to us that our next step was to pray faithfully for those who had to stay behind, that they would indeed be kept by the power of God in whom they were all putting their trust.

13

New start

Hong Kong — shoppers' paradise and gate to the Far East for tourists — had now become a safe harbor for hordes of homeless refugees. Finding housing at this time when so many people were fleeing China was next to impossible. While the Lord's answer to the mission's dilemma of providing shelter for its missionary exiles pouring out of China didn't involve a swank hotel, He did provide — nine quonset huts, courtesy of the Hong Kong government. The location was not exactly ideal. But I think that of all the places I have ever stayed in my many travels, this place, dubbed "Free Haven", was best — certainly not because of comfort or beauty of surroundings, but because it was a very special haven prepared for us by God. As we settled in without privacy and without elbow room to spare, we shared our experiences, praised God for His faithfulness and safekeeping, and prayed for those still in China, missionaries and Chinese friends alike.

About the first thing I did on arrival was look for letters from home and, to my surprise and relief, there were letters from Dad. He was still living! What joyous news!

But then it was time for me to have another interview with Mr. Sinton! He kindly suggested that I go right home for a short furlough in view of the fact that my father was alone and not well; then I could return to the Far East after a few months. He assured me, too, that when I was ready and able to return there would be work for me to do. Having had such a rough beginning as a new missionary, I was comforted to hear that I wasn't considered a flop and that I could look forward to coming back.

And so, after only ten or eleven days in Hong Kong, I was bound for home and *flying*, thanks to a special gift. This was, of course, before the days of jets; so the trip was taken in stages, stopping for the night in places like Bangkok and Calcutta; and then an unexpected few weeks' vacation in London, lovingly provided by my family. Those few weeks were very good for me, giving me time to adjust and also to get some decent new clothes!

From England the last lap of my trip was by ship, another good opportunity to do some more thinking and praying. When we docked in New York, my two sisters came over from Pennsylvania to meet me. I was home! We phoned Dad from New York City to help him get used to the reality of my actually being back on American soil. I think we were all a bit afraid what the shock of reunion might do to his heart. (Some of my friends might tell me that my face would stop a clock, but how terrible it would be if my reappearance stopped my father's heart!)

But when we got home, I walked into the house casually and said, "Hi, Dad," kissing him.

His answer was a simple, "Hi, Hon," and that was that.

Perhaps I was the one who was shocked. Dad looked so old and feeble now. It was obvious that he was pining for Mother. I had to get used to her absence too, but very soon we all felt as though I had merely been off on a trip to Philadelphia, and we took up just where we'd left off. How I thanked the Lord for undertaking for us so graciously in this important relationship!

It was the middle of May now, and beautiful springtime in Pennsylvania — with dogwood trees, redbud, rhododendron and mountain laurel, fruit trees and flowers all in bloom. I had almost forgotten how beautiful they could be. The spring slipped by into hot, humid summer, and then came the glorious colorful fall with that nip in the air which makes one glad to be alive.

During these months Dad and I took many drives. We visited his favorite boyhood haunts, and he did a lot of reminiscing about things which happened many years ago. Mother, of course, still figured largely in his conversations, though she had been gone almost four years now; I'm sure it was good for him to be able to talk about her freely. At first he did not ask much about my life in China. But after four months he began asking questions which revealed that he had practically memorized my letters! We were truly enjoying each other and sharing things that mattered, and I was coming to know my father in a new way.

But the days were passing too quickly, and I knew I should be considering the future. We didn't talk about it but, as though reading my mind, one day in late October Dad turned to me as we were driving with, "You feel you should go back, don't you?"

I couldn't deny it, and I shot a quick glance at him to see how he was looking. "Yes, Dad, I feel I should," I answered simply.

"I feel you should too," he said confidently, and then added, "You know, when I was very sick, I asked the Lord to let me see you once more. He has given me that request, and I'm not asking any more. I don't love you more than I love the Lord, and I don't want you to love me than you love Him. Should the way open up for you to go, I feel you should go back."

Knowing that it couldn't be easy for him to say these things, I appreciated his attitude more than words could express. How easily he might have said, "I'm an old man now, and I need you; I think you should stay home."

Even though Dad felt so positive about my returning to the field, I prayed much about it and, on my birthday in January 1952, I had a special time of waiting on the Lord about it. As I had already been home about eight months, I felt that it was time to go back. I really didn't know enough about the new fields the mission was entering to have any definite preference as to a new place of work, but the Lord knew. So I was praying for a definite indication regarding His direction.

To my great surprise, the day after my birthday Mr. Griffin, our U.S.A. Home Director, telephoned from Philadelphia and asked if I would be willing to sail for Hong Kong in March! It was a very quick answer to my prayer! My reply was full of understandable curiosity. "Well, where am I going?"

"We're not sure about your final designation yet," he replied. "There is an invitation for you to go to a Bible school in Taiwan, but that's not been finalized; so for the present you will go to Hong Kong. We need to go slowly and be very clear that we're doing the right thing because of possible repercussions on those who acted as your guarantors." I understood what he meant. In order to get exit visas it had been necessary for each of us to have two Chinese who would guarantee against any indebtedness on our part, and also to be responsible for anything we might say. This latter item, needless to say, made us very careful to say nothing which might be displeasing to the communists.

My family received Mr. Griffin's news as from the Lord, and the next day I drove to Philadelphia to talk over details at C.I.M. headquarters. Booked to sail on the *Queen Mary* March 13, I had just six weeks now to get ready. The Lord made those busy days a special blessing to Dad and me, and we became closer than ever before.

When I got to Hong Kong, everyone seemed very curious about my being there. "What are you going to do here?" was a question I kept hearing. I could answer only that I was awaiting further instructions. Not for several weeks did I get the "green light" to go ahead to Taiwan.

The C.I.M. was not starting up a new work in Taiwan — there was already an established church on the island — but workers were going in by invitation to help existing groups. My invitation was from Andrew Gih, a Chinese evangelist I had known in Shanghai. He had recently opened a Bible school in Taiwan, and I was to be on the teaching staff.

My introduction to my new place of work was very pleasant indeed. The trip from Hong Kong to Taiwan across the Formosa[1] Strait went quickly and as the

Taiwan was previously known as Formosa.

S.S. Yung Sheng (Steamship of Eternal Life) edged her way into the harbor at the northern port city of Keelung, I thrilled at the green mountains I could see. Later, on the trip south by rail with friend and fellow-missionary Ruth Nowack, we traveled through these mountains, our train threading through fourteen tunnels, then bursting out of each one to a new and beautiful vista. As the terrain flattened out towards the center section of the island in the area where I was to live, the mountains gave way to well-groomed farms and carefully tended rice paddies. How green everything was — nothing like what I was used to in dusty inland China. I felt sure I was going to like Taiwan.

At the Taichung railroad station I was met by the whole student body of the Bible school, the pastor of the church and many of the church people. Their warm welcome made me feel I was really wanted.

The church was an independent Mandarin-speaking group composed of people who had all fled Mainland China. Started in the home of a Christian air force general and his wife, Grace Church had begun with about ten believers. Now the congregation of about two hundred had just moved into a new church building. No wonder that they had felt led to call themselves Grace Church, honoring the One whose grace had brought them into being! I was thrilled at being associated with this group.

A brand-new era in my life was beginning to take shape. In less than a year after leaving China I was back among the Chinese. The Lord had again led as He once promised me, step by step.

But my new start wasn't to be an easy one. I soon discovered that, because one of the teachers was ill, I was supposed to start teaching the very next day!

Inwardly gasping in horror at this news, I begged for a few days to sort myself out. However, in about three days' time I was teaching classes in Old Testament outlines — never mind time to make adjustments, to brush up on my Chinese, or to make lesson plans.

I was overwhelmed when I found out all that I was being asked to teach, *in Chinese* — Doctrine, New Testament Survey, Old Testament Outlines, Hebrews, and several of Paul's epistles! I had assumed that along with some Bible I would be teaching English. But when I mentioned this, staff members explained that getting Chinese to teach English was easy; it was finding Chinese-speaking Bible teachers that was hard! This rather amused me — especially when a government official who attended our church told me that I spoke English very well (and later asked me whether I was singular or plural!)

Barely able to keep more than a step or two ahead of my students as it was, I was a bit chagrined to discover very shortly that I was not only expected to teach in the school but to take on a fair portion of work in the church as well, such as helping with the young people and giving a hand in the women's work. And work it was, as I was soon to realize!

The young people's ministry was a rather new venture headed up by a lovely Chinese lady. As she and I began to plan and work together, we got the idea of holding a young people's conference. Sure that it was the right thing to do after we had prayed much about it, we began to make plans and to advertise our intentions. Instantly we met opposition. Some older people in the church could see no value in such a conference, suspecting our idea was to get the young people together in some sort of matrimonial scheme! One old gentleman in particular opposed us so strongly that he stopped attending services when we would not give in to his opinion. All we could do was pray for him as we went ahead with preparations, feeling sure the Lord did want us to hold the conference.

Before long everything was in readiness, or so we thought! We had speakers, the meeting place, and transportation promised for our final outing to Sun Moon Lake. But suddenly, just a few days before the conference was to open, we got the bad news that our main speaker couldn't come. Shaken by this setback, we were cast on the Lord more than ever, and even began to have qualms about going ahead. But as we prayed for God's clear direction, He moved us to believe that it was because He had rich blessing in store for us that we were getting such opposition. The devil wanted to stop these meetings. Now we made a firm decision that the conference would go ahead as planned, even if we had to take all of the meetings ourselves. But our problems were still there, and now we ran into difficulties about the location. It was just one thing after another!

A solution to our speaker problem came when we unexpectedly heard about two Americans wanting to hold meetings; they had just arrived in Taiwan after speaking in Japan. Though knowing next to nothing about them, the committee took a chance and invited them to come. When they accepted immediately, we felt they must indeed be God's choice. Perhaps we were too hasty.

The conference started on schedule, and opposition was apparent at once. The congregation just did not respond to the messages. The speakers, knowing no Chinese, had to be interpreted and, worse still, used illustrations that were not at all relevant to life in Taiwan! We felt sick; though some of us were always in the prayer room during the meetings asking the Lord to break down barriers and send His blessing on us, nothing happened. No blessing came. Instead we heard more and more grumbling. "We told you so. God doesn't want this kind of thing." Oh, it was a rugged time! And, unfortunately, I had to admit to myself that apart from the Bible studies and discussion groups there didn't seem to be very much worthwhile taking place.

The last day of conference came, the day we had planned our outing to Sun Moon Lake. This famous holiday resort up in the mountains was a four-hour bus ride away, and we needed to leave at six in the morning. Up there we would have a boat trip across the lake to visit an aboriginal village, and then finish off by playing games before returning for the testimony meeting in Taichung that night. Needless to say, this trip would be the highlight of the conference for most of the young people! We had especially included it as a reward for those attending the entire conference, to keep out those who just wanted the nice outing. Even the plans for this activity had been full of problems. Our transportation arrangements had fallen through, and the pastor was just about to announce that the trip was called off when, in answer to our very earnest prayers, someone had come offering three army trucks for the trip!

A happier, jollier group of young people could scarcely have been found than finally started out that morning. The weather was perfect. Somehow, however, we who were leaders and speakers were peculiarly burdened in spirit, feeling a heaviness like a dark cloud hanging over us. But we had had a special time of prayer before leaving, committing the whole party to the Lord's keeping, and now we were off.

As we bounced along in the trucks, steadily ascending the winding road, we all exclaimed over the ever-green-covered mountains. Most of us had never taken this trip before, and the mountains, shimmering in the hot August sun, were much higher than I had imagined. Just imagine the chattering and fun on these trucks! The sound of singing echoing through the hills brought curious folk out to the roadside as we passed through villages on our way. The young people were especially enjoying a new chorus they had learned at conference:

"With Christ in my vessel I can smile at the storm,
      Smile at the storm, smile at the storm,
      With Christ in my vessel I can smile at the storm
      Until the day is done.
      Sailing, sailing home; sailing, sailing home,
      With Christ in my vessel I can smile at the storm,
      Until He leads me home."

Little did anyone realize how prophetic these words were.

We were nearly two-thirds along our way now, the narrow road steeper, unpaved and often badly rutted. There was no guard rail and beyond the shoulder the road fell away, a sheer drop of nearly a hundred feet down to the rocky river bed below. Just now the river was dry, bare rocks and boulders jutting up all over the river bed. Suddenly, out of nowhere, an old man started to make his way across the road right in front of the first truck! Frantically the driver yanked his steering wheel, swerving the truck out of the man's way. But the old fellow, becoming panicky, began to totter now forward, now back, like a chicken in the road. Miraculously the driver would be about to miss him, only to have him step again right into the truck's path. Back and forth, back and forth he stumbled, zigzagging across the road, so dazed he didn't know what to do.

Eventually the driver lost control of the truck, and it headed for the edge of the road. From our place in the second truck we watched aghast as it veered towards the cliff edge. Thirty-six girls, the wife of a Chinese diplomat, and the driver were headed for certain death. As the cab of the truck pierced nothingness out over the precipice, and the rear wheels began to rise to plunge the vehicle and passengers onto the rocks below, suddenly there was a sharp screeching noise and, with a terrific lurch backward, the truck stopped! We stared at it with horror, so terrified we couldn't even scream, expecting any minute to hear the deafening crash as it hit those rocks, demolishing it and crushing the passengers. But no! As though a mighty hand had reached out and held it, the truck just stood still, perched precariously on the edge of the cliff.

Urgently we warned the girls on the truck to move very carefully to the back, so as to balance the vehicle while one of the other trucks was being hitched up to pull it back to safety. The next few moments were strained and tense, but at last the danger was past. The girls were permitted to get off, many of them weeping uncontrollably, all shaking like the leaves of an aspen. Some now stood with bowed head, thanking God for their deliverance.

Suddenly we noticed what had kept the truck from plunging over the precipice. There growing out of a crag in the rocky cliff was a small tree, no bigger than a balled fist, but just big enough to stay the truck's plunge to destruction. It was the only tree along that part of the cliff. At first we all felt numb as we reflected on the miracle which had saved our young people, and then we spontaneously joined together to thank God for that tree and for His mercy. It made us think of another tree, the bridge between life and death for those who are perishing, the cross where God's Son bore our sins in His body so that we, being dead to sin, might live to righteousness. We finished with a wonderful time of praising God right there on the road.

It was a very different, more sober group of travelers which climbed back into the trucks. As on our way home we phoned the church to tell them of the close call we had had, we were met by quite a sizeable crowd of parents and church folk. Among them were some who were saying, now with even more scorn, "Didn't we tell you no good would come of your conference? Didn't we warn you?"

We replied with much feeling, "The devil wanted to work destruction today, but God has used this near tragedy to break through the callousness and coldness of many hearts. He has been glorified in it all. Just about everyone who was on this trip now knows in a new way the reality of God and how very much He cares for them."

That night at the testimony meeting, all of the girls who were not yet Christians put their trust in Jesus as a result of that experience; some of the boys whose hearts had been very hard turned to the Lord; and many young people offered their lives to Him for service. Then with much gratitude we once again joined in our special chorus.

As I prepared for bed that night, I read the day's portion for *Daily Light*. It was about praise: "I will greatly rejoice in the Lord; my soul shall be joyful in my God. I will bless the Lord at all times; His praise shall continually be in my mouth. My soul shall make her boast in the Lord; the humble shall hear thereof and be glad. O magnify the Lord with me, and let us exalt His name together." I was terribly weary — it had been an exhausting day — but I went to sleep rejoicing. Many young people had become the Lord's own. God had won the victory, and He was worthy of all praise.

This event marked the real beginning of the young people's work at Grace Church. They now decided to call themselves Grace Youth Group, not because they were part of Grace Church, but because of what had nearly happened on the mountain road and God's gracious deliverance. The revival among the young people caused quite a stir in the church, and the one who had opposed most strongly soon came back, confessing publicly that he had been an obstacle to God's working. This youth group has gone on for 27 years now, and God has continued to bless it, with many young people going on to serve the Lord.

But that was not to be the end of obstacles.

14
A round-trip ticket

It was almost time to start the new term in the Bible
school. I felt better prepared this time as I had been
able to work on preparation during the summer, and I
felt too that at last I was really getting a grip on
the language. Somehow, however, although I was
enjoying my work and seeing encouragements among
both students and church young people, I just didn't
have my usual pep. I'd had two bouts of surgery that
year and was probably taking longer to recuperate
because of the heat, I thought. In my recent annual
physical nothing had seemed to be out of order, except
that I was running a slight fever. As the doctor hadn't
shown any real concern, I just chalked it up to the very
hot summer weather.

Then, just after the opening exercises of the new
term, I received a letter from Mr. Gordon Dunn, our
Taiwan Superintendent. It appeared the doctor wanted
me to have another physical and was prescribing six
weeks' complete rest beforehand. Whatever could be
wrong? I felt nothing but rebellion and anger at this

blow, for I was sure there was nothing serious to worry about. I was all prepared and eager to get on with my ministry. But obviously God purposed otherwise.

Much as I didn't want to stay in bed, there was nothing I could do but obey orders. My temperature wasn't high, but it followed a regular pattern, like the curve of tuberculosis. I guessed what they were thinking, though x-rays showed nothing. A friend had an extra bedroom and I spent my six weeks' rest with her; but the temperature didn't go away. Six more weeks' rest was ordered, and the doctor was beginning to talk about a trip to Hong Kong for further tests. I didn't want to go to Hong Kong; I'd been there twice already for operations that year. The young people had kidded me about it: "Once you've finally had everything taken out of you, you'll be able to live a normal life!" Fortunately I had a good sense of humor! But now I wasn't feeling like laughing. I just wanted to get on with my work.

Finally I had to commit the whole matter to the Lord, praying that if I was to go to Hong Kong He would provide money for the round-trip ticket from some unexpected source. If I was to go but not return, I asked that He would provide a one-way fare; and if I wasn't to go over at all, that no money would come! I didn't tell anyone about my prayer; but as I was reading my *Daily Light* portion that day, November 6th, God assured me that I had done the right thing to commit it all to Him: "Lead me in Thy truth and teach me," I read, and "I will guide thee and teach thee in the way that thou shalt go. I will guide thee with mine eye."

I went on with my work in time, and my temperature seemed to be coming down. Then, to my surprise, on December 12th I received a letter from America which had taken at least six weeks to come by surface mail. In the envelope was a check, all by itself, with no letter or return address, just the name of a church in Trenton, N.J., where I had spoken one time. The check was made out for $48.95. *What an odd amount!* I thought to myself. *Why wouldn't they make it out for $49.00 or $50.00 like most people?* The date on the check was November 6th!

The very next day the doctor came to see me. "After conferring with several other doctors, I feel you should go to Hong Kong as soon as possible." When I changed the check into local currency, I had just enough for a round-trip air ticket to Hong Kong, plus my pedicab fare to the air company office!

And so, before I knew it, I was in Hong Kong again. At the hospital I underwent a very thorough battery of examinations including those for parrot fever, monkey fever and undulant fever. All tests were negative. And the x-rays were clear. It was a mystery to me what I was doing in Hong Kong.

Then one evening in the hospital our supper menu included greasy sausages. Not long after eating I got really sick, losing my supper all over the bed. The nurse called the doctor, and he came running.

"Whatever happened?" he asked.

"My stomach simply rebelled against those sausages. Do you think my problem might be gall bladder?"

Sure enough, the next day after a series of gall bladder tests the puzzle seemed to be solved. Normally my diet was fat free since I lived with a missionary who had sprue. The sausages with their high fat content, however, had unmasked the culprit. Although the doctors would have preferred not to operate on me again so soon after my previous surgeries, they decided they had to and put me on the table on January 25th.

I made a good recovery, and when friends came to visit me one Sunday afternoon about two weeks later I was feeling fine. They left assured that I would be discharged any day now. But supper brought a terrific relapse. Again I started vomiting, but this time I couldn't stop. In a few hours I became thoroughly dehydrated, and my whole body ached so much that I couldn't stand someone even touching the bed. In spite of injections, the pain was excruciating. When tests showed that my red blood cells were breaking, I began getting blood transfusions. By two o'clock in the morning I had lapsed into a coma.

None of my friends in Hong Kong, of course, knew a thing about my condition. As far as they knew I was doing just fine.

Sometime in the wee hours, through the mists of my unconsciousness, I heard the doctor tell a nurse that my family in America ought to be cabled that I was dying. I'd be gone by morning, I heard him tell her — there was absolutely nothing more they could do for me.

I understood what they were saying — my mind was quite alert. *No!* I wanted to shout. *Not that! Such a cable might kill Dad, with his bad heart!* But I couldn't even let the doctor know I realized what was going on.

Then a wonderful thought popped into my mind: *I can't die — I have a round-trip ticket!* The Lord had provided that round-trip ticket; surely that meant He purposed that I should return to Taiwan. I tried to muster enough strength to say something. Apparently noticing my efforts, the doctor stooped over to moisten my lips, then leaned closer to hear what I suppose he thought were my last words. "You can go off duty," I told him, "because I'm not going to die."

The doctor wasn't convinced.

But I did rally. Not that the doctors had been able to do anything for me — they knew the situation was out of their hands. Though I continued to vomit for three more days, I began to show improvement.

When the vomiting stopped, hiccoughing started and continued for days on end. Warm glucose helped, and it was also the only thing I could keep down. I was existing on warm glucose and the promises of God — but I was existing. How, the doctors still couldn't make out — I should have died.

Then one day the mystery began to unfold, in a couple of letters from Taiwan which arrived shortly after I started to improve; one was from my missionary friend Ruth Nowack, and the other from Mrs. Chu, my good Chinese friend and fellow worker. Ruth wanted to tell me about the strange experience she had had on the night of February 5th, the night I was at death's door. About two a.m. she was awakened suddenly with the compulsion that she must pray for me — something was wrong. The Lord not only urged her to pray, but to get out of bed and pray on her knees.

"I can pray in bed," she argued with the Lord. After all, it can be quite cold in Taiwan in February — damp, penetrating cold that goes right to the bones.

But it was as though the Lord said to her, "You can't pray in bed. You'll fall asleep."

"But, Lord," Ruth continued to reason, "Pauline's out of the hospital now, surely." But she still had no peace and, at last, got out of bed, knelt down and committed me to the Lord. She climbed back into bed then and fell right off to sleep.

The letter from Mrs. Chu told of a similar experience. And in the course of a week I received two more letters, one from a missionary friend in Tokyo and one from America. Each one explained the special burden they had had to pray for me and, taking into consideration the time changes, I worked it out that these four people had all been earnestly praying for me on that night of February 5th. What a prayer meeting!

When I shared this news with the doctors, they gladly gave God the credit for my restoration, for they knew they had done all they could to no avail. The miraculous healing had come from Him and, I knew, according to His foreordained plan. This whole experience was so obviously under His control that I wasn't even allowed to pay the bill, though I tried for more than a year! "To see you alive and healthy means more to us than the money," was how they expressed it. "We knew the situation was out of our hands."

And so my gall bladder was not, after all, the source of one more interruption to *my* work, but the means of God's receiving much glory.

15
Haunted house

While in Hong Kong I naturally thought and prayed about the work I had left at the Bible school, but somehow I didn't sense the Lord leading me back there. Instead I had an increasing burden for university students. While I was on bed rest before my gall bladder surgery, two university students from church had come in regularly for times of prayer with me. They were eager to get some sort of witness started on their campus. While I was away they contacted several other Christians in their school, and by the time I got back to Taichung the little group had grown to ten.

Learning while still in hospital that a fine Chinese person was teaching my courses in the Bible school, I was more convinced than ever that I should not return there. So when the Bible school very kindly wrote to invite me to return, I began my answer by reminding them that they had managed quite well without me all year, and then shared with them my burden for university students. Not only did *they* approve of my moving over to student work, so did the church. Then when I got back to Taiwan the students came around right away to ask for my help, and so it seemed the Lord was really putting His seal on this as His way for me.

Twice a week the small group of students and I had prayer together, with the students taking charge and growing in the doing of it. Numbers increased steadily. At last they came to ask me if we could begin a Bible study. I had been praying for this very thing and was delighted that the suggestion had come from them.

One day a delegation came to ask me another question. "Would you be able to move closer to the university? Your home is so far away," they explained. "It would be so much more convenient if you were on our side of the city; then more students would be able to come to see you."

It just so happened that the missionary I lived with was getting ready to go on furlough, and I was going to have to find new lodgings anyway. When our super-intendent gave his approval to the idea, house-hunting began in earnest.

Before too long we discovered just the place — a small house in a row of Japanese-style houses, about five minutes' walk from the university and with very low rent. The landlord promised to repair the place as it was in rather bad shape. I guess we did wonder at the time why the rent was so cheap and why he was so willing to fix up the house, but we didn't ask questions as it seemed just perfect. It even had sliding paper doors so that two rooms could be opened up into a large area for meetings.

Soon the students were finding their way to my new place and both the prayer meetings and Bible studies grew in numbers as they brought their friends along. Many began to seek me out for counseling too.

I was so very happy to be working among college students once again — it was almost like coming home to Nanking or Shanghai.

Almost. When I moved into my house, neighbors were bewildered. "Are you going to *live* in that house?" my close neighbor wanted to know.

"Yes," I answered, puzzled, "Why?" I wondered if maybe there was anti-foreign feeling in the area, or at least suspicion of westerners.

"That house is haunted," she replied unexpectedly, her eyes betraying genuine fear. She was incredulous that anyone would dare to move into a house inhabited by evil spirits. *So that was why the rent was so cheap!* I thought.

My house was indeed in a section of the city where the worship of the powers of darkness was concentrated. Temples were everywhere. At times I could sense the evil of the place, particularly during religious festivals.

A few days later my neighbor called over the fence, "Have you seen any ghosts?"

"No, I haven't," I replied calmly.

"Haven't you heard lots of queer sounds and un-explainable noises?" she persisted.

"Oh yes, there are those," I agreed, "but that's just the scratching and bumping of rats in the loft. I'll get some good rat poison and we'll have all the spooks out in no time. You know, I'm a Christian, and God has told us that He that is in us is greater than he that is in the world. I'm not afraid."

I was glad for this opportunity to share my confidence in God with her. These poor people were so terrified of evil spirits that they lived each day in dread, forced to appease the demons at every turn lest some calamity befall them.

But after this I had to confess to myself that there did seem to be queer things going on in my house. At first it was annoying when little things in the house moved from one place to another. I thought perhaps those rats in the loft were the pack-rat variety, or maybe with so much going on I was just getting forgetful. But there never was any satisfactory solution to this queer business.

Anyway, there was no time to dwell on it. It soon became obvious that God was answering prayer. The students were becoming more and more burdened for their unsaved classmates, and one of them suggested praying toward a special evangelistic outreach. Others, though a bit skeptical about whether non-Christians would come, were open-minded enough to pray about it. And as we kept praying over the next several months, the students were openly growing in the Lord and boldly witnessing on campus. Finally we felt the time had come to organize our evangelistic campaign. As such meetings as we envisioned could not be held on campus, we arranged to borrow a hall not too far from the university. The speaker we invited for our three-day campaign was a medical doctor from Taipei, a man the students highly respected and loved. We laid our plans with much prayer, and turned the Bible study into a class on personal evangelism. The Christian students themselves were going to do all of the personal work at the meetings.

When the day came for our first meeting, we couldn't help but wonder if anyone would come. Not that we hadn't advertised. Invitations had been sent out and posters placed on all the bulletin boards (though some were torn down). Yet by 7.15 p.m., with the meetings scheduled to start at 7.30, only a handful had dribbled in. Then all of a sudden at about 7.20

the students began to pour into the little hall until it was fairly bursting at the seams. Some even had to stand outside.

We were beside ourselves with joy at what the Lord was doing. All through the meeting Christian students were taking turns in a little side room set apart for prayer. The message was a very clear presentation of the Gospel, simple enough for the many who had no concept what the Gospel was all about, but at the same time deep enough to challenge those with some background in Christian things. When an invitation was given at the close, our joy soared as a number expressed their desire to accept the Lord Jesus as personal Savior. Some of these we had earnestly and specifically prayed for! The Christian students entered wholeheartedly into the personal work, and all three nights we witnessed the effect of the Holy Spirit's moving in people's hearts.

Even the university felt the impact. In fact, so many students came off campus to attend the meetings that the Dean of Student Affairs himself came along to see what was going on. He was very impressed with what he saw and heard.

Thirty students in all came to the Lord during those meetings. We decided that new believers should each be discipled by the person who had invited them — studying the Bible together, sharing about how to have a "quiet time," and going to church together. Both those leading and those being led benefited from this arrangement. Disciplers grew noticeably as they helped the new-born Christians, encouraged to be used of God and rejoicing to see their charges established.

But the devil does not stand idle while Christians go about zealously serving the Lord, and some of his schemes were about to be uncovered.

One day while I was preparing for the church young people's meeting, my dog Cinderella began to behave very strangely, running back and forth and jumping up at me. When she had continued this long enough to get me really annoyed, I shouted, "Oh, Cindy, stop it! What's gotten into you? I don't have time to play with you now. Just let me finish this preparation, and then we'll play." But with a loud whine and a hurt expression, Cindy continued her running, back and forth, back and forth, now almost frenzied. Fortunately this behavior triggered a new thought: *Maybe she's trying to get me to look at something.* My annoyance turned into curiosity, and I let her lead me.

When we got to the back door I looked out and there, just about four feet from my house, a roaring fire was licking up everything in its path! As I heard some very faint, but frantic, *gobble-gobbles*, I realized suddenly what had happened. My neighbor's turkeys had evidently overturned the warming stove in their pen, setting their house afire. I ran and called in an alarm, and thankfully the fire company was on the scene in a short time. Miraculously there was no wind; otherwise the whole block of wooden houses might have gone up in flames, mine included. All the houses were old, some even dating back to the days of Japanese occupation in the early 1900s. Not only was the wood dry, but all the homes had *tatami* (straw-mat) floors. As the firemen extinguished the flames, I said a grateful *thank you* to the Lord and immediately went out to buy a special treat of liver for little Cinderella, my faithful canine fellow-worker and protector.

It wasn't long before another incident occurred that further convinced me that the enemy was working hard to squelch my ministry for God. I had my own strawberry patch in my little yard, and each morning I'd go out to pick a few berries to have on my breakfast cereal. What a treat! (How's that for the hardships of missionary life?) One day, however, as I was on my way out to the strawberry patch, Cinderella planted herself in front of me and started to snarl and snap at me. As she had never done anything like this before, I didn't know what to make of it, but decided not to tangle with her in this mood. When I turned to go back into the house, Cindy bolted directly into the strawberry bed, attacking something fiercely. In minutes she was back, carrying a dead snake in her jaws. When she laid it at my feet, I saw that it was not very long, and its bright green color blended in perfectly with the green of the plants. It looked too pretty to be harmful, but in fact I recognized it as the deadly bamboo snake, one of the most poisonous in all Taiwan. Once again Cindy got her liver!

I wasn't frightened at these happenings, though they were evidently attacks from the enemy. Yet it was unsettling wondering what would happen next.

Soon after I settled into my new home I had begun a meeting for neighborhood women. I was surprised how many came right from the first. True, every Thursday afternoon women from Grace Church went from door to door inviting my neighbors to come. Still I suspected that some were coming just to get a look at the foreigner's house — and I later found that some wanted to see how the foreigner was faring in her haunted house!

Anyway, by this time the Lord was really blessing these Thursday meetings. Several of the women had put their faith in Jesus. The church women who came to help were now completely in charge — leading, speaking and doing the personal work. They would come early for a time of prayer and then go out visiting to remind the women to come. How thrilling it was to see these neighbors of mine coming to the Lord out of heathen worship, to watch their lives change, and to hear them tell how God was answering their prayers now that they had learned to take their burdens and needs to Him!

The women who came to the Bible study were a varied group, from old grannies to mothers with babies. A number of them were connected with either government service or the military, and had lived very differently back on the mainland. "We thought we had everything back there. Life was very comfortable," one lady explained. "I even had a servant to comb my hair. You foreigners went to preach to the poor and so we were miles apart. When we had to evacuate and settle over here, leaving just about everything behind, we began to discover that we really had nothing."

It is another woman who stands out most vividly in my memory. I first noticed her as I was passing by her little makeshift shanty down the alley from my house. This woman was quite small and looked undernourished. Though she must have been only in her mid to late thirties, she was so drawn and haggard-looking that she seemed much older. She had that blank, hopeless look often observed in the faces of those steeped in idolatry, eyes so empty and so full of darkness that they are hard to forget. *What a sad, pathetic woman!* I thought.

Hers seemed a peculiar situation. If the weather was good, her husband was always sitting out in front of the house. But he seemed bound to his chair! He had a vacant stare on his face, never responding to any kind of greeting; it was as if he saw no one. I wondered if he were blind, but on closer observation I noticed that he was indeed bound to the chair, by a combination of chains and leather thongs. I wondered why. Their place was swarming with children, but I wasn't sure whose they were.

We began to pray for this sad household in our Thursday meetings, and after quite a time the woman was persuaded to join us. The truth of the Gospel began to penetrate, its light shining into her darkened heart. With it hope began to dawn where there had been only despair. Eventually she began to attend regularly, in spite of much persecution and many beatings. And one day she made the decision that she would no longer go to the temples with offerings for the idols; neither would she make the daily offerings in her home. At last she made an open confession of her faith in Christ.

Now things became worse than ever for her. Yet she continued steadfast, the joy of the Lord giving her strength. She didn't understand very much, nor could she read — but she knew God loved her and had saved her, and she knew how to pray. As she poured out her heart to the Lord, telling Him about the cares of her life, she revealed much of her sufferings — and of her victory.

The devil could not allow this victory of the Lord to stand uncontested. I was all alone in my little house one day when I heard my gate suddenly crash open, followed by what sounded like a mob bursting into my small yard. I jumped up to look out of my window, and there pushing through my gate was an excited jumble of people, with the man who was usually bound to the chair in the lead. "Teacher, teacher, close your door!" the crowd yelled frantically. "Teacher, bolt your door!" Though at first I couldn't comprehend what was happening, I quickly obeyed instructions and slammed the door shut.

By now Cinderella was just about going wild. Venturing a quick glance out of the window, I understood in a flash — the neighbor man had become a raving maniac and with superhuman strength was now trying to break down my door to get into the house. Four or five men were struggling ineffectually to get control of him. He simply broke loose with a shrug and continued attacking my door with terrible force.

Now I panicked. I knew the door wouldn't take much more of his battering and smashing. Hardly knowing what I was doing, I hurried into the inner room, vainly closing the paper doors behind me. Those doors would be no protection at all should the madman get into the house! Scared to death, I just fell down on my knees and cried, "Lord, undertake for me now and cover me and this place with the blood of Jesus! Cast out Satan, for You have overcome him on Calvary!"

I don't know how long I was in there, but suddenly I realized that everything was quiet. Cindy had even stopped barking. Trembling, I got up from my knees and looked out into my front yard. It was absolutely empty. The gate was pulled shut, though hanging on one hinge, a small reminder of the devastation which had nearly come over my home. God had truly undertaken for me. (Later, by the way, in answer to much prayer, this man was delivered and never had any further seizures.)

Very shaken, I took time to wait quietly before the Lord and then took a long ride into the country on my bicycle. As I rode, I thought about the close call I had just had. Surely the devil was retaliating because my neighbor would no longer worship him, having destroyed her idols and related paraphernalia in order to worship the Lord Jesus. Satan had used her husband like a helpless pawn, giving him awful strength to try to destroy me. If I ever doubted it before, I knew now that I was involved in a war with powers and strategies in the heavenlies, but the battlefield was right down here on earth.

16
No man's debtor

Soon after these dramatic events, it was again time for me to go home on furlough. I arrived in early fall, and since Dad was now almost 83 I spent most of my time with him, once again enjoying our favorite drives in the surrounding countryside. Not long after Christmas, however, he began to go steadily downhill physically.

One day he said to me, "You're going back." Not sure whether this was a question or a statement, I answered cautiously, "Well, Dad, if you'd like me to stay with you, I'll stay home."

"Oh no you won't!" he exclaimed. "I won't have it! I know when your sailing date is, and you're going back on time."

I didn't say any more about this, and the subject didn't come up again for a while. Then in the early spring Arnold Lea, one of our directors from Singapore, was at a conference nearby and, knowing my father was ill, took the opportunity to visit us. I took him in to see Dad, stayed a while, and then excused myself to get some refreshments. As I was in the other room talking to the friend who had brought Mr. Lea, I became aware of Dad's voice getting louder and louder! *What's going on?* I wondered uneasily. Before long Mr. Lea came out. "Well, Pauline," he said, chuckling, "I can understand you a bit better now. You're a chip off the old block!"

"What makes you say that?" I asked. "What was going on in there? My dad sounded as though he really had his dander up."

"Well," Mr. Lea explained, "I was simply telling him that you could have an extension of furlough — that it's quite a common thing to do, so that you could stay and be of help to him while he needs you."

"What did Dad say to that?"

"Well, he really bristled and came at me with full force," Mr. Lea answered a bit sheepishly. "He told me I wasn't fit to be a director of a mission!" I had to laugh at this. Mr. Lea continued, "Your dad said, 'We take our orders from above, not from people like you.' He insists that if you stay home, he can't die peacefully. He doesn't want you to love him more than you love the Lord. He says he doesn't love you more."

I had of course heard Dad express himself this way before, so I wasn't surprised.

"That wasn't all," Mr. Lea continued. "Your dad said that if we say we are soldiers of the Cross, we should act like soldiers; and he also told me about how when he was very sick he prayed to have one more chance to see you, and how God gave him his wish. Now he doesn't want to ask more lest there be leanness of soul for himself or for you, Pauline."

I don't know if Mr. Lea had then been told to get out of the room or not, but I'm afraid my father wasn't as courteous as he might have been. Fortunately Mr.

Lea seemed to find the visit refreshing! I'm afraid I found it a bit embarrassing.

Dad's condition continued to worsen after that. But each day he insisted that I read him the book of Revelation — the *whole book*. "We must read that book," Dad explained. "It's the only book in the Bible that promises a blessing to those who read it." So I read it every day while he sat in his rocking chair. When I saw his head droop as though he was dozing, I would lower my voice or maybe try to skip a bit, but he'd say, "Hey, you missed some." Then I'd have to back up and read it again! And that's how it went on every day — because, he said, "I don't want to miss the blessing."

The hardest thing was seeing one I loved go down, down, down — at times not himself, irrational in speech and action. For several days he was in a coma. When he rallied, he said to me, "What day is this?" When I told him he asked, "What happened to the other three days?"

"Dad, you were very ill," I explained.

Then he apologized, "I don't know what I might have done or said, but don't take it to heart. Please forgive me." I was glad he said that, for sometimes he said things that hurt.

It was a time of great strain as I knew I would be leaving him soon. I didn't want to go, but he was adamant. As time went on the question never left me: *Should I go or shouldn't I?* But when Dad was rational he would say, "You've got ten more days," or however many there were, and I'd know I had to go.

Well-meaning friends kept urging me to get a rest before returning to the field. "You're so tired," they said, "You should leave a couple of weeks early and rest in California before sailing."

"No," I said. "I could never forgive myself if I went ahead of time and something happened to Dad."

Knowing the day I had to leave for the west coast, my dad got up that day dressed in his best suit, and was looking very perky. He must have mustered all his strength to do this, not wanting me to feel bad and trying to show me how well he was. After a lovely time of prayer together, it was time for me to go. He went out on the front porch with me, kissed me and waved me off as though I was just going to the city. I *was* just going to the city — but then I'd be taking the train to the west coast, with a stopover in Chicago to see friends. That evening when I telephoned home, everything was fine and Dad and I had a nice chat. On arrival in California I phoned again. This time he was in the hospital! How tempted I was to return! But his words rang in my ears, "If you stay I can't die peacefully. We say we're soldiers — let's act like soldiers." I obeyed his wishes, though reluctantly.

The Lord had a big surprise for me on that journey back to Taiwan. I was booked to sail from the west coast on the *President Wilson*, a truly beautiful ship. When I arrived at Los Angeles Mr. Walton, our mission representative, met me at the station. "Before we do anything else," he advised, "I think we should go over to the shipping office and have you check in; your ship has probably left San Francisco already, and we have to book you in at least 24 hours ahead of time."

Over at the shipping office I told the clerk, a tall blond man with merry blue eyes, who I was and where I was going, and showed him my ticket. He said nothing but disappeared into an inner office, coming out again finally with a letter in his hand.

"Dr. Hamilton," he began, "there seems to be some change — your booking has been canceled."

My heart sank right down to the soles of my shoes. "But you can't do that!" I argued. "My ticket is paid for, and I'm here on time. It's not right."

"Well, here, I'll show you the letter. See, your tourist class passage has been canceled. You are to go *first class*!"

My heart sank all over again. "I can't go first class!" I blurted out. "I don't have that kind of clothing; why, I don't even own a dinner dress. I don't have anything fit for first class. Do I have to pay the difference in price?" The words all came tumbling out in my confusion. He handed me the letter. All it said was that I was to be given first-class passage, and it gave my room number. There was no explanation, and not a word about the increase in price.

"I don't know what's happened," he said. "This is the order I've received — so you just go and enjoy yourself. You don't really need to worry about clothing. I'm sure you have some nice dresses. Besides, this is more of a cruise trip and people will not be dressing formally — you probably won't need a dinner dress."

I was now really rather in a daze. Just then Mr. Walton spoke up. "Well, Pauline, this is one time I guess you'll be a missionary to the 'up and outers'!"

"Yes," I answered, laughing. "It must be one of those times to feast when I feast, rather than fast when I fast." I thought of something else then. "You know, Mr. Walton, this is probably the Lord's way of giving me the rest I need!" And that is exactly the way it turned out. It was one of those extras the Lord often gives us when we least expect it and surely don't deserve it.

Mr. and Mrs. Walton and some other friends came down to the dock to see me off, and who else should be there but the clerk from the shipping office! He and his wife were traveling as far as Hawaii for a holiday. Knowing I felt rather strange about my change of status, they very kindly took a special interest in me, introducing me to everybody who was anybody on the ship, including the captain. They told him I was a C.I.M. missionary which I thought both interesting and strange, until I learned that he was a keen Christian and very interested in missions.

Everywhere the clerk and his attractive young wife escorted me, they introduced me as Dr. Hamilton — I've never been so "doctored" in all my life. But I just figured there's a time and a place for everything; after all, when Paul thought it would be to his advantage and would commend the Gospel to say he was a Roman, he said he was a Roman! Why shouldn't I admit I was a doctor? It did open up a good many opportunities to talk about my work, as most people at first assumed I was a medical missionary.

I was given a lovely outside cabin, which I shared with a very congenial woman who didn't smoke or drink either. I spent a lot of time up on the deck too, with my deck chair in a secluded area in the stern of the ship away from the wind and in a position to get the warming effects of the spring sun. It wasn't long before I realized that ours was a ship full of hungry souls, and indeed I did begin to feel like a missionary to the "up and outers", as Mr. Walton had said. There was one very nice older couple, for example, with whom I sat for meals. They must have been in their sixties, a homey pair and down to earth. Though he had a very high position in one of the big automobile companies in

Detroit, they did not put on any airs or advertise their wealth in any way. One day at dinner he said, "I understand that you are a missionary doctor. What hospital do you work in?"

"Well," I said, "I don't rise to that. I'm not the kind of doctor that does any good!"

"What do you mean by that?" he asked, smiling.

"I'm a physiologist by training. I did research work for about five years and also taught in college before I gave it up to go out to China as a missionary."

"Where did you get your doctorate?"

"University of Pennsylvania." I could see that this bit of information sent my percentage up considerably.

"Oh," he said, "that's Ivy League. Well, where did you do research work?"

"At the University of Pennsylvania," I replied. "I was working under a Rockefeller Grant."

"Oh, that was really something for a woman to have back in those days," he exclaimed, making me feel as if we were discussing some prehistoric period. Anyway, he was impressed when I explained how the Lord had given it.

"Where did you teach in college?" he asked next.

When I replied that I had taught at Smith College, they looked at each other meaningfully and told me, "We have one daughter. All her life she wanted to go to Smith College, but she couldn't make the grade. She wasn't accepted. All my money couldn't get her in there. But you, you throw a teaching position there overboard to go to the mission field with a mission that doesn't even offer a definite salary, promises you nothing!" As a businessman, he couldn't make any sense of this at all.

"Well, cheer up," I said. "I couldn't have gotten into Smith College as a student either, I'm sure. I just went in by the back door, on the teaching staff!" We laughed about that.

"You've just got to be out of your mind," he concluded.

"Well," I replied pleasantly, "if I am, I've been out of it for about ten years now and enjoying it very much! You're not the first to tell me that; but really, though the mission board makes no promises, I have had all the promises of God to count on."

Unknown to me, this couple was to be severely tested in the course of the next year. I wonder if they remembered anything I'd said to them.

The trip wasn't all resting and mingling with the other passengers; we called at Hawaii, Japan and the Philippines, and in each place I met O.M.F. friends and experienced more lovely extras from the Lord.

Last we called in at Hong Kong where I would transship for Taiwan. By this time I was certainly well rested. Out of curiosity I enquired at the shipping office about the extra expense of my luxury trip, and found that the first-class passage had cost three times as much as my tourist ticket! To this day I have no idea where the first-class booking actually came from, but the timing was perfect. Not only was I able to arrive back on the field with many new friends and my heart full of praise and gratitude — I arrived with a body and mind relaxed and resting in the Lord.

Just a month after my arrival in Taiwan I received a cable saying that God had called Dad Home. Many friends wrote letters and cards with nice verses and words of comfort, but there were also words of criticism. It was hard to take. I was criticized for not staying with

Dad yet in my heart I knew that this was one time I really had obeyed him. I'm sure it would have broken his heart if I hadn't returned to Taiwan, for he would have felt that he was the hindrance. I thank God for a parent like my dad, who was so one with me in the call and commitment that had been made. I had to learn in those days to live above the criticism of others who could not understand, as they knew nothing of the background of my going back at that time. I learned the precious lesson of trusting the Lord with the whole decision, realizing that He understood and that we live our lives before Him.

17
Does God still provide?

I arrived back in Taiwan to new opportunities and wide-open doors among students and young people. Not only were churches all over the city now sending young people with problems to see me, but the student work was going forward, and some young people from my earlier Bible classes were growing and getting a vision for student work. The idea of summer conference programs for university students was also becoming more popular, so that gradually leaders were able to unite and have an All-Taiwan summer conference rather than individual ones for each college and university. A student magazine had also started, and I was asked to write the daily Bible study notes for it, to help students with their quiet time.

In addition I had good contact with fellows in the military. On graduation from college all young men in Taiwan have to go for a year or so of military training, and the "boot camp" for basic training was located near Taichung where I lived. The recruits were free for most of Sunday and when word got around that there was always a welcome they started coming to my house. They knew they could bring their friends too — we called it the "Open door policy". The lads did the cooking, and though their concoctions were often weird and wonderful everyone claimed the food delicious even though they might not know what they were eating! And we had more than a variety of things to eat, we had discussions on a variety of subjects during which quite a few heard the Gospel for the first time.

Sometimes there seemed to be so many opportunities that it was hard for me to sort out my priorities. I had only so much time and energy. But seeing the students growing in the Lord and going on with Him in spite of opposition was a tremendous encouragement and thrill.

How often when the Lord is blessing, however, the devil does all he can to frustrate things! And so it happened that before very long he began to employ his devices not only to harass, but very nearly to wipe out the summer's work completely.

Plans were well under way for the second All-Taiwan Student Conference at which we expected between 150 and 200 students, considered quite a large group at that time. Good speakers had already accepted our invitation, we had a really fine program lined up and we were earnestly praying for God to be at work.

Since Taichung is in the center of Taiwan, it had been decided this was the best place to gather, and I had been able to obtain the use of a seminary's facilities for the conference. They had stipulated, however, that I bear sole responsibility. This put a lot of pressure on me. Ordinarily I would have turned over some of the details to students to care for, but instead I felt it best to care for them myself. And a conference for 200 students involves plenty of details, you can be sure.

At the same time Grace Church was preparing for their young people's conference, to be held just before the student one, and we were expecting 100 to 150 junior and senior high-schoolers to attend that. Again there was lots to be done, but fortunately the committee was working well and had a good spirit of cooperation among themselves. With their real sense of responsibility I could breathe a bit easier, which was good since I still had my ministry among women; and then the troubled young people coming to me seemed to be on the increase, especially during these summer months when they had more time on their hands.

So we were all working hard and praying hard, believing that God would really bless in the two conferences. And then the devil tried to disrupt everything. It was over the matter of money.

We were having to trust the Lord to bring in the funds to cover the expenses of both conferences. Initially there had been some discussion about whether to charge a fee, but most felt that this would keep young people from large families from attending. So it was decided to trust God to supply all our needs. This was indeed a real venture of faith.

One Saturday about two weeks before the church conference, several people came to my house with money half an hour or so after the banks had closed. One had a gift for the All-Taiwan Student Conference, another money for the young people's conference, while a third was bringing me my OMF board and personal allowance for the next three months. Our secretary was to be away, so as I would not be able to draw cash from him I got the lump sum in advance.

My question, of course, was what to do with all this money over the weekend! As I was rushing off to a meeting that afternoon, I hastily hid it in all sorts of places around the house. But somehow I did not feel at all happy about this arrangement and had an uncomfortable feeling that something was going to happen; so after the meeting I hurried home, changed all the hiding places and snapped another padlock on the door. Then, leaving the lights on in the house as if I were at home, I was off again to the evening young people's meeting.

After that meeting the president of the group — a tall, good-looking boy who was a commissioned officer in the Taiwan air force — came up to me greatly concerned about the financial needs for the conference. To encourage him, I told him about the gifts that had just come to me from students and young people who were out of town. This, I said, was God's seal that every penny would be supplied, reminding him of the verse, "My God shall supply all your needs according to His riches in glory by Christ Jesus" (Philippians 4:19).

"God has given us His promise," I continued, "and His promises never fail. I am willing to place my hand on the Bible and affirm my faith in His promise," and this I did. Then we had a word of prayer together, committing the whole matter to the Lord. I had absolute peace in my heart, sure that the Lord was going to meet every need.

What I did not know was that at that very moment someone was in my house taking every last penny!

I went along home from the meeting, a little earlier than usual, and spent a few minutes chatting with a neighbor outside the house. I shot a glance over at my house as we talked and everything seemed in order —

I could see that the lights were still on. When at last I unlatched my front gate, however, Cinderella came bounding down the path to meet me.

"Your little dog has come to meet you," my neighbor remarked pleasantly. But I realized immediately that Cinderella's enthusiastic welcome meant only one thing — trouble. She had been securely locked inside the house when I left.

Not wanting to raise a false alarm, I said nothing to my neighbor, who didn't know there was no one home. The thought passed through my mind that the girl who helped around the house might have come back for some reason. But since I was unsure of what I might find, I left the gate unlatched and made my way toward my front door.

Suddenly it dawned on me that the outside light was now turned off! Next I noticed the sliding door open about a foot, the locks broken! Oh, how my heart pounded as I looked around the bedroom and living room, where just hours before I had rehidden the money. In a flash I knew it was all gone. Things had been moved about, many items piled onto my bed. I could almost hear the old devil laughing, "Now do you believe that every last penny for the conferences will be supplied?"

But along with that insidious question came the Lord's word, "And we *know* that all things work together for good to them that love God, to them who are called according to His purpose" (Romans 8:28). Surely I could bring myself to echo with my own: "I *know*" — so I stood there literally kicking as I shouted, "Get out of here, you old devil. He that is in me is greater than he that is in the world; so you get out of here!" Then I began to look through the house, everywhere someone could possibly hide — under the bed, inside the big Japanese cupboards ... I wondered later what I would have done if I had found someone!

After this vain search I went out and called my neighbor, asking him to report the theft to the nearby police station. Then I went back inside to wait and think.

It seemed evident that when I had arrived at my front gate the thief had still been in the house. Most likely when he heard voices he turned off the light, slipped out the door, and hid in the darkness in my little back garden until I went into the house. Then later he slipped out through the front gate which I had not yet closed. There was no sign that anyone had climbed over the fence.

The job had obviously been done hurriedly and yet, oddly, with consideration, since things were not thrown helter-skelter but neatly piled on my bed. Surely the thief was familiar with the house! He also knew that I had a lot money around just at this particular time. And in addition, he must have known my dog very well, for Cinderella had not barked though she was usually very alert and didn't let people touch my things. And a common thief would probably have done away with her. As for poor Cinderella, she seemed full of remorse about the whole affair and wouldn't eat for days. She just didn't know how to express her sorrow, and in my state I appreciated her sympathy!

As I assessed the damages, I found I was left with fifty dollars local currency (worth about U.S.$1.50 at that time). All the money for the two conferences was gone as well as my personal money and living allowance. Everything was gone except, oddly, the envelope marked "Servant's salary." I immediately tried to put out of my mind the thought that my househelper might have done it, lest I falsely incriminate her. But how strange!

Now the police came on the scene, took fingerprints and made a thorough investigation. By the time they left it was 2 a.m. I proceeded to fix the lock so no one would know anything had happened. As I tidied up a bit more, I was struck again with the tight fix I was now in — a real opportunity for me to see if I really did live by faith as we in the C.I.M./O.M.F. say we do. Could I honestly say, "The God of Abraham, Isaac, Jacob and Hudson Taylor is my God too"? Of course I had proved this earlier while in university and also during those lean days in Nanking — but did I truly still trust Him for my needs, or was I merely looking to our mission for my supply?

My tidying up took until 4 a.m., when I lay down on my bed exhausted. I awoke early, nonetheless, as I had to make some adjustments in the day's plans. I was supposed to take three meetings that day; but since I now had to be home in the afternoon when the police were expected, I had to go out to find a substitute. The friend I asked to help me out was not only happy to do what she could, but promised to keep quiet about my predicament.

Arriving back home shortly, I was surprised to discover a bicycle now parked in my garden. Although this was Sunday morning, my househelper Iu-lan seemed to be on the scene and, what's more, her reaction on seeing me was one of anger. "Where did you come from?" she asked brusquely.

"I've just been out to see someone," I replied.

"But where've you been?" she insisted.

"I had to see someone," I repeated, though it wasn't any of her business.

"But I thought you were at the orphanage."

"I'm at the orphanage the last Sunday of the month; this is only the second, you know." Iu-lan had missed her cue on that one. So far the conversation had made me feel increasingly sure that somehow she was involved in the robbery; I didn't say a word about it, though, and she left shortly.

That afternoon Iu-lan returned much earlier than usual, and as she came in she remarked, watching me closely as she spoke, "They say *Han Pao-lien* (my Chinese name) has been robbed."

"Who says so?" I asked.

"The neighbors," Iu-lan replied simply.

I admitted then that I had been robbed, and told her that as the police were wanting to interview her as a matter of routine, she should go over to the police station at once.

And now I started to live my life of faith, praying that the Lord would prove His faithfulness to me as He had to Abraham, Isaac, Jacob and Hudson Taylor; and especially I asked Him to prove it to Iu-lan, for whom I felt very concerned.

In a way it would be easy enough to trust the Lord for my own needs — they weren't that many — but what about when the time came to hand over the money for the two conferences? I must admit my faith really did waver as I thought about that. Yet the Lord gave complete rest of heart about the whole matter, and the calm assurance that He knew all about it. I believed He would work it all out to His glory in some wonderful way.

In fact, He had been working even before the theft! He had laid it on the heart of a friend in far-off Philadelphia to spend time in special prayer for me.

She wrote me about it, and as I read her letter I could sense the tremendous burden she had that I was going to go through a difficult and dangerous experience. But she, too, had received assurance that the Lord was going to work for blessing and His glory. When I got that letter I could understand why I, the world's champion scaredy-cat, was not overwhelmed when the testing came.

Now it became a thrilling experience for me to watch, as from the sidelines, how the Lord provided day by day, for my own needs and then the greater needs of the conferences.

I was living on an all-Chinese diet those days. So, in typical Chinese fashion, I had no great supply of stores on hand, not even canned goods. We bought our vegetables and meat for each day and kept nothing over. I didn't even have a refrigerator, just an old Chinese "wind cupboard" (a small food cabinet made with wire mesh in the top and three sides, placed so that a good breeze went through it). So with almost no reserve supply of food in the house, it was not long before everything but the rice was used up.

About the third day after the robbery Iu-lan came to me saying, "There's nothing to make for breakfast."

"Well, set the table anyway," I told her.

"Why should I set the table when there is nothing to eat," she grumbled.

"Set the table," I repeated, rather sternly I'm afraid. "It's hardly even eight o'clock yet, and I usually don't eat till 8.30."

She mumbled and grumbled, slamming things down on the table. Slipping out, I went to my room and, closing the door behind me, knelt down by my bed. "Lord," I said, "I don't care if I don't eat, if that's your will; but I am asking you to show Iu-lan that YOU can provide for me."

When I went back, Iu-lan was still fussing and complaining. Just then — it was about 8.20 — I heard someone knocking. Wondering who would be calling so early, I went out to open the gate, and there stood my neighbor Mr. Li. He comes from Shantung, where the best steamed bread you ever tasted is made, and what do you suppose he was holding — a great big platter of steaming hot bread! "We know how much you like *mantou*," he explained, "so we made a specially big batch this morning in order to give you some." I thanked him and took my "bread from heaven" into the house.

When Iu-lan saw what I was carrying she asked with much curiosity, "Where'd you get that?"

"The Li's down the lane made it," I answered simply.

"You can't eat just steamed bread," she pouted.

"Well, lots of people do," I replied quietly, "and anyway, it will hold body and soul together."

Even as we were talking there came another knock, this time at the back gate, which we didn't normally use. On opening it, I was surprised to find little Mrs. Wang with a good-sized parcel in her hands. She was always a bit nervous and excited, and now as she handed me the parcel her hands trembled. With a quivering voice she explained, "*Wo tze-chi sheng-ti*" which literally means "I laid them myself." The parcel contained twenty eggs!

When I took them into the house Iu-lan's eyes fairly popped.

"Who brought those?" she asked, her voice lacking some of its earlier scorn.

"Little Mrs. Wang who has the seven daughters. She said she laid these eggs herself. Rather special, I'd say," I replied, laughing.

"Well, you don't have any fruit or coffee," my girl persisted.

Feeling quite bold now I replied, "We don't really need fruit every day, Iu-lan, and if the Lord thinks I should have coffee, I'll have it."

I suggested that she start preparing my breakfast, and cook two eggs instead of my usual one. But before she even had time to break the eggs, there was another knock at the front gate. I went out really wondering what further development this might prove to be. There at the gate stood a lad from the large boys' high school just around the corner. He was holding the biggest papaya I have ever seen!

"This papaya comes from one of our own trees," he explained. "Mother thought it was much too nice for us to keep for ourselves, and she wanted you to have it." He thrust the golden fruit into my hands and rode away on his bicycle.

Praising the Lord for what He had done in the last ten minutes, I walked back inside chuckling to myself.

Once again Iu-lan was full of questions. "Mrs. Chang's son just brought it on his way to school," I explained. "Comes from their own tree. Isn't it a beauty!"

Though everything was now in order for a real feast, Iu-lan was chafing and reminded me that I was still lacking coffee.

"If God thinks I should have coffee, He will give me coffee too," I repeated what I had said earlier, and even as I spoke there came another knock on the front gate! This time Iu-lan decided she would go and see what was happening, and I followed. The visitor this time turned out to be another Mrs. Wang, from another part of the city. She had pedaled quite a distance on her bicycle, and I wondered why she had come so early to see me. Just then, to my utter amazement, I noticed the big jar of instant coffee in her hands! Now in those days instant coffee was pretty hard to find, and Mrs. Wang was already explaining her story. "You know," she began, "my husband is an aviator, and sometimes he flies to Tokyo, Manila or Hong Kong. He often brings back gifts — and just look what he brought this time!"

I was indeed looking — I hoped without too much longing!

"Do you drink it?" Mrs. Wang was inquiring politely.

I didn't like to say yes and appear greedy, but I didn't want to lie by saying no either.

Mrs. Wang just carried on, "No one in our family drinks it. I don't know what possessed him to bring it. Do you drink it?"

"Mrs. Wang," I replied, "You should take that coffee down the street to the store that sells foreign things; they'll buy it, I'm sure, and you can use the money to get something for your children."

"No! No! You do drink it, don't you?" she persisted.

I admitted that I did, whereupon Mrs. Wang pressed the jar into my hands, slipped back onto her bike and rode away.

As we went into the house Iu-lan commented, "Imagine Mrs. Wang liking you so much! That's a very big gift. She could have sold that coffee for at least five U.S. dollars."

I hardly heard her, as I was still trying to get over this wonderful answer to my prayers. God surely was proving to be my *Jehovah-jireh*[1]. With this supply I had breakfast several times a day for several days!

---

[1] "The Lord will provide" (Genesis 22:14). One of Hudson Taylor's mottos.

18
Loaves and fishes

Even as I was rejoicing at the way the Lord had met my personal needs, I was aware that Wednesday was looming up, when I would have to put cash down for purchasing rice for the first conference — $1,000 in local currency that I didn't have. Getting out all the money I possessed, I found as I spread it out on my bed that it had dwindled quite a bit, to about ten dollars! *Not much to start a conference on,* I thought. But I knelt down and prayed, "Lord, you are the One who can multiply the fishes and the loaves and feed five thousand people; now this is all I've got, ten Taiwanese dollars, to feed about 150 young people for ten days. I've got to have a thousand dollars by the evening, Lord, to buy the rice. I ask you to give this for Your glory." As I got up from my knees, I had not the foggiest idea where the money would come from, but somehow I had assurance that it would come, so I didn't panic as I might have done.

In a matter of minutes a telegram arrived from Sun Moon Lake, where some missionary friends from Hong Kong were having a vacation. Today they would be coming down to Taichung and were wondering if we could have lunch together. Oh, and she had her four children with her. *Oh no!* I thought. This telegram wasn't exactly one of those miraculous answers to prayer. In fact it just presented me with another problem — what was I to feed them?

I went back into my bedroom, where the money was still spread out on my bed. Again I knelt down. "Lord, what do we do now? I don't have any money for eating out, and I sure don't have any food here to offer them." By now even my supply of steamed bread was getting very low, and there was no rice left in the house.

While I was still there chewing over my situation, there came another telegram from the same woman. "I forgot to tell you," she had wired, "I want you to go over to that restaurant where we had such good food before and order the best dinner they have for us all. We're treating!"

Immediately I thanked the Lord that the fishes and loaves were beginning to divide! And, believe me, I did order the best dinner that restaurant had, and plenty of it. I knew that in a Chinese restaurant, if you couldn't eat everything they would pack it up for you to take home, even the rice!

Later, as we were enjoying our meal together, my friend turned to me and said, "My daughter and I were talking together as we came down the mountain and we both felt you have some problem, some need that you're not telling anyone about. Is that true?"

Reluctantly I answered, "Yes, it's true. Since you're not from Taiwan, I guess I can tell you. I've been robbed." And I proceeded to tell her how serious the situation was.

"Well," she answered as she was getting over the shock of my story, "we had already decided that we would give you this Taiwan money instead of changing it back into Hong Kong currency. We won't be needing it any more since we're flying out of Taipei this afternoon," and she handed me the packet of money. I could see right away by the size of the packet that it must be at least a thousand dollars in Taiwan currency.

"This is very un-Chinese," I said, "but may I open it now?"

"Of course."

I opened the package and counted out exactly one thousand Taiwan dollars — just the amount I needed to pay for the rice for the first conference.

When I arrived at church that evening for the prayer meeting, the president of the youth group came up to me wearing a very worried expression on his handsome face. I had confided in him about the robbery, trusting God to show His faithfulness to this developing young leader, the only Christian in his family.

"What are we going to do, *Han Po Po* (Grandma Han)?" he moaned. "We've got to give the money for the rice right after the meeting — where are we going to get it? We'll just have to admit that the money was stolen and call the whole conference off."

"Oh blow it!" I blurted out, unable to contain my excitement any longer. "Don't wait till after the meeting, give the money to them now!"

"But, *Han Po Po*, where do you expect to get hold of all that money?"

"I'm getting it right out of my handbag," I said, and pulled the fat packet out for him to see. "Here!" I said gleefully. "Go give it to them!"

"Where'd you get this?" he asked, worry now turned to astonishment.

"Well, I didn't rob a bank, you can be sure," I chuckled. As I told him the story, we had a time of rejoicing together, praising God that He had gotten us over the first hurdle. At least we would have rice for the first conference, and our faith had been strengthened to believe He would now supply the needed things to go with the rice.

Meanwhile, my own situation was once more looking grim. The restaurant food gone after two meals, I was facing an almost empty cupboard again. But the Lord was not unaware of my needs. Again He used His people to share for His sake. While I was out calling on some young folks, urging them to attend the conference, the Lord laid it on several people's hearts to give me something to eat. Then another lady had made some jam. She was quite pleased with her first effort at jam-making and insisted that I take home a jar. Actually I never quite figured out what flavor it was supposed to be, but I think it was the best jam I've ever eaten since it was given in true love and at a time of need.

But the pressure was still on — electricity and water bills were coming due in just a few days. *Ai ya!* There was no end to it. To top it all off, the next day was Communion Sunday, when there would be the customary special offering. After the service everyone would go up to the front of the church to put their special offering in the big offering box, and what would *I* do?

Next morning I sat through the whole service arguing with the Lord about that little bit of money in my pocket, with the result that I have no recollection of who preached or what was said. My mind was working hard — *should I give this money or shouldn't I?*

And then, *You know, Lord, this is all the money I've got, and besides it really isn't Your money! Your money was stolen.* Thus I tried to reason my way out of giving those few dollars. But I had no peace. Finally I realized that since this was not nearly the amount I usually gave, I had better go up and put all of it into the box. And that's what I did. That day I could really sing the offertory hymn, *All for Jesus*, with all my heart. My pocket was completely empty.

Immediately after the service I was approached by a young couple, she slim and petite in her straight Chinese gown and he neat in his waist-length windbreaker and crisp trousers. "Grandma," they said, "We were praying for you this morning, and it was just as though the Lord told us we should give you something. Please don't feel offended. We felt you must have a special need." Rather new believers, they had never given me anything like this before, and were very apologetic as they handed me an envelope and hurried away.

Just then another older woman from the Mainland made her way over to me and thrust an envelope into my hand, saying she must give it to me. Before I could say a word she was gone. When I got home and opened the envelopes, I found the contents came to about $250 local currency — magnificent interest for the ten dollars I had given to the Lord! I had not had so much money of my own since the time of the robbery two weeks earlier!

That afternoon I had a visit from a schoolteacher, and as we were talking she asked if I could use some rice. Could I! I'd been out of rice for days, but of course I didn't tell her that. I just replied, "Why do you ask?"

"I just got my ration of rice," she explained, "and since my husband isn't home I don't need so much." Like other government employees she was provided with staples such as rice, oil and salt. "I thought maybe you could use some. I've got more than I need now, and soon a new allotment will be coming. I brought it along with me, and if you can use it I'll bring it in."

She went and fetched a big bag weighing twenty *jin*, or about 44 pounds. Starvation would not stalk my door, of that I was sure, for this amount of rice should tide me over until our financial secretary returned and I could again draw money. Some time later I explained to my teacher friend how the Lord had used her in my time of need.

Just when I was rejoicing at the way the Lord was caring for my big needs, I began to run into a succession of niggly little problems. Of all times for it to go out of whack, my watch stopped, and nothing could persuade it to run again. Just when I needed it most! But as I was out visiting at the home of another Chinese schoolteacher, something called her attention to the fact that my watch was not running, and she asked me about it.

"Oh," I replied lightly, "something just snapped in it the other day, and now it won't go."

"Well, you surely don't have time to bother about repairing watches, *Han Po Po*, with two conferences on your doorstep and all the other things you're doing. Here, take this watch and use it till you have time to get yours fixed." She had no inkling, of course, that I hadn't a cent for watch repairs.

The very next day my electric fan went dead. Since it was a very hot day, probably the hottest we had had all summer, and I was having a meeting at the house in the evening, I felt we couldn't get along without something to move the air. I thought about borrowing a fan, but finally decided I would first see if I could do anything to fix it myself. That afternoon, all alone in the house, I knelt down to ask the Lord for wisdom to repair the fan. I assure you, I know nothing about a fan's anatomy, but I opened it up and looked in. Then I fiddled with a few things here and there, ignoring completely the little inscriptions written for my instruction, unfortunately in Japanese. Finally I dropped in some oil where I thought it might do some good, and in the space of about ten minutes "Operation Fan" was completed as far as I was concerned. I closed her up and turned her on. To my amazement she worked, and continued to do so better than ever!

During all these days of seeing the Lord meet my needs I still had a really uneasy feeling about my servant, Iu-lan. Since the thief had left the money for her wages, I paid her right on the dot of time whenever her salary was due. Not once, however, did she ask me where I got the money from. But if I came home with something I'd bought, she would immediately ask, "Where'd you get the money to buy that?" Strange. I had determined, of course, not to spent one cent of that salary money on anything but her wages, and since this also included a food allowance *she* was never short of food. But I hadn't enough hard evidence to accuse her of the robbery; so we just carried on with our touch-and-go housekeeping.

One incident really was a trial. I came back from a meeting one day to find Iu-lan waiting for me at the gate, very upset. "There are some people here," she said. "I don't know who they are, but they just walked in and took over your bedroom, and have put your bedding on the *tatami* in the living room."

"What!" I exclaimed. "Well, who are they?"

"They're two women, not too old. I think they are from Taipei. I've never seen them before."

As we walked into the house and I looked at the two American ladies seated in my living room, I realized that I had never laid eyes on them before either.

As politely and discreetly as I could, remembering that we might be entertaining angels (though somehow I doubted it) I asked, "Who are you?" They told me, but this didn't help. I'd never so much as heard of them before, and though they mentioned the mission organization they were connected with I'd not heard of it either.

"How did you know about me?" I ventured now, wanting somehow to get to the bottom of this mystery. They had found my name, it seemed, in an old directory listing Taiwan missionaries. And apparently feeling that no further invitation was needed, they had moved right in. It looked as though I would be sleeping on my own living room floor!

Whew! I shot up a prayer. "Lord, give me grace and help me now, for I don't know what to do. This one beats me!"

Of course, in no time Iu-lan came asking the obvious question, "What are we going to do for food?"

"Just wait," I said quietly. "We'll stall off a bit and see what happens. Maybe they'll suggest taking me out to eat." But it wasn't to be; rather, the ladies began to hint about the hour for supper. I didn't answer. I just continued busily preparing for the meeting I was to take that evening. But I thought plenty! *This surely is going too far. These gals act like they plan on staying a while; I've never met people like this before. The nerve — what kind of upbringing did they have anyway!*

When I'd cooled down a little I tried casually to pry out of them some information about their plans, though I really would have liked to put it right to them, "Hey, when are you leaving, anyway?"

I don't know when I have ever been so rattled or annoyed in all my life. I was so upset that it was good news to hear someone at the front gate. "I'll go!" I called to the girl — anything to get out of the house for a bit.

I opened the gate, and there stood a young boy with a large wooden tray. He was the grandson of a woman I had gone to see that morning on her 80th birthday. We had had a lovely chat, read some Scriptures and had a time of prayer together; but before leaving I had apologized that I would not be able to attend her birthday feast that evening. "I'm sorry, but I have a meeting tonight, Granny, so I came to wish you happy birthday this morning instead." I gave her a little gift and left. Later, when the family were setting out the food for her feast, Granny had thought of me. "Grandma Han can't come; we should send some food over to her." And they had done so, nothing skimpy either but a portion from each one of the luscious dishes, and even some rice. Here it was, steaming and smelling so good, right at my front door. So my mysterious visitors and I were to be fed that night after all, not by the ravens but by a lad on his bicycle.

Taking a little forethought, I suggested that Iu-lan not put all that food on the table for supper. "We don't need all this," I told her, "and we'd better save some for tomorrow because who knows how long these people will stay."

The ladies stayed on for three days, and left as they had come; no explanation, not even a thank-you note. I've never seen them or heard from them again.

Now that there was just one week before the young people's conference, I was very busy preparing Bible studies and other sessions. Just at this time my old friend and fellow-worker, Ruth Nowack, was having to return home to America because of her failing health. My Chinese friends all urged me to go up to Taipei to see her off, not knowing of course that I didn't have money for such a trip.

"I'm awfully busy," I responded. "I simply can't take the time. I've got three meetings on that day too." At that, one person volunteered to take a meeting, someone else another.

"But I'd have to go up on the first train in the morning and come back late at night," I argued, "and you know how impossible it is to get a round-trip ticket these days. Actually, it's so late now that I probably couldn't even get a one-way ticket."

"Oh, that's no problem," put in another woman. "My husband's chauffeur can get one for you. He can get tickets anytime."

I went off to a meeting then, hoping that was the end of the business. When I arrived home, to my surprise I found a *round-trip* ticket to Taipei lying on my dining table.

Next morning I had to get up very early to catch the 5.30 a.m. train. I had to walk down to the station because paying the electric and water bills had strained my pocketbook so much I had just about three Taiwan dollars left, not enough for a pedicab. But that was just the beginning of my worries. Although I tried to sleep on the four-hour journey to Taipei, all the way my thoughts were struggling with the next problem — *how was I to get from the station all the way out to the airport on three dollars!* I needn't have lost sleep worrying about it; the Lord knew all about my need.

As I got off the train in Taipei station, a man walked up to me and said, "Aren't you Teacher Han from Taichung?"

"Yes, I am," I replied, a bit embarrassed since I could not think of his name, though his face looked familiar.

"Have you come to see Teacher Lo off?" the man continued.

"Why, yes!"

"That's fine. Come to the airport with us. My car is at the door!" I could hardly believe my ears. In all this big city of Taipei how could someone come along just at that moment who knew me, knew where I was going, and was going there too — by car! Obviously the Lord had gone ahead once again. How slow I was to learn to trust! This friend, a government official, not only provided a chauffeured ride to the airport but he and his wife took me out for a lovely dinner beforehand.

Then at the airport another strange thing happened. Several people had given Ruth gold rings as farewell gifts. Two of these she suddenly pulled off and handed to me. "I won't know what to do with these in America," she said, "but maybe sometime when you are in a spot and need money, you could sell them!" They were the sort of pure gold bands that Chinese buy as part of their dowry or just as savings, since they are always negotiable.

Ruth had said I could use the rings when I was in a tight spot and needed money. *Boy,* I thought, *if I was ever in a hot spot, I am now!* I put the rings on my hand, thinking as I did so, *Funny, isn't it, I have gold on my fingers but no cash in my pocket!*

Just then the people who had taken me to the airport very thoughtfully asked what train I was returning on, and on hearing my answer decided that there was time enough for another meal together before depositing me back at the station. Wow, with those two lovely meals under my belt, I'd have enough to last several days! And when I returned to Taichung, I went to a broker and sold my two precious rings for over eight hundred Taiwan dollars, a small fortune for me at that time.

Well, it was after midnight before I got home, since once again I walked from the station. It had been a long day, though it had been wonderful to see how the Lord provided all the way. Now, however, after Iu-lan had let me in I sank down in a chair, exhausted. "I'm just dead tired," I said, half talking out loud to myself. "What I wouldn't give for some chocolates to munch on right now!" (Chocolates are another of my weaknesses — especially when I'm tired.)

"You want some chocolates?" Iu-lan responded, brightly for a change.

"Yes, but where are you going to get any!"

"Just wait," she said, walking out of the room. She was back in a minute with a big box of chocolates.

"Iu-lan, where did these come from?" I asked, full of curiosity.

"There's a note on them. Some woman brought them in; I know her face but not her name."

Looking at the note, I discovered that these "heaven-sent" candies were from a Chinese friend just back from a trip to America. Knowing my love for chocolates, she had brought this big box for me. She had been in Taichung for just that one day, so it was many weeks before I could tell her how wonderful those chocolates were; how I'd gotten right down on the *tatami* mat floor with my canine pal Cinderella beside me and eaten them like a happy little kid. What a Father! He cares so much that He gives His children extras — even chocolates.

The following Monday the first of the conferences opened at last. The person in charge asked me if the remaining money for miscellaneous expenses such as honoraria for the speakers and chartering buses for our outing could possibly be handed over on Tuesday evening.

"I'll give it to you right after the evening meeting," I said, wondering even as I spoke where it was going to come from. I had a deep peace in my heart, however, and a calm assurance that the Lord was not going to let us down now.

I had been so busy these days I hadn't remembered to get my mail; so while the young people were having their recreation time on Tuesday afternoon I decided to run downtown to the post office. Not that I was expecting anything — I guess I just wanted to get away from the mob for a while. There was plenty of stuff in my box; but as it seemed to be mostly "junk mail" I stuffed the whole lot into my bag and went back to the conference.

Finding a quiet spot in the church, I began to go through the pile. Yes, most of it was just second-class mail as I'd suspected, but in the lot was an envelope from the U.S. Treasury Department. *Oh dear,* I thought, *now what's up? Are they after more money?* When I opened the envelope, however, out fell a check for several hundred dollars! "What has happened to my government," I spluttered with unbelief, "that they are sending me a check?" As I read the letter I discovered the answer.

Ten years earlier when I left for China, I had filled out all the tax papers for that year and should have been reimbursed for tax withheld. Now here it was, turning up ten years later when I needed it most. What perfect timing!

But even as I looked at the wonderful check, I immediately thought of a snag. Checks weren't easy to cash in Taiwan at that time. I did know someone whom I thought might cash it, but when I went to ask him he refused. After all, the situation was a bit shaky in Taiwan then, with heavy fighting on the offshore islands. I felt I should show him the check anyway and, lo and behold, when he saw it was a government bank money order, he brightened up. "Oh, that's different. I'll cash that kind," he said. Terribly relieved, I asked him when I could get the cash.

"I'll give it to you right now if you'll take local currency." I assured him that that was what I wanted. In about five minutes, with the money safely in my hands, I was walking away feeling like a millionaire!

Back at the church, I was met by the troubled youth group president. What a joy it was to be able to remind him that the Lord had promised to give every last penny, and then to amaze him by pulling the money right out of my bag! I counted out the amount due and gave it to him saying, "We'll even give it to them before the meeting, not after."

He was sure that I must have borrowed it. But when I explained to him the wonderful way the Lord had provided it, he was as thrilled as I was.

"But that money is really yours," he said, a concerned look coming over his face.

"No, it's not mine. I wasn't aware that it was due to me all these years, and the absolutely perfect timing of the whole thing makes it very clear that this is God's handiwork. The money's not mine, but the Lord's. He was the One who kept it for just this time, and what's more we got interest on it!"

The money carried us right through the first conference and part of the second, and enabled me to replenish my larder as well.

The Lord richly blessed that church young people's conference, despite the many efforts of the enemy to hinder His work. How wonderful it is to know that He that is in us is greater than he that is in the world! Thirty young people either accepted the Lord Jesus as Savior for the first time or came into assurance of salvation during those days. Then fifteen gave their lives to the Lord for His service, while others set matters straight that had gone wrong.

I had hoped for a few days' rest between the two conferences, but it was not to be. Instead the devil once again came in like a flood, now doing what he could to spoil the All-Taiwan Student Conference. His scheme this time was to use misunderstanding, and I was a victim. This was a more painful and wearing experience than losing the money had been. Of course it is not pleasant to hear all your faults and sins recounted by others. Yet it is an opportunity for the Lord to do a deep work, cutting and pruning for our spiritual good. As in many misunderstandings, much was false and even malicious. Still the Lord gave me grace to go to the people involved, talk it over and apologize where they felt I was wrong and had wronged them. After that I felt as light as a feather, as though I could fly, for I knew I had done what I could, and I left the rest with the Lord to work out.

But any hope for a rest had been shattered. By the time this situation had cleared up, I had to get busy with preparations for the student conference. There were a myriad of details to attend to, many which only I could handle since the seminary had made me responsible.

There were still the Bible study notes to prepare for the Campus Fellowship magazine — ninety or more studies for each issue, a reading and questions for each day of the three-month period. I had nearly finished this mammoth job when, just two days before conference began, I woke in the middle of the night with a terrific pain in my abdomen, a warning sign that my old ulcer was beginning to trouble me again. The stress of the past few weeks was apparently having a physical effect. My doctor was away, but I decided the wise thing to do was to go back on the bland diet he had given me. However, this was not too easy since I didn't have any dry milk powder, nor money to buy any! The Lord's word to me in my devotions that day was, "The Lord is on my side; I will not fear." This really encouraged me; I was sure the Lord knew all about this new test. And He did indeed, for that very morning He guided one of His faithful servants to bring along a gift of a big can of milk powder! No one at the conference suspected that I was not feeling up to par, and fortunately in a few days my symptoms were gone.

Once again, however, I was now faced with having to hand over more than a thousand Taiwan dollars for the supplies for the student conference. This time I had the amount in hand from the reimbursed tax money — but that wasn't going to cover all the expense that would be incurred before the end of conference for it was nowhere as much as had been stolen. So once again I was wondering what channel the Lord would use to supply our need.

The very Sunday before conference started, four different people came to my house with special gifts designated for the conference, bringing the total to the full amount needed. How good of the Lord to do that before conference started! Although my own personal needs were still outstanding, I would be at the conference for five days and would get my meals there — and I did still have plenty of milk!

Since the conference was held in Taichung, I was able to dash home now and then. One day, remembering the unfinished Bible study notes, I decided that as I already had about two months' material finished, I would take it out to my Chinese secretary. She could start copying now and save time and a rush later.

I went home to fetch the notes. But when I looked in the place where I always put them, they were not there! I hunted a bit more, but there was no sign of them. I couldn't remember having put them anywhere else either. These were my original rough copies, there were no duplicates. *Woe is me!* If they were truly gone, this would be in many ways a greater loss than the money. I couldn't take more time to look now as I had to hurry back to the conference. Although I was really puzzled, I didn't mention it to anyone, hoping above hope that after the conference I would be able to find those notes.

Before long the conference came to an end, with the Lord having indeed poured out His blessing on the gathering. Many who attended have since become leaders in various avenues of the Lord's work. No wonder we met such resistance!

But where were those notes? Now that question was again uppermost in my mind. Yet it is a question that is still unanswered as I write. I just had to go back and start from scratch and do the whole thing over, meeting the deadline in twenty days. The student magazine came out on time with 91 days of Bible study notes in it. I can only say that the Lord poured in strength, wisdom, and insight such as I had never experienced before. Though I saw little of my bed in those days, at least the ulcer didn't trouble me again. The Lord continued to care for my personal needs in wonderful ways, too many to record. Yet, when this period was over and the O.M.F. secretary returned so that I could draw money again, gifts stopped coming in as suddenly as they had started.

In spite of knowing I was living under attack these days, I was feeling very encouraged by the way God was working in the lives of the students and young people as well as caring for me. My faith was really being strengthened, and I felt a new deeper knowledge of God's love. How wonderful it was to see His hands at work in so many impossible situations during those eleven or twelve weeks, and to enjoy even closer fellowship with my Chinese friends, who were often God's channels to meet my needs. Now I had no more doubts. I could indeed say "I know" to Romans 8:28, and I had complete confidence that the God of Abraham, Isaac, Jacob and Hudson Taylor is indeed the God of Pauline Hamilton too. The lessons I learned were more precious than the money that was stolen or the missing Bible study notes. They came as a fresh reminder of the battle that was going on and how God's soldiers need always to be on the alert.

A while later when I shared this testimony with several groups, they asked, "Why didn't you let us know your need? We could have helped you."

"Had I done that," I replied, "I would have missed one of the most precious experiences of my whole life."

Yet at this point I was still wondering if Iu-lan had anything to do with the robbery and if so, what to do about it — especially when I heard that her brother was a gangster.

Now that the conferences were all over, I began to pray in earnest about dismissing my househelper Iu-lan. I should have done it before the robbery — I had plenty of reason. Yet I hated to. Iu-lan had been with me for three years, and up to a few months before the money was stolen she had been an almost ideal helper. A graduate of the local home economics school, she always went right ahead very capably managing my household, even making my clothes, thus freeing me for other work.

Trouble began, however, after an evening in which we had had a long talk. Iu-lan was under deep conviction of sin and had a real sense of her spiritual need. She seemed to want to accept the Lord, but couldn't. "My mother won't let me! My mother won't let me!" she kept saying over and over. She did have a problem there, I knew. While her father lived in Taichung and was a fine man, her mother lived out in the country and from all reports was a very evil woman — a sorceress, I was told later. Truth or fiction, I do not know, but to me she certainly did have the appearance of a woman given

over to evil, right to the core. Anyway, though Iu-lan
and I had talked until very late, and though God
seemed to be doing a deep work in her heart, she seemed
bound. In the end she closed the door tightly against
the Lord.

From that time on Iu-lan began to change. While
previously she hadn't gone out much in the evening,
preferring to stay in to sew or do embroidery, making
all sorts of lovely things for her dowry, now she began
going out every evening. If I asked where she was
going, she responded angrily. I also began to miss
things around the house. Gradually she came home
later and later, worrying me about what she was doing
and keeping me up to let her in.

One night Iu-lan didn't come in until after two a.m.
When I opened the gate, I made a simple inquiry as to
where she had been. "I've been worried," I explained.

Iu-lan's response was fury. As I finished bolting
the front gate, she sped into the house. I came along
behind her, secured the lock on the house door, and then
as I turned around, Iu-lan grabbed hold of me with a
powerful grip. She clenched my big, shiny Chinese
cleaver in her other hand, raised to strike, her face
white with rage. Cleverly she had secured my dog
Cinderella in the upper level of my Japanese house —
I could just see Cindy's little black nose at the tiny open
crack of the sliding door. The rest of the house was
tightly closed now, and calling for help would do no
good. I was trapped.

Just then I noticed that Cinderella, sensing trouble,
was trying frantically to push open the door with her
paw, and to widen the crack with her nose. She just
might make it. I felt my only chance was to play for time.

I started preaching to Iu-lan, whose strong grip on me by this time was really hurting. She didn't weaken. A large, brawny country girl, more than a head taller than I, she was very strong and still very angry. I was at her mercy.

I tried reasoning with her: "Look! You go ahead and kill me! It's all right because I'll go right to Heaven. But you won't get away with this." I knew even as I spoke that I couldn't hold out much longer against her. About ready to collapse, I called out to God to help me.

Cinderella's nose was soon protruding a bit further, and just when I felt I couldn't resist Iu-lan another second, the dog's soft body came writhing through the door. Instantly she lunged for the girl, sinking her teeth into Iu-lan's leg. Iu-lan, screaming with pain, released her grip on me. Quickly I wrenched the cleaver from her hands.

"Now you get in there, Iu-lan, and go to bed!" I ordered, not stopping to attend to her wounds. "It's okay; the dog's been injected so you won't get rabies. You just go to bed!"

I was feeling a bit shaky, but my mind was working all right; so I ran right out to the kitchen and grabbed every knife I could find, then going quickly back to my bedroom I slipped those knives under my mattress and pillow. Then I pulled Cinderella up onto the bed with me, tucked in the mosquito net and tried to call it a night. Later, when Iu-lan tip-toed through my room on her way to the bathroom, Cinderella growled so fiercely I could tell Iu-lan was pretty scared.

I hadn't shared the knife incident with anyone, and now that I knew that Iu-lan's big brother was a gangster I dared not for fear of retaliation. The robbery only added to my predicament. Though many things, including her attitude and the sparing of the envelope containing her salary, pointed to Iu-lan's involvement, evidence was all too circumstantial. I couldn't be sure. What I needed was an excuse to dismiss the girl that involved neither the murder attempt nor the robbery. How I prayed!

Then one day someone came to tell me that Iu-lan was engaged to be married. When I asked her about this she denied it at first. Then she admitted it, covering her failure to tell me with, "But it's only a *little* engagement." In Taiwan a so-called "little engagement" gives the couple the freedom to be seen together and go out on dates. If everything goes well and both families are satisfied, the next step is a "big engagement" which is as binding as marriage.

Now I had my excuse to dismiss Iu-lan, one that would save face all around. Not that I was against the marriage. The fellow she was engaged to was a university graduate who said he knew me as he had attended a conference where I was a speaker. I figured that if Iu-lan could get out of her mother's clutches and free from her brother's influence, there was still hope for her. No, I wasn't against the marriage. But she had not only failed to tell me of her engagement as she should have, a little engagement though it be, but she had lied about it when confronted with the fact. In letting her go, I gave her the extra salary due in such circumstances, then when she was ready ordered a taxi to take her and her things back home to the country.

When Iu-lan was packing, she should have asked me to come to watch, but she didn't. The middleman — in this case a woman — was there, however, and every once in a while I could hear her ask Iu-lan, "Is this yours, or is it Grandma Han's?"

"It's Grandma's."

"Then take it out." And so it went until Iu-lan was all packed.

While the middleman escorted Iu-lan back home to explain things, I quickly went out and hired oxcarts to move my things out of the house that same afternoon. Though I had been planning to move for some time, now I felt it would be best to get out of there before nightfall. Iu-lan knew I was planning to move, but she didn't know where, though it was actually only two lanes away. Not many people could have realized I had moved out, since I left by the back gate. The only thing I left behind was Cinderella.

I slept peacefully that night in my new home, no knives under my mattress either! Next morning I went over to the old house to get Cinderella — and found holes bashed through the front gate, a window broken, and all sorts of other damage!

The neighbors came out, inquiring, "Whatever was going on at your house last night?"

"I don't know," I answered. "I wasn't here because I moved out yesterday." Then they told me something that made me have cold chills. A large gang of men had come to the house (probably Iu-lan's brother and some of his gangmen, I guessed, paying me back for dismissing her). When they found I wasn't home they went away, but they came back several times and eventually took out their vegeance on the house. I hadn't moved any too soon.

But I was still very concerned for Iu-lan. Having to dismiss her had been very hard after she had helped me for three years. I wrote to five friends who prayed faithfully for me as well as for people I was concerned for; I knew they would keep confidence and would pray. But though we prayed, nothing seemed to happen. Eventually I lost all trace of Iu-lan and had no idea of her situation. We prayed on, however, for the Lord knew her whereabouts and her needs.

Five years later, on Chinese New Year's Day, among the other visitors a couple rode up to my gate on a motorcycle. They looked very much like some friends who worked at an orphanage where I went regularly. But as I opened the gate, I was really taken aback to see Iu-lan with her younger brother! She wouldn't accept my invitation to come in but just stood there at the gate. Then, without any of the usual polite formalities, she began blurting out what was on her mind. "I have come to make confession of everything. I got married and now have two lovely little boys — and am expecting another child, too. But I can't live another day like this! I've told my husband the whole story and said that he can divorce me if he wants to since I'm not fit to be his wife. I took your money. I took all sorts of things," and Iu-lan named a whole string of items she had stolen from me. "If you want to take me to court and send me to prison, it's okay with me. That's where I belong — I ... I just can't go on another day like this!"

"Well, Iu-lan," I said, "I'm not wanting to send you to jail or take you to court. Your little boys need their mother."

"But when I look at them, I know I'm not fit to be their mother," she sighed.

We did go into the house then and had a good talk. Iu-lan accepted the Lord that day, and a while later her husband believed as well. Today they are a lovely little Christian family with three sons — and, oh, yes, she paid back all the money, with compound interest.

20
A bloodstained boy

One of the greatest thrills of my whole missionary life was seeing Christian student work in Taiwan become nationalized. Various Christian groups had existed in universities all over the island for several years now, and from them was formed an indigenous organization called Campus Evangelical Fellowship. Now the work would be unified and in the control of the Chinese, led by young men willing to give themselves in this way to the evangelism of their fellow students. This was not an easy step for them and meant no little sacrifice. Some faced real opposition from parents who had great plans for them, hoping they would go abroad to study for higher degrees. In fact, some of these young people already had scholarships to some of the best universities in America, and gave these up to enter the Lord's work full time. Against terrific opposition they stood firm in the call they had from Him.

When the student work was nationalized, I turned over to C.E.F. the work I had been doing in running conferences and so on among students, while offering my

help in any way they might request. The new organization did call on us missionaries in many ways, the
difference being that now we were working under them
rather than running the show. Some missionaries rather
shook their heads, saying, "Well, if you're going to
work under the Chinese, you'll probably not have
anything to do." But I didn't find that the case — quite
the opposite, in fact. We have been asked to do much
more than we might have thought of doing ourselves,
such as helping with Bible teaching and conferences,
training staff and counseling.

I thoroughly enjoyed my new freedom from ad-
ministrative responsibilities. I was at last free to teach
and to counsel in a new way, and before I knew it
furlough time was rolling around again. How time flies
when you are happily busy in the work! I was really
praying about this furlough, however, as there was not
the same urgency to go home now since Dad had gone,
and my sister had been to visit me in Taiwan. As I
asked the Lord about this question of furlough and what
I would be doing next term, He began answering in a
rather unsettling way. In my daily reading, in ser-
mons, and in letters there continuously appeared a
verse: 2 Chronicles 25:9 — "The Lord is able to give
you much more than this." I couldn't seem to get away
from it! Did this verse have special significance for me,
or was I trying to read something into it? If it had special
meaning, what was God up to now? Well, it wasn't
very long before I began finding out and then any
thought of furlough went right down the drain.

It all began with a special visitor. I had just returned
from a conference over on the east coast of Taiwan, and
was dead on my feet. The bus trip through the craggy
mountains from Hualien to Taichung, which should

have taken only ten hours, had dragged on and on due to road work, landslides and bus breakdowns. As I pulled open my gate and went on into the house, setting down my case, my thoughts were all of a nice hot bath, a bite to eat, and an early bed. But just then there commenced such a great banging on the front gate that I stifled my feelings of annoyance and called out inquiringly, "Who's there?" The voice that answered was so full of urgency and had such a familiar ring to it that, despite my desire for bath and bed, I ran out to open the gate.

I was not prepared for the sight which presented itself. There stood a teenage boy, his clothing torn, grimy and bloodstained. His hands and face were encrusted with sores, some festering, and his matted hair had not seen a comb in days. Out of his wan face frightened eyes peered searchingly at me as though questioning, "Don't you remember me?" Hesitating a little, he finally mumbled, "May I come in?"

A name flashed into my mind — Ted. "Are you by any chance Ted? Little Ted?" I asked dubiously, since this boy's condition almost defied recognition. Ted nodded in assent. He was a boy I had known ever since he was very young. His mother was a Christian and his father, who was high up in the Chinese Army, claimed to be too, but never showed anything of Christ in his life. Of the several sons in the family, this one even at age six or seven showed signs that he would probably turn out to be a problem youth. I had pointed out some of the warning signs in his behavior to his parents at that time, suggesting they would be wise to nip trouble in the bud. But since I was not married and had no children of my own they felt I couldn't possibly understand these things, and did nothing about Ted's behavior.

Now here he stood on my doorstep, and goodness knows what trouble he was in. But I didn't take time to make inquiries. "C'mon in, Ted," I said. "Go along and have a good bath; there's hot water on tap. I'll get some towels and see if I can find clean clothes to fit you. After you've cleaned up a bit we'll have some supper, and then I want to hear your story."

As I prepared some food, my thoughts were filled with questions. *What's happened to bring Ted to this sort of life? Does his family know about it?* I hadn't seen him for seven or eight years, but I knew his home background very well. It was what people would call a good home, comfortable, with more income than most and all the amenities of life. His family was well respected in the community but the home seemed to be missing something of warmth and love, and there was definite partiality. The oldest son and heir seemed infallible in his parents' sight, whereas little Ted could never do anything right. From his youngest days he seemed to get blamed for all the misdemeanors of the other boys. For some reason he never told tales on the others, possibly because no one would believe what he said anyway. Before he was very old Ted had decided, "They always blame me; so I might just as well do it."

My thoughts were interrupted as Ted came bursting out of the bathroom, all scrubbed and groomed, yelling in a loud voice, "When do we eat? I'm starved! I could eat everything in the house."

He almost did! It was a long time since I had seen anyone consume so much. How different he looked all cleaned up — a handsome lad of fifteen or sixteen, with charming manners when he chose to turn them on!

Here's what he told me that night: "Since I saw you last I finished primary school. I was kicked out several times, but Dad seemed to know somebody, and so they took me back. I think they let me graduate because they wanted to get rid of me. Then I took the entrance examination for junior high school, but of course I failed. Dad beat me up — still got some scars from that one. Yet somehow Dad worked it so I would go to the best boys' junior high school in the city. That only accelerated my backward slide as it was way beyond me, and because I knew I could never measure up to their standards I didn't even try. I was in and out of that school until they lost patience with me and wouldn't have me back again.

"Since then I've been the rounds of all the schools in Taichung. Now, as none of them will admit me as a student, I'm trying schools in neighboring cities. I never can attain Dad's goals for me, and I've long since stopped trying. I've got my own gang of boys now — I'm their big brother. There are about seventy of us altogether. We have a lot of fun — you know, fighting with other gangs, stealing, picking pockets, running from the police. Well, that's been my story in part — lots more I can't tell you." He sighed as though relieved at his admission.

Then after a few minutes he started in again: "Several weeks ago Dad got really angry with me. We had a big fight. Then he literally threw me out of the house and told me never to come back again. I have gone back, several times, but no one answers the door. If Dad's home, Mom can't do anything to help me."

"You surely looked terrible when I opened the gate," I said. "Where have you lived these past few weeks? What have you been eating?"

"Oh, just been living with some of the gang out in air-raid shelters or under the stands in the athletic fields. The weather's been bad. It's not been much fun either since we met with another gang who outnumbered us so that we got the worst of it. Our food — well, we stole it from the little food stands on the streets, sometimes mugging the attendants before helping ourselves to what we wanted. The other fellows got tired of this after a while; so I sent them home. These last few days I've been all alone; it's been grim, pretty bad and scarey. I hate being alone." After this dissertation he fell silent for a time. Then he began again, "Got a lot of good boys though. We're really blood brothers and help each other. Got lots of secret things in our setup and even have our own language." Then he looked around in an embarrassed sort of way and said, "Gee — I've talked a lot! May I stay for the night? I can't go home."

"Well," I answered, "I could put you up in our little garden house." Hurriedly I went and fixed it up for him.

"Mind if I go to bed? I'm dead tired!" Ted said with a yawn.

"You may go to bed as soon as we've had prayers. This is a missionary's home," I explained, "and we have devotions before going to bed."

"Prayers? Devotions? What's all that? Okay, whatever you say. I'll try it and see. Sure sounds weird to me."

That evening the reading was from John's Gospel about Lazarus. Ted let me know right off he didn't think much of the gang Jesus had with Him. Too small, for one thing, and not very faithful. "I've got over seventy in my gang," he said, "and they do what I tell them, and we all stick together. Not like Jesus. He wasn't much of a big brother. Why, when that guy Laz... what's his name? — got sick and was dying, Jesus didn't even go to see him. I'd never do that! Why do you bother reading that stuff?"

"Off to bed! I'm tired," I said. I could hardly believe so much had happened in one evening but I refused to think any more that night about Ted and his affairs. I was out like a light in no time.

Next morning I was greeted cheerfully by Ted. "Hey!" he said, "You know, that's a good story. Jesus wasn't such a bad guy after all. Imagine Him making Lazarus live again!" Then he explained that as he hadn't been able to sleep he had gotten up, found John's Gospel in the Bible and finished reading about Lazarus.

This took me a bit by surprise, but I capitalized on the opportunity and discussed the story briefly. Then I gave him some work to do as I was going out on some errands.

"Where are you going?" he challenged me. "No point in going to see my parents — they won't have me back!"

But I did go to see his parents, hoping that his father would be away. Unfortunately he was very much at home and steaming and fuming about Ted, quite unaware that he was in my home. I could see this was no time to speak to him about Ted, so went home discouraged, realizing more and more the grave problem that had fallen on my shoulders. I sat down at my desk and wrote to three faithful prayer partners to ask their help in carrying this burden.

Ted stayed for days, days that soon turned into weeks. Gradually he seemed to be developing a feeling of security and began to respond to the love shown him. As far as I could tell, he didn't go out anywhere during this time, but daily he was asking questions which showed a growing interest in our devotional times.

Then came my "much more" from 2 Chronicles 25:9. One by one other boys from Ted's gang began turning up. How he had contacted them I don't know, but in the course of a week five came! Daily in my private devotions the Lord repeated His promise, "I am able to give you much more than this." *But I don't want any more of these boys,* I thought. I was starting to get criticism from people in Grace Church for having these boys in my house all the time. Because of their reaction, I couldn't be sure that this snowballing of things was from the Lord.

I prayed a lot about it, and the Lord's answer came, giving me the assurance that I needed — a very surprising answer. Our church youth conference was to start in just a few weeks, and I had a leading part in it as well as many other responsibilities. Besides that, I was very tired from my daily fight with the devil over these boys whom he wanted as badly as I did. I felt ill-prepared for the conference. Ted was upset about what was going to happen to him while I was away. "What'll I do while you're gone? May I stay here alone?" he asked.

My answer was an emphatic, "No!"

"Well, may I go with you to the conference?" he countered. "You said it was for young people. I'm young, and I'm a person. May I, please?"

I hardly knew what to say as I knew others would be worried about his presence there. As I prayed about it, it did seem wrong to turn him down when he was really wanting to attend; as well as showing some interest in our devotional time he had asked me to pray about certain things, his mother especially. He wanted God to comfort her so that she wouldn't cry so much. It seemed God had started a softening of his heart, but still I did not feel that I could give him an answer that night.

The next day at breakfast Ted brought up the subject again. "May I go? May I?"

"I'll have to talk it over with the committee and see how they feel," I replied.

That evening the young people's committee reluctantly agreed that Ted could attend — provided that I would bear full responsibility for him at the conference.

Ted was delighted when he heard the news. "May I take some of my gang with me to the conference?" was his next question. I was startled even at the thought of such a possibility.

"Hmm," I said, stalling for time. "I'll have to talk it over with the committee again."

That evening Ted, via his special grapevine system, contacted some of his gang, and they came over to see us. Surprisingly they seemed a lovely group of well-mannered, handsome young fellows — to look at them you would never have thought they were really a bunch of hoodlums. Five of them wanted to attend the conference along with Ted.

When I brought up this new request to the conference committee, they showed no enthusiasm whatsoever, as I had feared! Immediately some gave a flat NO! However, after we had prayed someone said, "Christ came for sinners. Do we have any right to say that these boys cannot come?" Again the stipulation was made that I must take full responsibility for the boys' actions. But at least they could come.

Fortunately most in the youth group knew nothing about "the gang." My boys promised me they would keep all the rules, attend all the meetings, and join in games and discussions.

Conference began and the speakers were super. Even the boys thought so. They participated in question and answer times and discussion groups wholeheartedly, which encouraged me no end. The evening messages were especially heart-searching. Yet, although by the fourth evening quite a few young people had accepted Christ, neither Ted nor his friends seemed to have been touched.

But then in the wee hours of the morning one of the gang members came to see me, under such deep conviction of sin that he couldn't sleep. "I have to talk to you *now*," he said urgently. Just as this boy was about finished recounting to me his unlovely story of sin, Ted arrived on the scene. "Hurry up," he said to his pal in his gruff way. "I want to take Jesus as my Savior too."

I could hardly believe my ears, but it was a very sober young man who stood there. "Don't bother telling me I have sin," he told me. "I know that. Just tell me what to do about it."

My heart was rejoicing as I answered his questions and we looked up passages of Scripture together. Then Ted said to me, "I'll pray tonight." Without hesitation he started in, "Hey God, are You tuned in on me? This is Ted. I'm dead like that man said tonight. I need You to clean up things. I've made an awful mess of my life. Can You do anything to help me? I'm here, God. Save me now like You said You would. I don't know how You do it, but go to it, God. Goodbye, Ted."

During the next few days we had many talks about the cost of being a Christian and about how to live the Christian life. Ted knew very well that he would be facing many battles and temptations, that this was just the beginning of living as a Christian.

After conference Ted's father allowed him to come home but was very angry when he found he had become a Christian. Not only did Ted face all kinds of persecution for this, but his father treated his mother even worse than before. Though Ted was forbidden to come to see me, he found ways to send along other boys, asking me to tell them what I had told him.

At last he managed to come himself, bringing along one of his best friends, second leader of another gang. "Here, Grandma, I just led him to the Lord. Now you see if I did it right." He seemed to have done a good job of it, which was a great encouragement to him.

I soon found that in this work it was easy to become too emotionally involved in the problems of the boys. Yet I knew that I didn't dare let this happen. So I asked the Lord for two things: that He would give me special wisdom to be balanced, and that He would make this new work acceptable to the church. Even so I slipped several times on the emotional angle.

On top of that, I never knew what would happen next; there just never seemed to be a dull moment. One afternoon, for instance, a young man whom I had been counseling arrived at the house very discouraged and depressed, yet for some reason unable to open up and talk. He came back again in the evening, stood at the gate but wouldn't come in. I thought this very odd behavior for him. Suddenly I looked at him and said,

"If you should die tonight, where would you go? Heaven or Hell?"

"Why do you ask that?" he shot back.

"You know why. Give me those pills."

"What pills?"

"You know what pills. You're not ready to die. You don't know Jesus as your Savior," I told him. Then lovingly but firmly I demanded that he turn the pills over to me.

"I don't have any," he insisted.

When I asked him to allow me to search him, he refused. "Give them to me," I repeated. By this time my friend had gone as weak as water. Slowly he reached into his pocket and pulled out a bottle of a hundred sleeping pills. Obviously he had intended to take the lot.

Today that boy, now grown up, is a bright and happy Christian, not perfect but growing and witnessing to the love of Christ.

The boys didn't find it easy to break away from the gangs in which they were involved. The devil doesn't give up his bid for a life without struggle. Bill, for example, accepted the Lord and really wanted to go straight and grow as a Christian. However, just at that time he was going to be expelled from school again for an earlier offence; so we made this a definite matter of prayer and then presented the case to the school authorities. After some persuasion, and an assurance that the boy really wanted to go straight, they agreed to give him another chance.

Not long after this Bill arrived at my home just a mass of blood. On his way home from school, he explained, he had suddenly been surrounded by his former gang. (Because these gangs have many secrets and consider themselves blood brothers, to leave or break away is viewed as a very serious thing.) There he was all alone against the whole gang. He didn't have a chance and took a terrific beating. Now that he had been involved in another fight — in spite of the circumstances — he knew it meant expulsion from school again. Naturally he was too scared to go home, but after cleaning up his wounds and having his school uniform washed and ironed I went with him, and we were able to explain the matter to his parents. Subsequently I went out to Bill's house every day to help him with English, to prepare him for the entrance examinations for senior high school — education in Taiwan is very competitive, and these examinations are very stringent. I also arranged for several university students to tutor him in other subjects. Eventually he was able to get into a good school and, in the process of my nearly daily contacts with his mother and sister, they also came to trust in Jesus. So the whole family is now one in Christ.

21
Monkeys and black eyes

By this time so many street boys were coming to my house that I simply didn't have time enough in the course of a day to have Bible study with each one. I was still helping with some of the outreach to university students, writing Bible study notes for the student magazine, and being involved with both the young people's and women's groups at church. My days were full. Yet these boys had a limited knowledge of the Gospel, and they really needed time for prayer and counseling, and an opportunity to talk over their particular problems. So I began to think about a Bible class for them.

My friends and co-workers laughed at the idea. "You're crazy if you think that kind of fellow will ever attend a Bible class. You're just wasting your time on that bunch of hoodlums. They'll never amount to anything," was the tone of their response.

But, in spite of this lack of encouragement, I did a lot of praying about the matter, and my friends at home did too. After a time I decided to put the idea of a class to the boys themselves, to see what they felt about it. Without hesitation they had an answer for me. "Sure, let's have a class," they chimed, then added quite in character, "then we can really heckle you!"

The boys called it "The Monkey Class." I must admit it was very descriptive, but I didn't think it set very high goals for the kids. "Look, fellows," I challenged them one day, "if you call yourselves 'The Monkey Class' you are just going to continue acting like monkeys. I've got a new name to suggest — see how you like it." In the middle of some special lessons on the Christian life, I had gotten a vision of these fellows really committing themselves to Christ. "Let's call this class 'The Hope of China Band'."

Immediately the room filled with the babble of the boys discussing the proposal among themselves. Could they live up to such a name? was the question. Some weren't sure. Yet in the end the group decided to adopt the new name.

In this kind of work one thing tends to lead to another, and "The Monkey Class" — now "The Hope of China Band" — was no exception. It was just about this time that I first heard rumors about government plans to build a school for the kind of troubled youth that were wearing a path to my door. The school, I gathered, was to be built on the outskirts of Changhua, the neighboring city where I went weekly to teach a Bible class at a Christian hospital. Immediately I felt led to ask a Chinese friend to pray with me that the Lord would open a door there for me to do something. "That's an absolute impossibility, and you know it," she said, laughing, a hint of scorn in her voice. "They would never ask a foreigner to go into a school like that." After a moment's thought she added halfheartedly,

"Well, all right — let's pray about it."

I was irritated. "There's no point in praying with you about this," I complained. "You don't believe God can do it." She argued. "No," I said, unmoved. "You wouldn't be praying the prayer of faith ... If you want to pray about it, you pray down here and I'll pray upstairs." And that's what we did.

I continued to pray. So did several of my faithful prayer partners. And every week on my way to the hospital for my Bible class, I would check on the progress at the new school as the brick walls rose higher and higher. When the roof took shape, I knew it could not be long before school would start. I tried to find out when, but no one I asked knew anything about it. I guess people thought I was crazy to be so interested in a school for problem boys.

Eventually, with no information at all to go on and no idea how to go about applying for the job, I gave up the idea of a ministry to the students at the new school. Since furlough was long overdue, I decided perhaps I had better just consider that the time had come. My sister was coming out for her third visit that summer, and we could travel home together.

I was in for a surprise, however. One day, as I was in the process of writing a letter requesting furlough, an invitation to tea at the governor's mansion arrived. *Must be some special Chinese holiday celebration*, I thought, since at times we foreigners were special guests at such occasions. But we hadn't had such an invitation in a long time.

I dashed around to discover who else among my friends had received an invitation. None had. What in the world was up?

With my curiosity in high gear, I set about to prepare to attend the affair on my own. I got out my best dress and looked over my shoes. The shoes had definitely seen better days; so I went out and bought a new pair. But my new shoes made my handbag look shabby; so I had to get a new handbag. *Can't go to the governor's tea looking like a tramp*, I thought. And, as one thing led to another, by the time the great day arrived I was quite decked out in new finery! Before I left the house, my househelper briefed me on how to behave in the presence of governors and other high officials!

I had no sooner parked my bike in front of the pillared edifice than I was ushered inside. To my astonishment, 'as my steps echoed in the expanses of the mansion's interior I discovered that I was not just the only foreigner, but the only outside guest at all. I was surrounded by Chinese officials, all looking very important.

My hosts wasted no time telling me why they had invited me to tea. Having heard about my work with the boys, they wanted to express their appreciation. It seems that some of those who had been helped came from families of the official class. It was just as well in this situation that I personally didn't know or care exactly who the boys were. As they usually gave aliases when they first came to me, sometimes it was a long time before I learned their full identities.

Now, on the recommendation of several high officials whose sons had been helped, my hosts were actually inviting me to do counseling in that new school I had been watching go up. I was to teach English as well.

I was speechless. Even though I had prayed specifically for this opening, I was completely unprepared for this moment. Before long, however, I rallied enough to ask politely, "You do know that I'm a missionary, don't you?"

"Yes, we do."

"Well," I said, jumping in with both feet, "since I am a missionary, I know that the only thing that will change these boys is the Gospel of Jesus Christ. If you have heard of any success in my work, it has not been because of anything I have done — it has been through the power of the Gospel of Jesus Christ." I wanted to state my case frankly so that they would be clear from the beginning about my position. I knew that most of the officials there were Buddhists, one was a Muslim and at least one other was an agnostic. I knew of not one Christian in the group.

"And as a Christian missionary," I continued, "I would like your permission to use the Bible, God's Word, in my counseling — because no change in the boys' environment, no pressure on them from the outside, and no new restrictions will change them for the good. No, change has to be in the heart, and this is what God does through His Word. In my counseling I must be permitted to use the Bible."

It was interesting to watch the expressions on their faces as I spoke. My ideas weren't going down very well, that was for sure, but I carried on. "My second request is that I not be required to put anything in writing to go into the boys' files which might later get into print."

"What is your third point?" someone then asked coolly.

"My third point is that I must keep absolute confidence about anything they say to me," and I turned to the governor, saying, "Even if you should ask me what any boy has said to me, I will not be able to tell you. These boys need to know that someone cares enough for them to keep her mouth shut." Though obviously taken aback by my proposals so far, my listeners still signaled to me to continue.

"My last point is that I will not accept a salary."

"Oh!" they protested, "but we were prepared to give you a good salary!"

"No," I persisted, "and I'm not asking for transportation expenses either. If this is something God wants me to do, He will provide the means for my travel expenses to the school."

"But why won't you take a salary?"

"Simply because one of the things these boys need to know is that someone cares enough to put herself out."

I don't remember whether I drank any of the tea or ate any of the goodies that were laid out on the long polished table. But once the interview was over I left as soon as it seemed polite to do so. As I rode home on my bike I thought, *Well, you've really cooked your own goose on that one!* I was sure those men would never invite me after all I had said. The only thing to do was to get on with plans for furlough.

Several weeks later the principal of the new school came to see me. Would I please come to the school regularly to do counseling? I could also teach as much English as I wanted to. What a moment of joy and victory! God had done it! He had answered our prayers of faith.

From my first day at the school it was obvious that, since eight of us had to share one office, most of my counseling would be done on the playing field. The boys would not open up if they thought others might be listening. So outside I went. When the boys were out on the playing field, I would amble around out there with an old camera slung over my shoulder. I wouldn't be alone for long. Singly, in pairs or in groups the boys would join me. Before they realized it they were opening up to me, spilling out the things that troubled them — problems, loves, hates. Then we would sit down on the ground as if to watch the game or competition, but actually we would continue talking over things that mattered, with no eavesdroppers.

With English classes meant to focus on conversational skills, we talked about almost anything. Sometimes the boys asked very direct questions:

"Grandma, why are you a missionary?"

"What does a missionary do?"

"Are you a nun?"

"What's Jesus?"

"Why do you come to our school?"

"Did you have any problems when you were young?"

My answers always contained some of my own testimony — things that had bothered me as a young person, something of my own wayward ways. Sharing how I had felt and how miserable I had been helped them to know that I could understand their yearnings, fears and misery. Ever so gradually I was able to get close to one and another of these troubled kids. They needed much time — and the kind of patience that only love could generate.

"Grandma," a group of them asked one day out of the blue, "may we go to your house on Sundays?" Though a bit taken aback, I knew the background to this request. If they maintained good behaviour during the week, they were permitted several hours out on Sunday afternoon. The problem often was, where to go.

"Sure, you can come to my house," I answered, hiding my reservations. "Come along — my door is always open."

"If we come," they warned, "we're going to steal everything you've got."

"That's all right," I told them. "Just steal my things according to your conscience. And I'm not going to hide anything away either." And I never did — nor did I ever miss anything as a result of their visits.

These kids had very bad records for the most part, and they delighted in trying to shock me. Once a group even passed on some pointers in the art of pickpocketing! I never put my new-found knowledge into practice, of course, but it did help me later on to detect someone trying to pick *my* pocket!

At school I spent time watching them taking judo lessons as part of their physical education program. I even agreed when they asked me one day to give it a try myself. After a few lessons I caught on to the various holds, and one day I managed to throw two people! I suspect that the two were really cooperating with me, but they wouldn't admit it, and the show was apparently convincing enough that the spectators decided never again to try any tricks on me.

My being willing to enter both the nonsense and no-nonsense areas of the boys' lives was, I felt, beginning to pay off. I was encouraged. At least I had my foot in the door. Still, when God worked to bring the real breakthrough I longed for, it was not something I planned and certainly not a way I would have chosen.

Running late for the meeting I was to take, I was cycling toward the university through the lengthening shadows, racing along the always-busy streets at a pretty good clip. Cresting a hill and heading with the traffic down a long grade, I suddenly spotted not far ahead of me a little boy of about two or three, breaking into the street headed for the other side. I braked, swerved deftly to thread my bike behind the youngster, and was just about to sigh my relief when like lightning he turned around and headed straight into my path.

I had nowhere to go. On one side I faced heavy on-coming traffic, on the other parked trucks. I knew if I hit the child it would be right in the center of his body, and would surely kill him. My thoughts in a frenzy of fear, I veered my front wheel toward the parked trucks, brakes on hard and screeching. People standing along the side looked on in horror.

But my wheel didn't touch the child. Instead he struck my thigh and plunked down on the road on his seat, hard. A great yowl rose from a fear-contorted face, and tears soon gushed. Yet the little jaywalker was not hurt. Not at all.

As for me — well, I was like the man on the flying trapeze, flying through the air with the greatest of ease. Over the handlebars I went, crashing flat on my face. Oh, the crunch as I hit the road! Gone, I was sure, was any beauty I might ever have had. Almost immediately I knew I was now without my front teeth. From the pain in my jaw I judged that it was dislocated, and as I felt gingerly the big gash in my upper lip I discovered the lip dangling freely, probably sliced by the teeth. I guessed my nose must be broken, and a wound by my left eye was spurting blood like a geyser. And oh, how my legs hurt, especially the left one which was still twisted in the bicycle framework. Painfully I worked myself free.

By now people were crowding around me, offering to take me to the hospital. Just down the road, I managed to tell them, were some missionaries with a car who would get me to a doctor.

Fifteen stitches zipped up my lip and a quick maneuver put my jaw back into place, neither procedure a pleasant experience! Next day my leg and feet were x-rayed, and the left leg went into a walking cast to mend the broken foot bones and cracked ankle. Finally I had a look in the mirror. What a sight! There I stood toothless, bandaged, and with two of the most beautiful black eyes ever seen! However, tragedy had been averted, and how I praised the Lord for that!

Soon I was hobbling around again. When the day came for me to go to the boys' school, my eyes were still black and my friends were horrified that I planned to go along as usual. "You can't go over there looking like that!" they exclaimed. But I did.

The minute I got out of the taxi, some of the boys came running up to me. "Grandma, whatever has happened to you?"

"Oh," I said, "the other night my gang got messin' around this other gang — but you should see *them*!" We had a good laugh, and then I explained about my accident. After this the boys seemed more approachable and more willing to come and talk with me than ever before. I suppose they felt I really must care if I would put out such an effort to come over to see them. However they interpreted it, my accident seemed to go over big with them! The Lord had used it for good.

However, about two months later, when all the abrasions were healed and I had new front teeth in my mouth, I began to experience excruciating pains down my right arm and left leg. Since I was already over fifty by this time, I just put it down to getting old, never dreaming that it might be related to the accident. *Anyone over fifty has a right to few aches and pains,* I thought. Yet daily the pain got worse, making it impossible for me to sleep at night. Aspirin didn't help — in fact nothing helped. Then suddenly I realized I was losing mobility and sensitivity in both limbs. That frightened me.

The next time I went to teach my class at the hospital I took the opportunity to look up the doctor and describe what was happening. He sent me up to the neurologist, who was convinced that there was some nerve damage. X-rays showed some changes in the vertebrae of the lower back, impinging on several of the root nerves. As x-rays of the neck area didn't show anything, however, I was told I'd have to go into hospital for more observation of that area and for treatment of my back.

Being in the hospital didn't help. The pain just got worse and worse while doctors tried to find the place of injury by taking x-rays from every possible angle. I couldn't understand why all this was happening, since I had a very busy summer schedule ahead of me, with eight different conferences coming up. After the first few days in the hospital, I very reluctantly canceled my part in all eight.

Then one day an x-ray taken through my open mouth revealed the problem — a break in the bodies of three vertebrae in the cervical region, most likely cracked in the bicycle accident. They had begun to separate and get more out of position. As the separation had been gradual, the pressure on the nerves was not sudden, but both pain and paralysis grew slowly and progressively worse. By now my right arm was absolutely useless, like a stick of wood hanging at my side. I lay in my bed wondering if I would ever use it again.

I had a new kind of life to adjust to now as I was put in traction for 23 hours a day. I felt like an elastic band stretched to its greatest limit. In the beginning the doctor told me I'd be all right in about two weeks. But those two weeks stretched into almost four months. When I was moved into a private room to ensure proper rest, it meant no limit on the number of people who could come to visit me. Naturally having visitors helped take my mind off my near immobility, and I had already said to the Lord, "I don't care how many people come as long as they don't tell me how their great uncle or somebody had this same sort of trouble and died a horrible death! Lord," I continued, "please keep the Job's comforters away and just send people with prepared hearts."

And that is exactly what the Lord did! Every day there were visitors, some coming out of curiosity to see how I was strung up, some coming with burdens needing help. I didn't care about their motives, for I had a deep assurance that each was prepared by the Lord and that He had some purpose to bringing them. I longed to give a helpful word to each one. People who had previously shied away from me came now, feeling that maybe I could understand their problems and needs. Boys from the school, which was not far from the hospital, sneaked out to see me and talk, even though they knew that when they got back they would be punished. Surprisingly, many of the staff from the school, who had previously been rather distant because I was a missionary, came pouring out their hearts' needs. Since I was in such difficulty they seemed to feel I could understand their needs, and barriers were broken down.

I was even able to continue my Bible classes with the nurses-in-training from my hospital room. I wonder if I am the only person who ever conducted Bible classes while hanging!

My hours of immobility were being turned into blessing, for me and others as well. In fact I think I can honestly say that this time in the hospital was the most fruitful part of my whole life in China. So many came to see me that the nurses decided to keep a guest record, and at the end of my stay when they totaled the number of different individuals who had come, to our astonishment the total was 1,253. Had I been able to go to the eight scheduled conferences, it is doubtful that I could have personally contacted as many people as I did in these weeks. As most came alone and without the pressure of time were willing to open up, we often got down to business spiritually.

But my time in the hospital bed was only the beginning of this episode, for I had to learn to walk again. Sometimes I wondered as I tried to walk, *How on earth did I ever make my feet and legs work before?* Physiotherapy treatment lasted a long time, until gradually the muscles were reeducated and began to do what they were supposed to once again. As I was finally leaving the hospital, however, I got the news that I would have to return daily for physiotherapy treatments.

"I can't possibly make the trip over to the hospital every day," I balked. Then suddenly I thought of one of the Chinese martial arts called "shadow boxing," that very slow, deliberate exercise with its over 250 body movements supposed to include every muscle in the body.

"If I took up Chinese shadow boxing, would that take the place of daily physiotherapy?" I asked the doctor abruptly.

His answer was a laugh, probably prompted by a mental picture of me going through those contortions! Then he replied, "I guess you could give it a try, but do come in once a week for physiotherapy when you come to teach. I don't know where you'll find a shadow boxing teacher, though."

"That's easy," I said. "The man who teaches me Chinese painting has been after me about this for a long time."

And so it was arranged, and Mr. Han began instructing me at 5.30 a.m. in my garden. From the second day four other women joined me in the class. Though neither the teacher nor the other ladies were Christians, as we sat around and talked after the class the conversation would often turn to the things of God.

The shadow boxing in my yard even caught the attention of an American serviceman living nearby. Each morning as he came down his stairs on the way to the air base he could see us performing! Then all along his way to work he saw other Chinese people shadow boxing in parks and yards. One day he could stand it no longer, and seeing me out in my yard on a Sunday afternoon he called over to me, "Ma'am, may I ask you a question? Are you Chinese, or are you a foreigner?"

"Oh," I laughed, "I'm a foreigner. I'm an American." No wonder he was a bit confused, since most of the time I wore Chinese dress because of working with the boys, and for the shadow boxing I wore a regular Chinese pajama suit.

"Ma'am," he continued, 'just one more question. What is it that you people are doing in the garden every morning? Is that some kind of a religious dance?"

"No, it's not," I laughed. "Why don't you come on in for a cup of coffee and we can chat a bit." We had a nice talk that day, and from that time he came often, sometimes bringing his buddies. He was flying in and out of Vietnam, so he always came to tell me when he was going and ask me to be sure to pray for him.

And so little by little I came to realize all that God was accomplishing through my accident, and I could only praise Him for His plan.

22
Diamonds in the rough

As the boys who were taking up my life those days in Taichung were troubled, problem boys, whose maddeningly unpredictable ways sometimes more than hid their potential, I got to thinking of them as diamonds in the rough. Once in Amsterdam, Holland, on my way home for furlough I had watched a master diamond cutter at work on a gem. The uncut crystal lying before him did not look much like a diamond; it certainly was not yet a thing of beauty. At first the master craftsman just studied the stone. I don't know how long he had already studied it — perhaps for days or even weeks. Suddenly, however, he dealt the gray-white stone a sharp blow. This was no random blow, but well planned and well aimed. And the crude crystal fell apart along the lines he knew it would, and a thing of dazzling beauty began to be revealed.

Like that crude diamond in the rough, my boys in all their unloveliness needed the right blow from the Master to break their resistance and to begin to reveal the beauty locked within. I never knew as I worked with them exactly what the blow might be; it was different for each boy. All of them, however, had missed out somewhere in the matter of love. God confirmed this to me one day while I was praying especially for some whom I was finding very difficult. As clearly as if He had spoken audibly, the Lord said, "All you can do is to love them and to let them know that someone cares." Not that I was to be soft with them. But, just like the blow that the diamond cutter gave the rough diamond in Amsterdam, dealings with these rough young characters had to be guided by the One who knows when and where to strike and how to do it in love.

One boy, I remember, seemed to be responding quite well to counseling and to be getting his behavior problems solved, when suddenly he went flop. He forgot all his commitments and was spiritually flat on his face. Of course this meant he was scared to come to see me. But one day, to my surprise, he arrived at my gate. Angry with him, I guess, for the way he had scuttled his advances, I just blew my top when I saw him. Oh, did I explode! Then I did something I don't easily do — I burst out crying. His condition must really have been getting to me. He looked at me, absolutely stunned. "Grandma!" he exclaimed. "Why do you care so much? Nobody else cares about me!"

My outburst did something to that boy. It was the "blow" he needed — for from that day he began to leave his old ways and habits behind. In time, in fact, he went on to university and became one of the leaders in the Christian group there. Though I had had little hope for that rough diamond, the Lord was teaching me that with Him there are no hopeless cases and that He knows how and when to touch people.

Not knowing what God might use to reach a boy, I was always in for surprises. As the words of Zechariah 4:6 explain — "Not by might, nor by power, but by My Spirit" — it was not what I did which brought about miracles, but what God did by His Holy Spirit, often through the smallest of things. One lad, for example, suddenly became very responsive and started coming often to see me about his problems. He was so eager to hear more about the Gospel that I was frankly puzzled by the sudden change. One day, however, he let me in on the secret: "You remembered my name!" he said with feeling. "You remembered my name!"

That this foreign lady had remembered his name out of a class of over thirty meant to him that I cared, that he was important to me. It was a small blow — but a skilful blow in the hands of the Master Diamond Cutter, a blow that opened his life to the Lord Jesus.

Well-aimed blows used on other rough diamonds were Scripture verses, hand-picked by the Lord. It was my practice at the end of each Hope of China Bible Class to give each student a little card with a Scripture verse on it — Chinese on one side, English on the other. Each Sunday morning I would go over to the church early to check that everything was in order for my class and, going from chair to chair around the classroom, I would pray for the fellow who would be sitting in each one. I would pray for God to work in his heart during the study time and to make sure he got the verse that would most help and bless him in the week to come. God wonderfully answered those prayers over the years — but when Stephen picked up his card on his way out of the class, I had no idea which verse he received nor the effect it would have on his life.

For some time I had been missing things around the house. Since my home was like Grand Central Station, with people coming and going all the time, I had no idea who the culprit was. When one day a sizable sum of money disappeared that I knew I hadn't misplaced I told no one, but went to the Lord about the problem.

About a month after the money disappeared I had been working late to finish the Bible studies for the student magazine, and had just wearily switched off my light at about 3 a.m. when I heard a car pull into my lane and stop. Next the outer gate creaked open and the sound of muffled voices came to me. In a few seconds my doorbell rang. Whatever was going on?

I shuffled to the door, and as I opened it I saw a woman standing there with a very downcast, sorry-looking lad at her side. It was Stephen and his mother. Rather bewildered, I ushered them into my living room, and before long they were pouring out their story.

It seemed that it was Stephen who had stolen my money. Though under such deep conviction of sin that he had been feeling physically unwell for some time, he hadn't been willing to give in to what he knew God would have him do. But the previous Sunday he had attended our Bible class, and the verse he received was, "Be sure your sin will find you out." It wasn't the kind of verse a thief could easily put out of his mind! He knew God was speaking directly to him.

Two or three days after attending the Bible class, Stephen had run away. "Don't look for me," he had written his mother in a note. "You won't find me." She was terrified. Where had he gone, and why? What was he doing?

Yesterday he had reappeared, however, explaining that he had gone off to think about important things such as what kind of a person he wanted to be. But when he went to bed, he couldn't sleep. In desperation he had gotten up, called his mother and told her what he had done.

"Gather up all the things you have taken from Grandma Han, and we will take them back — tonight," she told him.

Just as they were leaving the house, she had called to her husband to tell him where they were going. "You're crazy!" he growled, and tried to stop them. But the mother insisted, convincing him that I would understand.

And of course I did understand, and was very thankful for that wise Christian mother and the stand she took that night. As for me, it was a night I shall never forget. Stephen was truly broken before the Lord and humbled before man as he poured out his confession and made restitution.

Stephen didn't have an easy time of it after that — there was much to straighten out. But, standing with him in loving support, we encouraged him to leave no loopholes for the devil. Having to stand up against much opposition in his school, he had a hard climb back to the straight path, and he slipped many a time. Yet in the years since, as far as I know, he has continued on well against many odds.

Jim was another in whose life God used the Scripture text cards in a very dramatic way. Jim, a really lovable kid, came to the class regularly and at one point made a profession of faith in the Lord Jesus. In fact, he suffered a lot for his stand for Christ. But then all of a sudden he stopped coming to the class, and even for his tutoring. I was puzzled; it was so unlike him.

After several weeks I asked some of the other fellows about his absence. "Is he sick?"

"He's not coming any more," was all they could say. No one would give me any more information, not even an inkling.

What did I do or say to hurt him? I wondered with a heavy heart, feeling sure that the problem must be something of this sort. I continued earnestly praying for Jim, for he was a boy who really needed help and encouragement in his Christian life.

But week after week went by and I still didn't see him or know where to find him. He didn't even answer the notes I sent to him, and the other boys still wouldn't venture any information about him. I was beginning to worry now that he might be in serious trouble.

One afternoon, as I was riding my bicycle down one of Taichung's main streets, I suddenly spied him up ahead. He was riding towards me; but he must have spotted me as well, for he suddenly veered into a side street. Between us was a traffic light, and it was red! As I sailed through it, I yelled to the dumbfounded policeman, "I'll be back and tell you what it's all about." Fortunately mine was a good three-speed bike while Jim's was an old beat-up one, overdue for the junk pile; so I quickly caught up with him.

"Hey, Jim," I called, "where have you been?"

"Nowhere," was his sullen, almost angry reply.

"Then why haven't you been to class?" I persisted.

"I'm not coming anymore," he said with finality, his black eyes showing defiance.

"Well, why not? What have I done? Just tell me what I've done," I pleaded. I loved this boy. But he was not talking. And now as we faced each other there on the street, people began to gather to see what the discussion was about and why the old foreign lady was carrying on such an argument with this young fellow. "Hey, look, now we've got a crowd gathering," I said, sure that he was no happier about it than I. "Why don't we ride out to my house and talk things over?"

Reluctantly Jim mounted his bike and we pedaled over to my house. Once we were settled in my sitting room I resumed my probe. "Now tell me what I have said or done that has hurt you or stumbled you. Please! There must be some reason. You used to come every Sunday, and during the week for help with your studies too. Now you don't even come in for your time with the tutors, and nobody knows why. What is it?"

"You always give me the same card," he finally blurted out, his fine features distorted with feelings welling up within him.

"What?" I responded incredulously. "I have no idea what card I give any of you. I just stand at the door and give them out as they come. I don't know who is going to be next in line the way you fellows push and shove each other. I don't know what verse I've been giving you," I went on. "What verse is it anyway?"

"I John 1:9."

"Well," I said, "next to John 3:16 I think that's just about the best verse in the Bible. 'If we confess our sins, He is faithful and just to forgive us our sins and to cleanse us from all unrighteousness.' What's better than that?" Then an idea came to me. "Maybe you have some unconfessed sin. Maybe you are hiding something."

He sat there very sullen for a long time, not willing to say anything.

"Well," I proposed at last, getting up from my chair, "I'll just let you sit here and think awhile. I've got some things to do so I'll be out in the other room. You can call me when you want me."

Jim didn't sit there very long. God the Holy Spirit was working in his heart. "*Han Po Po*," he summoned, and I came back to hear his tale. I have never seen anyone under such conviction of sin as he was. He beat his chest as he exclaimed in agony, "I killed a man in cold blood, and someone else is in prison for it." Perspiration was beading on his bronzed face. "That man has a wife and children — and he's already been in prison for about two years." The boy's spirit was pulverized.

I sat there praying silently for wisdom. "What do you think you ought to do?" I asked at last.

Jim stared at the floor. "Well," he stammered after a long silence, "I guess I ought to go and report myself."

"Before you do that you had better count the cost," I counseled. "You know if you report yourself, the authorities will probably put you in prison."

"That doesn't matter; anything is better than the way it's been," he groaned.

"It might even mean the firing squad," I warned, feeling that he needed to face the seriousness of what he proposed.

"I've got to go!" he cried, again beating his breast, his knuckles white. "I've go to! Anything is better than this!"

"Be sure that this is what you want to do," I advised "One thing is sure: if you go and confess this thing, you will have peace in your heart, for God will forgive you.

If you don't, you're going to have to live with yourself in misery."

"I know. I know," he blurted impatiently. "You don't need to tell me that." He looked at me resolutely and added, "I'm going over to the courts right away to tell them. Will you go with me?"

"No, I won't," I answered. It hurt to refuse him, but I explained, "If I go with you and they put you in jail or in the house of detention, when you are sitting there alone the devil is going to say to you, 'That old maid missionary made you do this. She got you into this mess. What a fool you were!' No, if you are going to do this, you've got to do it on your own ... I'll stay here and pray for you while you go over to make your confession. But don't do anything hastily. You've got to be sure," I added, urging that we both take time to pray. He agreed reluctantly, and we had prayer together before he went home.

Early the next morning Jim appeared on my doorstep looking very bedraggled. Obviously he hadn't slept any better than I. "I've got to go," he said.

"I'll be here praying," I promised. "The Lord will be with you and give you wisdom and strength. If they put you in the house of detention, I can bring you food."

I went into my bedroom and closed the door, kneeling down to pray for him. I don't know how long I had been there, but I was still on my knees when Jim returned. It seemed such a short time that I said, "You didn't go!"

"Sure, I went," he replied, rather pleased with himself. "They didn't know what to do with me, so they told me to go home. They said they would investigate and call me when they wanted me."

Days grew into weeks and weeks into months — so many months that I wondered whether the officials were doing anything or whether they had dropped the case. During this time of waiting, however, Jim came in nearly every day for Bible study and prayer and grew steadily in the Lord. He had a real burden for his unsaved family members, and we were praying for them. Neither they nor any of his friends knew anything about what had been going on. Soon he had the joy of leading a younger sister to the Lord, then another, and finally his mother.

After about eight months Jim came one day with an official-looking envelope in his hand and said stiffly, "Well, Grandma, this is it. I have to go to the law courts." Then he added, a bit more confidently, "I'll be like Paul in prison, preaching the Gospel."

I replied, smiling a little, "By the way, Paul, do you have a Bible?"

"Oh no, I forgot it," he confessed a bit sheepishly. So I gave him a Bible, and after we'd had a time of prayer he went off.

Again I was on my knees praying for him when he returned rather quickly. Once more I was sure he just hadn't gone. Perplexed, I asked, "Hey, what's up? Didn't you go? Don't you know that if you don't go on time you'll be in real trouble?"

"Oh," he said, "I went all right. It was a bit scarey facing all those stern officials, but they still don't know what to do with me. They've investigated everything, know exactly where I've been and what I've been doing all these months — even know how often I've been here at your place and what I've been doing here." That last bit of news really gave me the shivers!

Jim continued, "I sure was relieved when they told me that the man who was in prison has been released, and restitution has been made as far as possible. They've found that these months my life has been flawless. They said that I'm a useful citizen now and don't see much point to taking my life or putting me in prison. 'Nothing would be gained by that,' they said. They warned me that as long as I go straight I'm free; but if I do anything wrong I'm in real trouble. Then after that the judge — he was an old, kind of fatherly man — came down from the bench and put his arm around my shoulder. 'Now son, tell me what made you change like this?' he asked."

So Jim had had a marvelous opportunity to stand up in the court and tell what the Lord Jesus had done for him. Later through the help of various tutors he was able to pass the entrance exam to get into a good college. After graduation he married and now has a lovely Christian family. God used His Word on that rough diamond to bring out the beauty of the Lord Jesus in his life.

The polishing of these diamonds took years, of course, and sometimes faith had to strain to see progress. One Sunday, for example, I was teaching on the Christian life, stressing the responsibilities we have as Christians. Since they were called the Hope of China Class, I guess I was emphasizing the point that they were the hope of their country. In response one big brawny fellow, almost six feet tall and sitting on the first row, stood up. He said nothing at first — just looked around at his fellow students and then back at me. "Grandma," he began, "if the hope of China depends on us, I don't think there is much hope." But he was wrong. Many of those once-delinquent boys have turned out to be very useful citizens and are now leaders in their fields of work and in the churches in Taiwan and abroad.

Those boys really enjoyed singing and some of them had lovely voices. One day when we were lustily singing one of their favorites, "When the Roll is called up yonder," I noticed one boy not joining in. As we had a rule that everybody had to join in, I asked John, "Why aren't you singing?"

"I can't sing that because my name's not on the roll," he answered honestly. That day he stayed after class to accept Christ and to have his name added to God's roll of His own.

Peter had been a regular attender of the Bible Class, but although he knew a lot abut the Lord and was truly interested in the Bible study, he had made no personal profession of faith in Christ. One day I faced him with his position. "I'll believe," he said, looking me straight in the eye, "when I see someone who lives what he says he believes. I want to see it working in somebody's life."

It took a long time before the "blow" fell which caused this fellow to believe in the Jesus he knew so much about. But one day there was a knock at my gate and I called out, "Who is it?"

"It's me!" This was the usual response. The trick was that I was supposed to recognize the voice, some of the fellows getting upset if I didn't.

This time I recognized Peter's voice, relieved to hear its familiar ring. "Peter!" I said, "so glad you've come at last. What's on your mind?"

"I've come today because I want to accept Jesus as my Savior," he announced as we walked into the house.

"Are you kidding?" I probed. "This is no joking matter, you know."

"I know that," Peter replied seriously. "I've been watching someone these past few months, and now I know it works."

I have no idea who that person was. But it made me think about how often people may be watching us and how often we may make them stumble or cause them to disbelieve the Gospel.

I guess you could hardly call it a blow that made the change in Jerry's life. I found out only when he came back to visit me during his college days, just how the Lord had worked with this diamond in the rough. "The very first time I came here to your house," he explained, "it was with a friend of mine who wanted me to meet you. Then he had gone off somewhere, and just as he had left someone called at your gate. You went out to pay a bill, coming back inside with the change in your hand — but just then someone else called. You put the money down on the table, went out and stayed quite a while talking. Temptation got the better of me ... but just as I was in the act of reaching for the money, Cinderella jumped up, grabbed my hand and bit me!" Jerry couldn't have known that my dog Cindy was very jealous of my belongings and that no one could touch anything on that table; my househelper couldn't even dust it!

"If I had taken that money," Jerry continued, "I would never have come back again." But he had come back again and again till the Lord melted his heart and he put his trust in Christ as his Savior. No, it wasn't a blow exactly — it was a bite! Well, I say, by any means preach the Gospel, even if your dog has to bite a guest for you to get the chance!

Bob was a fellow who knew my dog Cindy much better. He had been many times to my home to pour out his problems. But that was the trouble. When he came one night, made his way into my living room and sat down as usual, I suspected nothing. What I didn't realize was that he had first gone into the back yard, enticing Cinderella to follow him and then shutting her out there. Suddenly, as we chatted, Bob jumped up and lunged at me, grabbing one shoulder and putting a knife to my throat. His scheme to kill me had been well planned! Faithful Cindy, who had come to my rescue on other occasions, could not now do so, and I realized all too well the seriousness of my predicament.

Wonderfully, however, the Lord took all fear from my heart, and I said to Bob, "Why do you want to kill the only friend you have?"

"You know too much," he answered gruffly, still holding my shoulder firmly, the knife not moving. "If you ever told any of the things I've told you, I'd probably be up for life or more."

"Have I ever broken confidence?" I asked him.

"No, but I can't take the chance," he growled.

"Well, if I have kept confidence, why do you want to kill me?"

"I'm afraid some day you might." His grip seemed to be a little less strong.

"Bob," I challenged, "do you think you will get away with this?" No answer. I continued, "Before you kill me, would you let me pray to commit myself to the Lord?"

"Well, yeh, I guess I could do that," he conceded.

So I just bowed my head, with Bob still holding me tightly. He was a big fellow and meant business, but the Lord seemed to be guiding me what to do. I honestly did not preach a sermon as I prayed that night. I just committed myself to the Lord and asked Him to have mercy on Bob. It was a very short prayer. When I raised my head and opened my eyes, his grip on my shoulder released completely and he laid the knife down on my table. Before me stood a broken boy.

Soon after this incident Bob came to trust the Lord. My prayer had been the blow God used. Bob didn't hate me; he was just one scared boy, scared stiff that I wouldn't keep confidence. Later he apologized for his actions and asked for my forgiveness, not once but many times. Several years later, when he had the opportunity to go to America for further study, he came to ask me for a letter of recommendation, and I wrote a good one for him. How could I write a good recommendation after he had tried to kill me? That was his old life; now Bob was a new man in Jesus Christ.

23
Not with my sickle!

One day some police plainclothesmen came to my door with a most unusual request. They often visited me, not to spy on any boy but rather in an effort to help. They would come just to the gate to talk so that any boy in the house would assume they were visitors, perhaps from the church. On this occasion my plain-clothed visitors came to tell me that they had gotten wind of a big gang fight scheduled for that night out on the edge of town. "Most of the boys on our list have never been taken in before," they told me, "and we're not interested in just picking them up, giving them a bad record. Would it be possible for you to ride out there this evening and somehow try to head them off?"

What an assignment! "Well," I replied slowly, "I do have a meeting tonight, but I think I could arrange to come home that way, probably just about the time they would be assembling for the fight."

These boys always picked a dark country road for their battles, and as I biked home from my meeting that night along the appointed night-shrouded lane I began to pick up fellows in my headlights. Some I knew. "Hi, Grandma! Where are you going?" one shouted.

"Oh, I'm just on my way home," I answered casually, getting off my bike. Since these boys were basically polite, they immediately got off their bikes too. And while we stood there in the road talking, other boys, kids from both gangs, sidled by.

"Hey," I called, "I haven't seen you fellows for a long time."

Too embarrassed not to stop, they dismounted from their bikes and joined the crowd. Before long we had quite a little gathering along that dark road. I could see that some were getting anxious to move on — but with this old woman keeping the conversation going, their upbringing wouldn't let them dash off impolitely.

After some time I looked at my watch and said, "Hey, fellows, it's cold out here, and it's getting late. What say you all come over to my house, and I'll make a kettle of hot soup or some hot chocolate to warm us up?" By now some who had passed by without stopping were making their way back. Since it looked as if the fight was off for the night the two gangs decided to take me up on my crazy invitation, and off we all trooped to my house. Later, as we sat drinking cocoa and eating cookies, no one could have guessed that the boys were from two warring gangs. "Well, maybe this is better than what we had planned," someone remarked.

"Oh," I asked with mock innocence, "did you have something planned?"

They all looked at each other and then burst out laughing as they explained what they had been up to. They had no idea that I was in on it!

However, the devil doesn't sit idly by when he is thwarted. When I involved myself with these boys, I knew I was engaged in a spiritual battle. And I was not "disappointed." Often in difficult situations I have claimed the promise of Romans 8:28, "We know that all things work together for good to them that love God, to them who are called according to His purpose." But sometimes in the heat of the battle I have found myself doubting. Such was the case in Tony's life.

Not feeling well one night, I came home from the young people's meeting early. But as I reached my house I was shocked to find the door standing wide open and the window beside it burned and smashed. Obviously someone had gone in through the window and then opened the door. The back door was also wide open and my dog at the time, Coca-Cola, was nowhere to be seen.

Cautiously I went inside, assessing the situation. I knew I had left the sliding door to the upper *tatami* level of my house open; now it was closed. As I thought about going up to investigate, an inner voice seemed to warn me against doing so. Instead I turned on my heel and hurried out of the house and over to my neighbor who had a telephone. "Please," I gasped, "would you call the police? Someone has broken into my house and I don't know if there's anyone still inside or not."

When the police came and we entered the house together the sliding door, shut before, was now open. Someone had indeed been inside! We found poor Coca-Cola in the bathroom. Stunned, he was just regaining consciousness and was staggering around as if to say, "What's going on around here?"

"Did you hear Coco bark?" I asked my neighbor, who was tagging along with me.

"No," she answered quite positively. "I'm sure I didn't hear him."

The intruder must be someone Coco knows, I concluded silently. We were looking around the upper section of the house now. Japanese houses are noted for their huge cupboards, and I guess missionaries are known for the wide array of stuff they store. Anyway, my cupboards had been ransacked, and everything from Bibles to clothes for orphans was now strewn every which way. But my annoyance turned to dismay when I realized that among the missing things were the three tape recorders I used for teaching English. In fact, anything that could be sold for cash — such as my camera, record player and radio — had disappeared.

But the disappearance of one other thing really puzzled me. My preaching Bible was missing from beside the pillow on the divan, where I had left it earlier in the day. Not feeling well, I had been lying down on the divan as I prepared for the next day's meeting. *Why would a thief move my Bible?* I wondered. Suddenly out of the corner of my eye I spotted that much-used copy of God's Word stuffed in the waste paper basket, way down under my working table.

Another thing I noticed having been disturbed was the cards with the boys' names on. I used these in praying for my charges, a certain number each day, and ordinarily the packet would be stacked in a neat pile with an elastic band around it. Now the band was off and the pile flipped to a certain name, that of a boy in the army. *No, he couldn't possibly have done this,* I thought.

The police were now dusting for fingerprints. When the detectives asked if I had any idea who might have done the job, I quite honestly had to answer "no." My suspicions were nothing to go on. I decided not to mention the name turned up on the card; I didn't want to point the finger at anyone.

A couple of days later an anti-Christian newspaper in Taichung came out with the headline: "God did not protect His servant Pauline Hamilton." I felt badly about this smear on God's name; besides, it was definitely unhealthy publicity for me.

The robbery had taken place on Saturday night. The following Monday evening I had a visitor — Tony, the boy whose name was turned up on the prayer card! He had brought a friend with him. I didn't mention a thing about my misfortune. Yet Tony was acting strangely — insisting, for instance, on sitting underneath the window rather than in the chair facing the window that I had indicated.

"How does it happen that you are out of the army?" I asked.

"Oh," he said, "I'm on the basketball team," producing a pass that gave him special leave. As the boys were always changing dates on permits and the like, I had become quite adept at spotting counterfeits. This pass, I was quite sure, had been altered.

We had a pleasant enough visit, but on Friday night, when I returned from the boys' school, a group of fellows were waiting for me on the other side of the street when I got off the bus. "Grandma!" they called. "Come over here — we want to see you!"

"What's up?" I asked, not happy with the fact that I didn't know any of them. "Who are you?" I probed.

They identified themselves, giving both their names and the gangs they belonged to. A bit uneasily I crossed over to where they were clustered.

"We hear that Tony is talking big," they began. "He's the one who robbed you, and he's hiding." *So it was Tony after all!* "He's really laying it in for you," my informants continued, "and means to kill you." Tony wasn't a gang member but a loner, and a loner can be more fearsome than gang boys, especially when he gets scared and feels cornered. I wondered if police suspicions were putting pressure on him.

"Tony's been talking real big," the boys repeated seriously.

"Oh, he's just a big bag of wind," I said, pooh-poohing their warning.

"No, not this time," they insisted. "He means business."

I swallowed dryly and was about to open my mouth when the spokesman continued, "We're going to protect you. You must promise us never to go anywhere by your usual shortcuts. He knows them all."

"Oh come now," I laughed. "How are you going to protect me?"

"We're going to set a watch every night at your gate and at each end of your front and back lanes. Eight of us gangs are working together on this and there will be eight different fellows every night." I was dumbfounded. These boys, usually enemies to each other, were so angry that anyone would rob me that they were uniting to protect me, and they had thought through their plan very thoroughly.

The eight gangs wanted to take complete charge of the situation, and would have had no compunction about killing Tony except that I insisted that they keep their hands off. "Look here, fellows," I warned, "you just let the law take care of this. They'll get the thief."

But the boys did set their watch every night — eight fellows at a go, two at either end of the front lane and two at either end of the back lane. Between 12.30 and 1.00 a.m. we had the changing of the guard, when they all came inside for hot chocolate or soup. It was a rare experience, and we had some really good gab sessions during those midnight snack times. Those gang boys, if you can imagine such determination, carried on their guard routine for five or six weeks!

Certainly Satan had overstepped himself this time, for God used the robbery to put me into sustained contact with all kinds of boys I would otherwise never have reached. I didn't even know some of those gangs existed.

But the heartache with Tony wasn't over. When the authorities caught up with him, he was tried and sent to prison. And from prison I received several very bitter letters from him. He blamed me for his imprisonment, for letting the police take him. Somehow my letters to him never reached him; so it was a time of real suffering for both of us.

I had known Tony since he was a little boy and was with his mother when she died of cancer after terrible suffering. That dreadful experience seemed to do something to Tony, for after it he became quite sadistic, finding delight in seeing others suffer. For example, one day while he was at my house for an English lesson, I suddenly heard a piercing cry from my dog Coca-Cola. I dashed out to find Tony with a large open safety pin thrust into Coco's mouth. I was so angry I didn't know what to do. Perhaps his robbing me had something to do with that day.

But I wasn't about to give up on Tony. Writing notes to my five most faithful prayers helpers, I asked them to concentrate prayer on this boy. As a child Tony had won more Scripture memory contests than anyone I had ever known, and with all that Word of God hidden in his heart the promise of Isaiah 55:11, that God's Word would accomplish His purpose, surely fit.

When he was released from prison after several years, friends suggested that I had better leave for furlough. "You don't know what he might do," they warned. Although it was time for furlough, I felt that to run away would be giving the devil the victory. So, trying to treat the whole thing as another test of my commitment, I plunged into a heavy summer program. And in fact nothing happened; little by little the whole incident was forgotten.

About two years later, during the Moon Festival in September when the moon is at its brightest, I had a caller. Earlier that evening I had spoken to a group at the Christian industrial center in the city. Afterwards I had joined the others eating the special moon cakes made just for that time of year and , according to custom, we had shared stories about the Lord's goodness during the past year. It was a lovely time and we finished late. But since everyone stays out late that night, no one would wonder about my arriving home between 12.30 and 1.00 a.m.

I was living at the time behind the United States Information Service building, and the guards there often kept an eye on my place when they knew I was away. When I got home that night they grilled me excitedly, "Where were you? Why are you so late?" Then they explained, "Someone has come all the way from Taipei on a motorbike to see you. The fellow has a girl with him, and they've been back at least three times tonight to see if you've gotten home."

I wondered who it could be. "Well," I said, "they won't come again. It's pretty late now," and I bid the guards good night.

Very tired after a full day and evening, I went inside to run the water for a good bath. I had just stepped into the tub when the doorbell rang. *Oh no!* I groaned. *Not now!* I "drip-dried," managing to grab some clothes. Fortunately Chinese-style clothes can be donned on the run, and by the time I reached the front door I was decent.

Though I didn't recognize the voice beyond the gate I opened it — and there stood Tony. The girl with him he introduced as his wife. I really didn't quite know what to expect next! But quickly I rallied and asked them to come in, apologizing for not being home when they called earlier.

Within minutes Tony was on his knees pouring out his heart, asking forgiveness. He had been out of jail for two years, and couldn't live any longer with the guilt of what he had done to me. When he had finally told the whole story to his wife, they immediately decided to come the several hours' drive to see me. Those wee morning hours were a very precious time, and both Tony and his wife came to the Lord before they left. Later they made restitution, not only paying back the money Tony had stolen, but with compound interest!

In tempting Tony to rob me, the devil had meant it for much evil and for my harm. But God had worked it all out for good and to His own glory. Seven of the gangs who protected me at that time disbanded, a number of the members coming to believe in the Lord. And Tony and his wife found Christ as Savior as well, and their lives were transformed.

One evening I was reveling in the thought of some rare free time — no meetings and no one wanting to come for counseling because it was final exam week.

The cat and dog had been fed, good music was playing on the phonograph, and I was just getting ready to settle down with a good book I had started long before. Then suddenly there was a terrific banging on my gate and someone urgently yelling, "Grandma! Grandma! Open up!" I didn't recognize the voice and was sorely tempted to pretend I wasn't home. But I picked up my weary bones and went to the gate to find out what this seeming emergency could be. There stood Mike, a boy who had only recently begun coming to class with a friend. He was clad only in undershorts and wooden clogs. And he had been beaten.

"Whatever happened to you?" I blurted out. I had my suspicions, for Mike had it rough at home. Though his father held a good position, he was a very hard man, a real despot in the home who drank heavily and terrorized the whole family with his temper. The mother escaped by spending a good bit of time away from home playing mahjong, an illegal gambling game in Taiwan.

"Sorry about the way I look," the big seventeen-year-old responded gloomily. "I just had a big fight with my father. He kicked me out of the house. Do you think you could go home for me and bring back my clothes and my residence certificate?"

"Well," I said, "come on inside first."

As we talked, it wasn't hard to sympathize with Mike's present situation. But since the Gospel was only just beginning to have an impact in his life, I wondered if he might be partly responsible for what had happened at home. Having never met his parents, I didn't feel I could just go there and ask for Mike's clothes. Finally by about midnight I had convinced Mike that we should go together to see what could be done to make peace. *What a nice quiet evening!* I thought ruefully. But the worst was yet to come.

As we got ready to leave for his house, Mike was still fuming threats against his father. Then, passing through the dining room, he spied the grass-cutting sickle my househelper had been using in my little bit of lawn. Grabbing it from the table, he began to run, heading for the gate. As soon as I realized what was happening, I tore right after him — I wasn't going to have him kill his father with *my* sickle! A lot of adrenalin must have surged into my short-legged, top-heavy, not-so-young-anymore body to give me the speed and strength to grab him in a flying tackle on my front lawn. I landed so hard that I smashed my good watch all to smithereens. But I got my prey!

"You're not going to kill your father with my sickle!" I scolded him as I yanked the weapon out of his hand. Then, helping him up, I said, "Now you get right back into the house!"

I put the sickle back where it belonged and locked it up. But Mike wasn't so easy to get where he belonged. Eventually, however, we set off again. I pushed my bicycle and Mike walked beside me as we made our way through the dark, deserted streets and the small patch of woods that led to the new housing area in which he lived. He was jumpy the whole two miles. Any sudden noise — the flapping of canvas in a puff of wind or the snap of a twig — made him start. "Who's there?" he half whispered. "What's that?"

"What's the matter, Mike?" I teased. "What are you afraid of?"

"Oh," he protested scornfully, "I'm not afraid. I'm just protecting you."

"Well," I laughed, "will you please not protect me so much and just keep going!" But he was like a frightened animal.

After what seemed a long time we reached his house, its thick mud-plastered walls and orange tile roof visible above the shorter wall that surrounded the tiny yard. I knocked but no one answered. I rapped several more times, each time louder than the last. Sensing movement inside I was sure the family was awake, so I pounded some more, then called.

"Who is it?" a gruff male voice bellowed from within the one-story home.

"It's Grandma Han. Your son has come home."

That brought an onslaught of very bad language from behind the locked door. Now angrier than ever, Mike started to run away. I grabbed him by his trunks and held him there until the embarrassed family finally opened the door.

Swearing profusely and emboldened by alcohol, Mike's father declared that he did not want his son back. Though my vocabulary in that angry man's kind of language was somewhat limited, I understood enough to feel the chills go up and down my spine. But I stood my ground, and when he had run out of things to say I again exhorted him to give his son another chance.

When at last I got the father to allow Mike inside, Mike wasn't willing to go in! After much convincing, however, the boy glumly edged through the door, and I followed. But before leaving the entry way and joining the unhappy group in the living room I closed and locked the door, slipping the key into my pocket. I wasn't taking any chances that anything would break up this nice little reunion party now!

As we stood there, our shadows grotesque against the white walls, I introduced myself to Mike's father, mother and two sisters, all in their night clothes. With Mike still only wearing his underclothes and clogs, I was the only one who was fully clothed, and by this point I questioned whether any of us were in our right minds! The air bristled with tension. The father was a frightening sight, his face black with rage. The trembling mother was as white as the refrigerator that held a prominent place there in the living room. The two girls sat huddled together on a reed and cane settee.

As I started talking with them, how I prayed in my heart for wisdom! I prayed also that God would move the hearts of others to pray for me right then, as I sensed the seriousness and the potential danger of the situation.

After we had talked for a while they all slowly began to relax. Mike now could admit to his wrongs and, amazingly, his father did too. Finally, when they seemed to have come to a point of mutual understanding where they could see the stupidity of their actions, I decided it was time for me to leave.

But before going I felt I should speak a word about the seriousness of their family problems. "Now, none of you here are Christians; you don't know the Lord Jesus Christ, and that's why you are having so many problems in your home," I said with feeling. "You have nowhere to go with your problems." After explaining the Gospel to them simply and emphasizing that they really needed Christ to be the head of their home, I suggested that we pray. "When we pray, we kneel," I explained, and down went all the knees onto the cold cement floor. I must have prayed for an hour or more. I don't remember exactly what I prayed; I only know it came from my heart's deep concern for that needy home.

The power of prayer began to show in Mike's personal life as not only did he stop hanging around and getting into fights all the time, but he developed a desire to excel in his studies and, with the help of some tutoring, passed exams into a good school. In time he came through to real faith in the Lord. So changed was his life, in fact, that his sisters began coming to our church young people's group and came to the Lord during our winter conference. His mother made the angels rejoice when she, too, put her trust in Christ a few weeks later.

Most wonderfully of all, just as I was preparing to leave for furlough I received a letter from Mike's father. It's a letter I treasure. "Grandma," he wrote, "I want you to know I'm a Christian now too. That makes us one family in the Lord. I am going to be baptized in three weeks as a testimony to my friends. I am sorry that you will have gone by then. I have never forgotten your prayer that night."

24
No teaching for Ned

"Has my son Ned been coming to your home?" the middle-aged man at my gate demanded.

"Yes, sir," I replied. I had seen the boy's father pull up in his jeep and strut up my path, and I had sensed that all was not well. Never having met him before, I was surprised when he tore into me without the customary polite Chinese preamble.

"Have you been teaching him about Christianity?" he continued crossly, his question more of a charge than a query.

"Yes, we have a Bible study. Why?"

"I don't mind my son coming here for English. As a matter of fact I appreciate your helping him with his English and also the help he is getting from fellow students in math, physics and chemistry. But," he went on, his voice rising, "you've got to promise me that you won't let my boy attend your Bible class."

What was I to say? Could I make such a promise? "I'll do my best to abide by your wishes," I replied reluctantly, and that was the end of our interview.

My concession to Ned's father did nothing to disarm him. Every day when Ned arived home from school, his father searched his school bag to see whether he had anything in it which pertained to Christianity. When he found a Bible a time or two, he destroyed it, then beat his son for disobedience.

True to my word, I avoided talking to Ned personally about the Lord. When the other boys were asking questions, though, I could be sure he was somewhere on the sidelines drinking it all in. If Ned asked a question I would say, "I'm sorry, Ned; I dare not talk to you about this." But then someone else would ask the same question. I'm not sure if this procedure was on the up and up or not, but Ned got his answers more or less second-hand.

One Sunday, however, Ned showed up at the Bible class with his school bag. "Ned, did you tell your father you were coming to class?" I challenged.

"No."

"Did you tell him that you were going to school?" Review classes for seniors were usually held on Sundays.

"Yes."

"Then," I said, "you go to school. You know your father's wish. I can't have you in class; it wouldn't do you any good ... nor our testimony for the Lord any good. You said you were going to school, so to school you go!"

The other boys thought not letting him come to class was terrible. I had to admit I felt horrible doing it; but I also felt in my heart that it was the right thing to do. Most of class that day, I'm afraid, was used up in discussing the problem.

Ned, however, was not to be left out, for the next day he came in with several friends who had missed

Sunday's class. "Grandma," he urged, "these fellows couldn't get to class yesterday; so would you tell them what you taught?" I did, and Ned listened from the sidelines.

Chinese New Year was fast approaching, and everyone was busy with preparations for the biggest festival of the year. As it is also a very idolatrous time, it posed a special problem for Ned. His father had never been much of an idol worshipper; he had, in fact, attended a church school somewhere in China. But having become embittered against Christianity and decided his son was to have nothing to do with it, he now went out and bought a number of idols and all the paraphernalia for a heathen celebration — joss sticks, paper money, vessels for food offerings, even a priest's robe. In this celebration he decided Ned would not only participate but would take the lead, which should really have fallen to his oldest brother. For this role he took Ned out to the barber to have his head shaved.

Ned came running over to my place for help. "Grandma," he pleaded, ignoring my stifled amusement at his appearance, "what can I do?"

I didn't know what to say. But then my sense of humor got the better of me, sparked by the sight of his shaven head looking for all the world like a light bulb. "Well," I teased, "one thing for sure, Ned, you'll be a bright and shining light for the Lord!" We had a good laugh, easing the tension a bit. Then seriously I told him, "I don't know what to tell you to do, Ned. But I know one thing: we can pray about the situation, and God will undertake."

"Is that *all* we can do?" he sputtered, clearly upset.

"That's the greatest thing we can do," I said. "God can change the whole picture." But this time my mouth was ahead of my heart — my faith felt shot full of holes. But we both got down and prayed.

Suddenly I began to pray a second time, rather surprising myself: "Lord, it would be so easy for You to call Ned's father out just before he has to start this horrible ritual, so that Your child will not have to go through with this thing. You know Ned's heart. You know he doesn't want to worship idols. He loves You, Lord. Please undertake for him now. We thank and praise You for what You are going to do. In Jesus' Name, amen."

As we got up from our knees Ned asked, "Grandma, what made you pray like that?"

I explained that I thought the Holy Spirit had prompted me to pray in that direction, and if so, that's how God would work. "Now get along home before your father misses you," I dismissed him. "I'll be praying for you. I never go anywhere on New Year's Eve, but stay home to pray because so many fellows like yourself are facing difficulty at this time. God answers prayer; you can bank on that."

Before settling for the evening I went out to do some last-minute shopping, as the stores would be closed for the next several days. I needed a supply of fruit and candies for the many visitors who would be dropping in to wish me a happy New Year. Already, I noticed as I pedaled down the street, people had pasted lucky sayings printed on strips of red paper onto the posts and lintels of their front doors. A few families had apparently only now finished the ritual New Year's housecleaning, and were in the process of carrying the furniture back into the house. Excited children skipped about, some already scrubbed and dressed in their new clothes, also a tradition. The women, who had been preparing food for several weeks, were now making final preparations for the feast. The aromas were tantalizing — almost stirring self-pity that I would be alone while everyone else was enjoying the luscious food that Chinese know how to prepare so wonderfully.

When I reached home it was already dark. Firecrackers were filling the air with noise and the smell of gunpowder. Once the evil spirits had been driven off by the racket, I knew, the doors of the houses would be shut and no one would go out lest the dragon eat him. Relatives by the score had returned to old family homes for joyous reunion. Grandparents would be telling stories to the younger generation, and games and feasting would keep most people up all night.

All evening I let my heart lay before the Lord its burdens for Ned and the other boys. The sound of activity throughout the neighborhood kept stirring fresh prayer for them. And I prayed that God would undertake for Ned in a special, obvious way.

Very weary and feeling a bit achy, I decided to have a good soak in Epsom salts before going to bed. No one would be coming to see me this night. Remembering Coca-Cola's terror of the firecrackers, I left the bathroom door unlatched in case the dog might want to come in to be comforted. But I wasn't prepared for what happened. I was reveling in the luxury of my bath and singing at the top of my voice, when all of a sudden there was a terrific *bang* in my yard, followed by a great splash as Coca-Cola leapt right into the tub with me. Worse than the dog's fright from the firecracker was his reaction to the heat of the water and the taste of Epsom salts! What a scramble to get the thrashing dog up and over the side of the tub! And, of course, the moment he hit the floor and got his equilibrium he shook himself violently. What a mess! I spent the rest of the evening cleaning up the bathroom and comforting a very unhappy dog. Fortunately that huge firecracker in my yard was the last for the night.

Very early in the morning, as I lay awake listening to the repeated *bang-bang-bangs* of more firecrackers, this time set off by squealing children, I heard, "Grandma! Grandma!" at my gate. I knew immediately who it was.

"What happened?" I asked Ned as I let him in.

"It happened just as you prayed!" he bubbled. "When I was about to start the ritual, someone came and rang the doorbell, calling for my father. He went off with the callers, while we waited and waited and waited. Finally, after quite a while, my mother said, 'The food is already cold; I have no idea where Father has gone or when he'll be back. We might as well eat.' So the whole idolatrous business was dropped, and since the food hadn't been offered to idols I was free to eat it!"

"What about when your father returned?" I asked.

"He just asked if everything had been taken care of, and my mother said it had!"

Ned's father continued to be unhappy with his son's interest in Christian things, however. "I'd like to have a talk with Grandma Han," he said to Ned one day quite a time later. "Ask her if she could come over on Sunday afternoon at two o'clock."

I agreed to the visit, though I knew it spelled trouble. But a group of young people from the church decided to come to my house to pray while I went to see Ned's father.

Because he was lying down when I arrived I waited in their metal-working factory next door, chatting with the workmen. I figured he was trying to irritate me; so when he appeared a half hour later, I responded to his apology with a light, "That's all right."

When we reached the living area of the unpainted Japanese-style house, I discovered that Ned's mother, sisters and all the other members of the household except Ned were away. My guess was that they didn't want to be around when the sparks flew!

Ned's father was indeed on the warpath. He wasted no time telling me exactly what he thought of Christians: all hypocrites — not a good one in the lot. He thought even less of the Gospel, saying that Christianity dulled the mind and killed ambition. At least he did admit I'd kept his rules regarding Ned.

Lord, help me keep my cool, I prayed as I lowered my weight carefully onto an old reed chair, its broad bamboo frame designed to avoid damaging tatami floors. *Don't let me show the least sign of irritation, no matter what this man says,* I cried to the Lord silently ... *and show me what to say if he ever gives me a chance to talk.*

Eventually my host did run out of things to say. "Do you have anything you want to say?" he asked finally.

"I have a few questions I would like to ask you," I replied. "Since your son has shown an interest in the things of God, has he been coming home on time?"

"Yes, yes — he's been much better about that than before," he admitted awkwardly.

"Has he been obedient and filial?"

"Yes, yes."

"Does he help around the house, or do you still have to nag at him continually to do things?"

"Oh, no. Come to think of it, he is much better

about that, and he even thinks of things that should be done. He is also much pleasanter to have around."

"What about Ned's grades — have they come up or gone down?" I knew they were considerably better, for I had seen his report card.

"Oh, his grades are much better than before," he had to admit.

I jumped in with both feet. "Your son has shown improvement in everything since he has become interested in the things of God," I pointed out. "Why then are you so vehement in opposing his going this way? Why are you so anti-Christian?"

He was honest enough to admit that he couldn't find anything negative in Ned's behavior. "I just don't want him to be a Christian," he said defensively. "It's not Chinese."

I was tempted to counter with, "Neither is Buddhism Chinese," but I felt it best not to antagonize him further.

Ned's father looked at me scornfully and said, "Now, Grandma, if you really want to sacrifice your life for God, I'll tell you what to do. Go out and buy a gallon of gasoline and a box of matches; pour the gasoline over yourself and set yourself afire. Then I'll believe in your Jesus."

That, I guess, was supposed to be the straw that broke the camel's back. "What good would that do?" I laughed. "I wouldn't even know if you did come to believe in Jesus. Besides, I wouldn't be around to help you grow as a Christian. That doesn't make sense."

The storm seemed to be over now, and he said a few nice things. Then he turned to me and invited, "It's getting late. Would you stay for supper?"

I knew I had to say yes. To refuse would be to admit anger. "I'd be delighted to stay," I replied.

Ned's mother was not at home, but as one of the workmen was preparing food for the others I presumed he would prepare ours as well. I could smell fresh rice cooking in the back. But to expand the meal, Ned's father retrieved some leftover dishes from the wind cupboard (they didn't have a refrigerator) and put them on the table in the factory entry without reheating them. One was a shrimp dish; I forget what the other was. When the meal was ready my antagonist gave me the lowest seat, the one nearest the door among the workmen. This was meant to "take away my face," since as a guest I should have been seated at his right, furthest from the door.

Before we started eating I said, "Do you mind if I ask a blessing? We Christians always thank God for our food."

"Oh, yes, if that's your custom." But as I prayed, he made all sorts of noises to annoy me.

According to custom, my host placed food in my bowl, carefully seeing to it that I got a full share of the leftover dishes. Though my nose told me that the shrimp dish was too far gone to be eaten safely, I knew I had to eat it. *Lord,* I prayed in my heart, *I'm eating this for your glory; so help me swallow it.* Somehow I got it down. No one else ate any of it.

The little old workman next to me was very sweet and even helped me to some of the freshly cooked vegetables. At the end of the meal Ned's father turned to me and said, "Now, Grandma, I hope you are not angry at anything I said today."

"No," I replied truthfully, "I'm glad we had this opportunity to talk things over. Now we know where we each stand. No, I'm not angry. If I were, I wouldn't have stayed and eaten your food."

At that the little man next to me leaned over and whispered, "You win! He lost! You win! He lost!" In my heart I knew he was right.

I got home to find the young people still at my house, worried that I had been gone so long. Sharing with them how the Lord had answered in keeping me calm and clear-thinking, I thanked them for being behind me in prayer and sent them off home.

About midnight an unhappy stomach began rumbling, then cramping. The pain was excruciating. Oh, I was sick! All alone without a telephone, I didn't know what to do. So I prayed, feeling very faint, clammy with sweat. *Lord*, I cried, *help me to get rid of everything!* He did, and immediately I felt better. But I was terribly weak for several days afterward. Well, now I knew what Ned had to live with daily.

Some time later when my birthday was coming up, Ned went to his father and asked him for $20 in local currency, the equivalent of U.S.$0.50. His father handed it over without question. But later he asked, "Say, son, what did you want that twenty dollars for?"

"Oh, Grandma Han had a birthday, and I wanted to buy her a gift."

"What did you get for her?"

"I got her a record of *The Messiah* — with The Hallelujah Chorus on it and other parts she likes."

"Why didn't you buy her a gallon of gasoline and a box of matches so that she could burn herself up?" he persisted with his idea. He and I certainly weren't getting anywhere with our relationship.

Ned continued to improve in his school work, however, so that when he sat for the university entrance exams he did better than any of his friends and was accepted into one of the national universities. So pleased was his father that he came to thank me for my help. Progress! But that wasn't all. To my amazement he continued, "My son may not be baptized until he is 21." No longer was he saying anything against Ned becoming a Christian! I think he realized now what a fine Christian Ned already was.

On his 21st birthday Ned came home for a visit and, of course, he came to see me. "I'm 21 now," he said. "May I be baptized this time?" Already he had gotten wind that we were preparing a group to be baptized at church. He passed the pre-baptism interview with flying colors. Most people in the church knew very well what he had gone through and the consistent life he had lived.

The night before the baptismal service Ned came to me to ask, "Do you think I ought to invite my father to the service?"

"I think it would be very nice if you did," I told him. "You have honored his request in waiting until now, so he shouldn't object." Down deep in my heart, though, I doubted that his father would come; perhaps I even hoped he wouldn't.

Next morning early Ned came running over to my house and reported, "He's coming, Grandma! What am I going to do?"

"Well," I said carefully, "if he's coming, that's fine. You invited him, and the Lord can keep His hand on him." We had a time of prayer, then hurried off to the church.

Seeing Ned's father as he came in the church gate, I went out to greet him and to introduce him to someone who could help him with the hymns and so forth. Also

I did not want him to find himself in the wrong section, since we women always sat on the left side and the men on the right according to Chinese custom.

Since our baptisms were by immersion, we had a baptistry up front. Before the service started Ned's father walked to the front of the church, then up onto the platform to inspect the baptistry! He even reached down to feel the water in the pool. By this time the church was almost full, but no one paid any attention to him; curiosity was nothing new. I sat, however, in fear and trembling. *What's going to happen now?* I worried. Ned's father stayed up there for a while — it seemed forever — then went back to his seat. I sighed with relief.

After the regular service of worship with all the usual hymns, Scripture reading and a message appropriate for the occasion, an exhortation was given to the baptismal candidates. Ned's father listened very attentively. Then, as those to be baptized filed up front, he walked up onto the platform so that he could really see what they were doing. When it was his son's turn, the boy gave a brief testimony while the father continued to stand there, taking it all in. Once Ned was immersed, the older man took his seat.

When immediately after the service a group photograph was to be taken, Ned's father insisted on being in it too, standing next to his son. It seemed that he was now quite proud of the stand his son had taken, though to this day he himself remains an unbeliever.

What a day!

25
More trouble with fathers

"Can I stay at your house for the holidays?" Bill pleaded. Although the only son of a very wealthy family in another city, he was in the school for bad boys where I went every week. The school had a break at New Year's time, long enough for the boys to go home. But Bill didn't want to go home.

I can't start this, I thought. *Why, I'd have the whole school moving in on me!* But out loud I asked, "Why don't you want to go home, Bill? Chinese New Year is the time when you can experience the warmth and fellowship of your family."

"What warmth?" Bill moaned. "There's no warmth or fellowship in *my* home." I wasn't surprised at his answer. From earlier conversations I gathered that his parents looked on him as excess baggage and showed very little interest in what he was doing. My guess was that he had got into trouble as one way of gaining their attention.

After much persuasion Bill did go home, very reluctantly.

Several days later, however, he was back knocking at my gate. "When I got home, Mother wasn't there," he explained, his face downcast and his voice tight with emotion. "She's out gambling, night and day — I haven't seen her." I knew his mother was addicted to playing mahjong. "My father came back while I was home and got angry with me because I was there. He gave me a pile of money and said, 'Go buy yourself some clothes and whoop it up. Just don't bother me'."

When Bill told me the amount of money his father had given him, it seemed a fabulous sum to me. But it wasn't money Bill wanted. A servant in the home had practically raised the boy. He had more respect for her, in fact, than for either of his parents. She was very concerned about Bill — but since it was New Year's time and she had time off to visit relatives, the best she could do was to take Bill along for a few days. But, embarrassed to be intruding into their family festival, he had left and come back to see me, not knowing where else to go.

Well, here he was, hurting and virtually homeless. I did have a spare bed in what I called my "Prophet's Chamber" — he could sleep there.

"What is it you really want?" I asked him one evening as we were talking together.

"A father! All I want is a father!" was his reply. His voice was filled with longing and pathos. To see this lovely boy being driven to a life of sin by his own parents because of a lack of love really hurt me.

Some weeks later I had occasion to go to Bill's home town on business so I went to see his father, a suave well-groomed man. It was hard to get through to him what parental love meant, for his reply to what I saw as Bill's need was, "Don't I give him money? Don't I pay for his schooling? Don't I ..."

"But that's not enough!" I broke in, perhaps a bit too impatiently. "There's no feeling in money. He doesn't want your money — he wants *you*! He wants you to give him time and to go places with him and do things with him like other fathers do."

At this Bill's father broke into very bad language and wouldn't hear any more from this meddling missionary. Now I understood better why my trying to get Bill to think of God as his heavenly Father so turned him off.

Although I had a great deal more contact with Bill, I don't know of his ever coming through for the Lord, and I often wonder what has become of him. Is he a father himself by now? And if so, what kind of a father? Since I don't know, he remains one of those boys for whom I claim the promise of Isaiah 55:11, that the Word of God will not return to Him empty but will accomplish the purpose for which it was sent.

Which is worse, a home where there is no love or one where harmful habits are taught by the example of parents? I knew Fred's family well, and of all the boys I knew Fred best, perhaps because he was always in trouble. High in the ranks of the military, Fred's father was a tall, heavy-set man with a nice face when he wasn't angry. Very strict, he was sometimes cruel in his discipline as it was usually meted out in the heat of anger. I think this anger was intensified because he saw his own weaknesses in this son. Often he came over to my house, his military posture in full bloom, to complain about how his son stole money from the house, and things he could pawn. Fred was helping himself to cigarettes and liquor as well. I knew that the boy was really doing these things, but I couldn't help asking myself, *Why should this father, who claims that he neither drinks nor smokes, have liquor and cigarettes in his home for his son to steal?*

One day when this big man came to my house in one of his rages, I took the opportunity to raise the issue. "You ask for my help," I began, "but ... are you willing to do your part in helping your son?"

"Yes, yes!" he promised eagerly.

"Well then, let me ask you this: Do you have anything in your home that might be stumbling him?"

"Oh, no." He was sure he didn't.

I decided to let the matter cool a bit and dropped the subject for the moment. Later, however, after much prayer, I went to pay the family a visit in their large Japanese-style house, with its lovely polished hardwood floors in both the entry way and living room. I was invited to stay for dinner, and after we had eaten we adults settled onto the bamboo and cane chairs there in the living room while the boys disappeared into their rooms to do homework. As we adults talked, no doubt the younger generation eavesdropped as the light paper-and-wood sliding doors separating the bedrooms from the living room did little to muffle sound.

"I have a feeling that your son tries to go straight, but can't," I told Fred's father. He was unconvinced, but I went on to explain, "There's too much temptation around him." As we chatted I had let my eyes feast on the lovely scrolls that hung on the walls; but in doing so I could not miss the large calendar of nudes displayed just as prominently, nor the cigarettes on the coffee table, nor the tall glass-fronted cabinet full of well-known brands of liquor. "If you mean business about cooperating with me, I'm going to ask you to do some things," I continued, perhaps too boldly. "You say

Fred steals your liquor — whiskey, brandy, gin and so forth — but why do you have this stuff in your home?" I took a breath. "Why are you putting temptation in front of the boy? If you didn't have it, he wouldn't steal it from you or have access to it. Is it possible that you are the one leading him to drink?"

Fred's father was getting angrier by the minute and his wife paler — the subject had been a sore spot in the home for many years. "I have to have it on hand for my friends," my host insisted hotly.

"But your friends are *Chinese*," I argued. "You don't need to have liquor for them. They don't expect it of you. Serve them tea!"

"Well, what do you want me to do with the liquor then?"

"I don't know — but get rid of it!"

"I'll give it away tomorrow," he proposed.

"No. Tomorrow never comes. If you mean business, you'd better do something tonight," I countered.

"But I can't give it away tonight," he complained.

"Forget about *giving* it away," I replied boldly. "Do you think it would be right to give it away· and make someone else fall through your gift? Would that be right?"

"What do you want me to do with it then — pour it down the drain?" he fought back.

"Now that you've suggested it — that's not a bad idea, is it?"

"You want me to pour all that liquor down the drain? Why, that cost ..."

"Which is more valuable," I plowed into the sputtering man, flushed with emotion, "your son or your money?" Silence. The struggle within was fierce.

"All right," he growled, "you pour it down the drain!"

"Oh, no! I'm not pouring it down the drain. If you mean business, you will do it yourself. I'll hand you the bottles."

So we began. I handed him bottle after bottle, and he tipped them — *blurp, blurp, blurp* — into the drain. As in that part of the city the drains were open, the neighborhood must have smelled like one big tavern. Pity any dog or cat who chose that time for a drink!

I was merciless. Once all we had left were empty bottles, I said, "Now, what about the cigarettes? What are you going to do about them? You say you don't smoke; so why do you have cigarettes in the house? You're going to stumble every last one of your children through these things. Just because one is more vulnerable than the others doesn't mean that the others aren't going to try smoking too."

"I've got to have those cigarettes when my friends come," the father argued.

"Put out some melon seeds for your friends," I suggested. "They can sit and crack and nibble melon seeds. It's the same sort of thing as puffing on a cigarette — just something to do."

"Then what do you want me to do with the cigarettes?" the big man growled. "I suppose I can't give those away either."

"What do you think? Do you want your friends to get lung cancer?" I prodded. "Say, have you started heating the water for baths tonight?"

"You mean you want me to use those cigarettes to heat the bath water?" His laugh was sarcastic.

"Not a bad idea," I replied calmly.

"Oh — all right!" he snapped.

"Are these all you have?" I asked, glancing at the carton on the table.

At this his wife looked at me, and I knew by her expression that there must be more stashed away somewhere. Reluctantly the father walked over to a cupboard and pulled out several more cartons, then led the way to the kitchen where a wood stove was heating water.

He stacked the cartons on a nearby surface and began feeding the fire. I handed the cigarettes to him, carton after carton. Soon the pungent smell of incinerating tobacco filled the whole place. I wonder what the neighbors thought!

Now that the dastardly deed was done, he seemed relieved. "Now it's all cleaned up," he smiled.

"Not really," I disagreed.

"Now what's wrong?" he asked incredulously.

"Look at that picture on the wall. That's not Chinese art." I was pointing to the offensive calendar. "Is that the sort of picture to have in a home where children are growing up?" I was well aware that these pictures too had long been a bone of contention between him and his wife.

"Well, that is a very good picture," he argued lamely. "That's art."

I wasn't about to back down now. "That picture is sensuous, and you know it. If you mean business, you'll take that picture and others like it down tonight."

"But if I take it down, there's going to be a spot on the wall that will look terrible," he complained.

"You take that picture down tonight, and tomorrow I'll bring you a scroll from home by a very famous Chinese artist, which will just cover that spot." I knew he appreciated Chinese art. So did I — Chinese painting is one of my hobbies. But now that I had promised I knew I would have to part with one of my favorite scrolls. I could sacrifice that much for the sake of this family. So the picture — and others like it — came down from the wall, and the whole lot were added to the fire.

The next day I delivered the promised scroll, and it covered the spot on the wall exactly. To hide another obvious rectangular scar, I had a well-known calligrapher write in character on a second scroll: "The Lord is the head of this house."

Not only did this "housecleaning" mark the beginning of a change in Fred's life, but it was only a matter of weeks before his father took a positive stand for the Lord. God had led, as at the time I was sure He had.

Many mothers and fathers, of course, saw the importance of working with me and were able eventually to rejoice at what God did for their boys. And where at first cooperation was lacking, I often saw the Lord break through the walls of opposition to His own glory.

26

Foot-washing

Gradually my work with boys was being taken up by national Christians, some of whom were boys I had helped in their teens, now mature servants of God. Though I was still doing some counseling, I had somewhat worked myself out of a job. And, like the proverbial mare, I wasn't as young as I used to be. So when I returned from furlough in 1969 I was looking for fresh direction.

Actually it came as rather a shock to me to realize that I was no longer one of the *young* missionaries. At 55 my days of running around on a bicycle or even on a motorbike were over. The doctor, in fact, had "grounded" me in that regard. Even this, however, was part of the circumstances crowding me to a very different style of ministry the Lord was planning.

I came back to the house I had lived in just before furlough, more of a foreign-style house than the Japanese one I had had earlier. This one had a good-sized yard, with the little guest house out back that we called "The Prophet's Chamber." It was only about five minutes' walk from the church and very handy to the train station and shopping district. My landlady, also my good friend, let me use the house for token rent and even provided me with a phone — in those days exorbitantly expensive and very difficult to obtain. The house was perfect for my new assignment. I also came back from furlough with a little Japanese station wagon. As the Lord had given it to me, I believed He wanted me to use it in some special ministry, particularly since at that time the mission had no vehicle of any kind.

By this time the China Inland Mission was known as the Overseas Missionary Fellowship, even in Taiwan. Up till now most of our missionaries in this island nation had begun their ministries in Mainland China. Now, however, the mission was being blessed with an influx of new missionaries wanting to be part of the Taiwan team. And this is where my "grandma" status (gray hair and all), my house and my little station wagon all came together, in what I called a "foot-washing ministry". While continuing to be on call to help both women and young people of the church, I could open my house and myself to ease the way for the new missionaries to understand the customs and culture of their adopted country.

Key to this ministry was Mrs. Chang, a lovely Christian widow with six sons and nine daughters, who looked on serving me as serving the Lord. She was a real fellow worker who stayed with me for nine years, never seeming to mind stretching her energies to put delicious food on the table for our frequent guests, both new workers and older fellow missionaries as well, who sometimes needed to get away to rest awhile.

One reason I invited new workers over was to introduce them to Chinese food. I wanted them to learn to like it — even to learn to cook it — as part of feeling at home in Taiwan.

And as the Overseas Missionary Fellowship was an international mission, mealtimes at my house were part of the adjusting process between fellow missionaries of widely varying backgrounds' as we shared stories, related interesting features about our own beloved countries, and discovered all kinds of differences in table etiquette. What a mixed group we sometimes were around the table! One noon I counted seven different nationalities.

But this was only the beginning. In Taiwan the O.M.F. was facing a new sort of problem — if you could call it that — single men! The young unmarried men who were joining O.M.F. to serve in Taiwan somehow always came one by one, and we soon discovered how very difficult it was for them to scrounge for meals, take care of their laundry and, with no real home life, work flat out learning the language. My heart went out to them.

One day when the field administration was holding a council meeting in my home, this subject came up. Perhaps my garden house could be fixed up to house someone, I suggested. It was an idea. So we stopped our talk, went outside and took a look at the little house. Yes, there was plumbing — a mini-bathroom. But how would Mrs. Chang react to having a "son" move in? It would mean a heavier workload for her. But as I talked it over with her I found her very willing — she was quite partial to boys, she said. Thanks to her, we were able to look after three young men, one after another, during their early years on the field.

As students, the gang boys and people from church continued to come in for counseling, I prayed that the Lord would be my Gatekeeper, bringing the ones He wanted to come; and that I would be so prepared that He could minister through me for each person's need. All over again I was realizing how important person-to-person work really is. We all need to know that someone cares, that someone is interested in what we are doing or going through.

Often at the end of the day I would wonder, *What did I do today?* I would feel like one big ear, as most of my time was spent listening. Many of those who came didn't necessarily want advice but to unburden their hearts. Once they had done this, we would have a time of prayer. It was usually as simple as that — yet the person would often go away. saying, "You have been such a help to me."

I often failed, of course. When plans are thwarted, it is easy to forget the well-known adage, "there are no interruptions, only opportunities." A person has to be free from himself and his own plans to be able to identify with people and really listen to what they are saying. "I sat where they sat," is how Ezekiel put what I wanted, but sometimes failed to do.

"Dr. Pauline," one of our mission leaders once asked as I was driving him to Taipei, "which do you think is the more important — doing or being?"

I considered the question for a bit, then replied, "*Being* is more important." Later I realized that this summed up exactly the lesson I was learning. My job was *being* available, *being* willing to give up my time to share the burdens of others, *being* myself in God's hands. In other words, I was learning anew what that Indian brother had told me in Toronto before I left for the mission field for the first time: "Man before business, because man *is* your business."

This was primarily a period of being available. I did less running around to meetings than in previous terms. But "Datsie" — as I called my little blue Datsun — and I covered plenty of miles. We helped move new workers to their places of appointment, we helped deliver babies — or rather we drove several missionary mothers-to-be to the hospital! Datsie and I had five or six such "stork races" in the wee hours, and once we almost lost, when the little one made her appearance about three minutes after we arrived at the hospital entrance!

We had sadder tasks too. On eight separate occasions Datsie and I were in the right place to pick up accident victims along the road and take them to the hospital. Then when two of our own veteran missionaries, Eric and Edith Liberty, were badly injured in a motorcycle accident just months before leaving for retirement, Datsie and I made the sixty-mile trip almost daily for a couple of months to look in on them in the hospital. When they could be moved, they were brought down to Taichung and installed in the larger of my two guest rooms. Two of our younger missionaries lived in the other guest room and did round-the-clock nursing.

Prayer was taking on new meaning for me in these days. A great deal of the follow-up work with my boys was now done through prayer. Many times the Lord would give me a special burden for a boy I hadn't seen for a long time — perhaps I didn't even know where he was. As I prayed, the Lord would work; then not many days later I would either meet the fellow on the street or he would come to see me, or perhaps I would get a letter telling how God was working.

People who knew I had been seriously ill on several occasions got the idea I had "dying grace"! As a result, when someone was very ill I frequently got called to the bedside. It was a precious and sacred ministry to be able to share some of the riches of Christ with them in their last moments. More than one said, "Grandma, I'm so glad you've come. You know what it is like because you've been through so much illness." At times like this I could understand, at least in part, why God had permitted me to go through some of the physical trials I've related in this book. I often remembered Paul's words about "the God of all comfort, who comforts us in all our affliction, so that we may be able to comfort those who are in any affliction, with the comfort with which we ourselves are comforted by God" (2 Cor. 1:4).

I was thrilled to see the student work in Taiwan, with which I had worked in its embryo stage, now flourishing in evangelism, in staff training and in publishing. Every Friday noon the Campus Evangelical Fellowship staff workers in Taichung came to my house to eat. The purpose was not only for fellowship, but also to help these student workers improve their English conversation. So we made a rule that only English was to be spoken while we ate. Oh, how quiet some of those mealtimes were! Then someone would forget the rule, and we would all at once realize that we were chattering away in Chinese, discussing the problems, the challenge, the blessings.

This term was different in many ways, not so tightly organized as far as daily program was concerned but very people-oriented, especially on the person-to-person basis. I came to appreciate more fully the variety of means God uses to draw people first to know Him, and then to live for Him, as I tried to follow His example in "foot-washing."

27
Fiery furnace

God still had a new syllabus for this old student, through which I was to learn in a new way myself what I had tried faithfully to teach others — God is there in the "lions' den" and in the "fiery furnace."

Dr. Monica Hogben, O.M.F.'s Medical Officer from international headquarters in Singapore, was in Taiwan in 1975 for biennial physicals. When she discovered a growth in my abdomen I was as surprised as anyone, as not a twinge of discomfort had indicated anything was wrong. That same afternoon Monica and I went over to see the doctor who usually attended me at the Christian hospital in nearby Changhua. Yes, surgery should be done, Dr. Wilkerson and two consulting doctors decided, but it should not be considered an emergency.

There was no room for me at the hospital anyway, so I decided to go ahead with my vacation plans. I was looking forward to going to my favorite spot, Goose's Nose at the southernmost tip of the island, in just a couple of weeks. This is a beautiful place with mountains going right down to the sea, lovely beaches, coral reefs, a lighthouse at the very tip, and nearby Kenting National Park.

I was three-fourths of the way to Goose's Nose, spending a night at a friend's home, when I got a telephone call to say there was now a room at the hospital if I wanted it. I did, for by now I realized that the tumor was growing alarmingly fast; already it could be seen as a bulge on my abdomen. So I turned around the next day and entered the hospital just twenty days after the initial examination.

That morning of September 4, the Lord spoke clearly to me as I read the collection of Scripture texts in *Daily Light*: "Sit still, my daughter; take heed and be quiet; fear not, neither be fainthearted. Be still and know that I am God. Said I not unto thee that if thou shouldst believe, thou shouldst see the glory of God? The Lord alone shall be exalted in that day. Rest in the Lord and wait patiently for Him. Fret not thyself because of him that prospereth in his way, because of the man that bringeth wicked devices to pass. He shall not be afraid of evil tidings. His heart is fixed, trusting in the Lord. His heart is established. He that believeth shall not make haste. What I do thou knowest not now, but thou shalt know hereafter." With these words in my heart I faced surgery — "Be quiet; be still; rest." It is not that easy for me to be still but that was what God was asking of me now — to trust Him so that He could glorify Himself.

I felt no strangeness in entering the hospital, since for years I had held a nurses' Bible study there each week, and had been a patient there several times before. My room faced west, and that first evening the sunset was spectacular. Several of the doctors and nurses who had dropped in to see me joined in singing the hymn, "Day is Dying in the West." Later, after the nurses had "prepped" me for tomorrow's surgery, they stayed to talk and pray before I went to sleep. How wonderful to be in a Christian hospital! Dr. Wilkerson came in early the next morning to check on things and to pray before I went under the anesthesia. As usual, I started my way through the 23rd Psalm, but before I got to "the valley of the shadow of death," I was out.

When I came to, sometime in the afternoon, a good friend who was a nurse from another mission was sitting beside me. I looked at her groggily; said, "Hi"; then turned over and went back to sleep.

As far as I knew, everything had gone well. I knew better than to ask the doctor anything — when the laboratory report came, he would tell me all I needed to know. Day by day I could feel my strength returning.

On about the eighth day Dr. Wilkerson came and took the stitches out. Then he sat down beside me and said, "Now I think we should talk about your operation." Nothing in his tone rang any bells of alarm. We knew each other well: I knew him to be a very straightforward person, and he knew that I would want the truth. But I was hardly prepared for what he had to say: "You have cancer, and it's terminal."

"Do I have to stay in the hospital?" I managed to ask.

"No, now that your stitches are out you may go home today if you wish."

"About how long do you give me to live?" I found myself asking.

He squared himself in his chair. "I removed as much as I could," he said. "But that wasn't much. The cancer has spread throughout your abdomen, enveloping several of your organs. During these weeks it has been growing very rapidly. The last case I saw like this lasted two months. I've discussed it with several other doctors, and the consensus of opinion is two or three months."

"Is there any therapy for this type of cancer?" I asked.

"As far as I know," he answered quietly, "there is none."

"Well, since I don't have to stay in the hospital, may I hitch a ride home with you tonight?" The Wilkersons also lived in Taichung.

"Yes, I'll be glad to take you home," he replied, then was gone.

I was amazed at the absolute peace in my heart. It was as though the Lord was saying to me, "It's all right — this is from Me." My heart response was, *Thy will be done, Lord!* Peace such as I have never known before flooded my heart.

In a few minutes Estelle Wilkerson, the doctor's wife, came to see me. "I'll take you home now, Pauline," she said. "The doctor has a meeting in the hospital. He'll return by train later." Estelle, a nurse, was a good friend of mine and a cheerful person to have around. She had heard the results of the examination and on our way home brought up the subject, telling me she and her husband were worried that the news had not really registered with me — my reaction had been too calm. I assured her to the contrary.

I got more than a warm welcome from my two dogs, Suzie and Snoopy, who could not contain their delight at seeing me again. With them prancing and dancing around me, I took a while to make my way into the house where we could sit on the sofa and have a "love-in" after our ten-day separation.

When Suzie and Snoopy had calmed down a bit, I phoned Mr. Draper, our Taiwan superintendant, and asked if he and his wife Jane could come over for a few minutes. I felt I should share the news with them immediately. Being so unexpected, it naturally came as quite a shock to them — but it was a shock I could ease with a testimony of the wonderful peace the Lord was giving me. (Not only have the Drapers been a strength through this whole experience, but Jane has also helped edit this book. I am grateful for both.)

A few days later Dr. and Mrs. Wilkerson dropped in to see how things were going. At first the doctor said little, but sat on my sofa playing with Suzie, who was being an absolute clown. "Now you do know the cancer is terminal?" he said finally, the poodle still wriggling in his lap.

"Look, I heard you the first time," I replied with a hint of irritation after he had repeated this several times.

"But you didn't react," he defended himself. "Most people break down and cry, or faint, but you had no reaction at all."

So I told him what had happened. "When you told me I had terminal cancer, I had a most wonderful experience. It was as though a great cloud came down over me, a cloud of peace from God, who assured me that this illness is part of His will — that it is not only good, but also acceptable and perfect.[1] This is hard for me to explain," I said, smiling, "but I think I could give a message on the peace that passeth all understanding now, for that is what He has given me."

Even as I write this, His peace has not left me. He knows what He is doing and is fulfilling the word that

Romans 12:1,2

He gave me the morning before the operation, "You don't know what I'm doing now, but you will know afterwards." He promised that He would be exalted and that He would get glory, and that was and is my prayer.

"According to all the books, cobalt doesn't touch this kind of cancer, nor does chemotherapy," Dr Wilkerson fretted, trying to hold Suzie still. "But it wouldn't do any harm to try the cobalt," he decided as an after-thought.

So I was sent for treatment to the modern, well-equipped veterans' hospital in Taipei. I had a hard time finding the imposing structure at first, as it was in a part of the city with which I was unfamiliar. Even so, I arrived before Dr. Wilkerson's letter did! Happily, however, it was Thursday afternoon, the time scheduled for doctors to see new patients. I was in the waiting room when a young doctor came out of the inner office and, seeing me sticking out like a sore thumb as the only foreigner, he came up and asked what I wanted. He turned out to be Dr. Chen, head of the radiology department and only recently returned from study in the United States. He took my copy of Dr. Wilkerson's referral letter along with the other medical papers I had brought with me, and perused them quietly, looking up at me now and again as he read, so that I wondered what was going on in his mind. Eventually he examined me, and decided to start treatment immediately.

When he inquired whether I planned to stay in the hospital or elsewhere, I answered, "I really don't have any plans — I'm at your mercy." I told him that I could stay at our mission headquarters, though it was a good fourteen miles away.

"Do you know anyone in this section of the city?" he asked.

"I'm afraid not."

"I would like you close by — just in case you have a bad reaction. We are going to have to give you very heavy doses of radiation, so unless you can find a place nearby I may have to ask you to stay in the hospital. Here's your appointment for tomorrow at three."

Driving across town through the heavy commuter traffic to our headquarters, I wondered where I could possibly stay. I hadn't even spotted a hotel in the vicinity of the hospital. I needn't have worried, for as usual the Lord had gone ahead. When I arrived at the O.M.F. office I was told that a Mr. Sun had telephoned and wanted me to call back as soon as I came in. I knew several people by that name, but was puzzled how any of them could know where I was. When I called the number, I was embarrassed to have to ask which Mr. Sun I was talking to.

"I'm Sun Chih-fang's father," the voice on the other end of the line replied, "and, as you know, I'm the business manager at Andrew Gih's orphanage here in Taipei. I understand that you have come to Taipei for treatment at the V.A. hospital."

Well, I thought, *news travels faster by the grapevine than by mail!* "Yes, that's right," I answered, "I just arrived this afternoon."

"Do you have any place to stay?" he asked.

I explained my problem.

"Well, that's why I'm calling," he said. I could hear the smile in his voice. "The orphanage is only about a five-minute drive from the hospital, and we would like you to stay with us while you are in Taipei. Dr. Gih, calling from Singapore, has said we should let you have his private apartment as it is not being used just now. It's ready for you anytime you choose to come."

"Praise the Lord!" I exploded into the phone. "Thank you! I'll try to move over in the early afternoon tomorrow, as I have my treatment at three." As I hung up, I thanked the Lord for His supply and for the kindness of Chinese friends.

The little apartment turned out to be ideal, and the people kindness itself. Not only was the refrigerator kept stocked with fresh fruit, milk and yogurt — things which my body seemed to crave during the treatment — but all during the ten weeks I stayed my breakfast was served in the apartment so that I could rest longer in the morning, and other meals too were brought to me if I did not feel up to par. When I was ready to leave, they would not accept anything for room and board. Surely the Lord has blessed them for their kindness.

As I began treatment the doctors all warned me of the possibility of hair loss, skin discoloration, nausea and diarrhea. We joked about the hair loss, deciding that if that should happen I could get myself wigs to match every outfit! However, after several days of observing fellow patients, I realized that these side effects were no joking matter.

On my third day in the waiting room I was talking with the Chinese lady beside me when I was summoned for treatment: "Grandma Han! Grandma Han!" As I got up, all the people in the waiting room looked at me and someone said, "But you're not sick!"

"Oh yes I am," I said as I disappeared into the treatment room.

Dr. Chen had heard, and after I was out of earshot he went out to put the record straight. "She's worse off than any of you," he told them. "She has only a few weeks to live."

When I reappeared, in true Chinese fashion those still waiting told me what the doctor had said.

"Yes, that's right," I replied, and sat down to talk with what was now an attentive audience.

"How can you be so calm?" they wanted to know. "How can you be so peaceful?" What a springboard for testimony to the lovingkindness of the Lord! And thereafter, as I came in day after day for treatment, I brought my Chinese Bible and some tracts, taking the opportunity to chat the Gospel to fellow patients. Each day there would be some new patients as well as some of the old-timers. Those I knew would say, "Have you told them what you told us yesterday?" or "Have you told them how to have peace?" What made those opportunities so poignant was the knowledge that many in that waiting room would be facing eternity within weeks or months. Already many were suffering terribly, their fear rising in proportion to their agony.

I was counting on going home soon, but the doctor decided he wanted to prolong the treatment. So far I had had none of the awful side effects. And even when my body was bombarded with the heaviest dosage of cobalt radiation I still suffered no more than a little bit of diarrhea. "You're a breed of your own," the doctors teased in amazement. Some of their patients, they confided, were so gripped by fear that it seemed they were dying more of fear than of the disease itself.

While I was still in Taipei, well-meaning friends wanted to anoint me and pray for my healing. "No, thank you," I refused. "While I appreciate your love and concern for me, God has not given me any freedom to ask for healing. When I was told that I had terminal cancer, I prayed, 'Thy will be done,' and afterwards His peace filled me in a very wonderful way. That's all I want — His will. I can't ask for any more. Many years ago when I was sick, I asked the Lord to heal me and He did. I am not free to ask now. I don't want leanness to my soul."

Not very happy with my attitude, some of my visitors that day wanted to insist on laying hands on me for healing. I remained firm. "No, His will is best," I argued. "God knows what He wants to do, and He is able to heal if it is His will. If it isn't, I'd rather go to be with Him."

"Just let *us* pray," they coaxed. "You don't need to."

"No," I shook my head wearily. "I don't feel up to it either emotionally or nervously ... If you want to pray for me, you can go home to pray."

I could feel the exasperation of some of them. It hurt, too, when it was suggested that I was trying to be super-spiritual, or that I had been wrong in having the radiation treatments if I wanted to trust the Lord. I reserved my comments on that subject as I was getting overly upset by the discussion. After my well-meaning visitors left, I was able to have a time of quiet waiting upon the Lord about the whole matter, and again He assured me of His abiding presence.

One marked change I saw in myself with the prognosis of only two to three months to live was in my attitude toward living. Things that had once seemed important became trivialities. When I returned to my home from the hospital, for instance, one of the first things I saw as I walked in the door was that the terrazzo floors were not gleaming with polished wax as I expected, but instead washed but dull. Then I found a stack of mending and several other things that Mrs. Chang had left undone in my absence. I found myself getting uptight. All I could see were dull floors and mending, not all that Mrs. Chang had done. Suddenly, when I was about at boiling point (fortunately Mrs. Chang wasn't home), the Lord seemed to say, "Floors don't matter. Things don't matter — *people* do." Of course He was right. In the light of eternity what did floors and mending matter? Actually Mrs. Chang had been busy looking after a string of guests. I suppose she got to those chores in time. I never worried about them again.

Although not expected to see Christmas 1975, I began trying to live as normal a life as possible. As activity increased gradually, so did strength. And ministering to others took my mind off myself. I guess I didn't look as well as I thought I did, however, for someone told me recently that those days I looked like "death warmed over."

People's reactions to my illness were interesting. As I had been sharing the news that I had terminal cancer quite frankly with friends and fellow workers right from the first, I took our next O.M.F. prayer meeting as an opportunity to explain what the doctors had told me and to testify to the peace the Lord had given. I began to hear a sniff here and a snuffle there. Suddenly the "down" atmosphere struck me as funny! Here was a group of fifteen or so missionaries who would all say, and mean it, that to be absent from the body and present with the Lord is far better. "We are a funny lot," I observed. "We say how wonderful it will be to go to be with the Lord, and now when someone has her ticket bought and is on the way — on the train, in fact — we sit and cry. Why, you should be *rejoicing* with me!"

Other friends didn't know how to act or what to say at all, and began evading me. Some blurted out irrelevant remarks simply because they were nervous.

Others were overly nice. Eventually it made me feel like yelling, "Hey, everybody — treat me normally! I'm still living and still me!" One day I did say to my fellow workers, "Don't pity me; that's the last thing I want. If you want to get mad at me, go ahead!" The kid-glove treatment was giving me more trouble than the cobalt treatments! Anyway, my sense of humor was intact and it helped me and others to make the adjustments needed to get life back to a sense of normalcy.

28
End of an era

Oh, was I angry! I was so rebellious that I could not
honestly pray. Mission leadership had directed that I
should take early retirement and be off the field by the
following summer. *Why?* my heart screamed. *Why now,
two years later, when I am so much better and able to carry on
my full program of work? It isn't fair!*

Besides, where would I live in the United States?
How would I be able to meet the high medical expenses
back home? I was under excellent medical care in
Taiwan and getting along quite well. I hated — even
feared, if I could have admitted it — the unknown.

I was amazed and horrified at my reactions and my
lack of faith, so different from my reaction to the news
of having terminal cancer. Why could I accept that
news and not this? Had I forgotten God's faithfulness
to me down through the years? The turmoil wouldn't
die down, however, even with all my self-lecturing.
This news I could not share with others, either Chinese
or westerners. I would have to fight it out alone before
the Lord.

After a week of misery, I heard the Lord's voice through Isaiah 54:10-11: "The mountains may depart and the hills be removed, but My steadfast love shall not depart from you and My covenant of peace shall not be removed, says the Lord, who has compassion on you. O afflicted one, storm-tossed, and not comforted, behold, I will set your stones in antimony and lay your foundations with sapphires ... In righteousness you shall be established." What a timely reminder that though everything be changed, God is still there! He understands my needs; He could be trusted to prepare a place for me. Peace and calm began to return to my heart, and I could again pray for His will to be done. I knew if it weren't His will that I retire, He could easily change the whole picture.

As life began to return to normal, I felt it wise to keep the retirement threat under my hat. Opportunities to serve abounded, and I saw the Lord working in many people's hearts.

On my birthday at the end of January 1978, I got up early for an uninterrupted time with the Lord. I knew that after ten o'clock there would be no hope for peace and quiet. People would be coming to wish me happy birthday in the morning, and in the late afternoon 35 or 40 women from the church were to come for a pot-luck supper, staying to make Chinese meat dumplings.

Again that day the Lord demonstrated His ability to apply His Word to my specific need. He spoke through Psalm 139: "O Lord, thou hast searched me and known me! Thou knowest when I sit down and when I rise up; thou discernest my thoughts from afar. Thou searchest out my path and my lying down, and art acquainted with all my ways. Even before a word is on my tongue, O Lord, thou knowest it altogether ... Such knowledge is too wonderful for me; it is high, I cannot attain it ... Search me, O God, and know my heart! Try me and lead me in the way everlasting!" Though I knew these truths and had taught this psalm many times, yet that day the Word came to me with freshness and new light. How well it applied to the doubts of my heart about my future! The Lord truly needed to search my heart and root out every wrong attitude.

It was hard to face leaving Asia. Now 63, I had spent half of my life in letting the Lord use me for His purposes among the Chinese. I had no regret about going from youth to old age in my 31½ years in Mainland China and in Taiwan. No, my heaviness of heart was due to the thought of leaving behind the familiarity of my adopted land and of parting from the many people who had become as dear as family to me. Whatever I had given up to follow the Lord, He had returned to me a hundredfold.

By early March my heart was settled enough for me to be able to share the news of my impending retirement with Chinese and missionary fellow workers. Besides, I needed to begin to wind down my affairs soon if I were to be gone before summer.

As farewells and feasts can be emotionally draining in these circumstances, I hoped to get away as quietly as possible. I still found social affairs a nervous strain. But it would have been easier to stop a runaway locomotive! The love that Chinese friends began to shower on me was simply overwhelming. Not only were there farewell gatherings in both Taichung and Taipei, but gifts poured in from all over Taiwan — much of it jewelry as people had realized I would be flying home with limited baggage. Besides lovely pieces of jade and settings that included pearls, opals, agate, ruby and coral, there were gifts of gold, much of it the yellow negotiable gold which is accompanied by a certificate of weight. Givers of gold reminded me that as the dollar goes down the price of gold goes up; their gifts were to assure me that I would not be in need.

At a farewell at Gracè Church in Taichung, the congregation with which I had been associated for 27 years, I was presented with a brass plaque inscribed with the words of Isaiah 54:10! No way could they have known how much that verse had come to mean to me! The people at Grace Church also gave me a money gift — the amazing equivalent of one thousand dollars in American currency. It should be used, they said, toward furnishing my apartment when I got to America. Today practically everything around me speaks to me of those dear people.

Not to be left out, fellow missionaries also planned a really hilarious farewell for me, the highlight of which was a side-splitting skit portraying my life's story. I don't think I ever laughed so much in my whole life. They also presented me with gifts I treasure.

The days were passing rapidly, with many things yet to care for. I needed to sell Datsie, for one thing. The paint on the little station wagon was in good shape, and the car had been serviced regularly. But who would want a nine-year-old vehicle with 98,000 miles on it? I remembered, though, that the garage man had once said that if I ever decided to part with it he wanted first refusal. *Perhaps he would give me as much as three hundred dollars for it.* So off I went to find him.

"How much do you want for it?" he asked when I explained the situation.

"I really don't know what to ask; I don't know what it's worth," I answered honestly.

"I'll give you 48,000 Taiwan dollars (equivalent to US$1,200!)," he offered. In my surprise I hesitated. Apparently taking my hesitation to mean I was expecting more, he jumped in with, "Okay, make it 60,000 dollars, and you can use it up to the time you leave Taichung." We parted company, both pleased. Surely the Lord meant this as a good start on His provision of a car when I reached America.

For many years I had been praying for a person who owed me a considerable sum of money. While studying in America twenty years earlier, he had had a real need because of a medical problem and I had helped him out in his emergency. Later he returned half of the amount of the loan, promising the rest in a couple of months. It never came. After about fifteen years he returned to Taiwan to take up a good position there in Taichung. Yet he never came to see me, and when we bumped into each other he always seemed in a hurry. I became burdened for him, more for his attitude than for the money he was withholding — I felt the sum was too large for him to forget. Now that I was about to leave Taiwan, I began to pray, "Lord, if I am to retire, please bring this man back to a close relationship with Yourself and as proof put it in his heart to repay this debt." Nothing happened, except that now when I met him he seemed more uncomfortable than ever.

Then, just two days before I was to say my last farewells in Taichung, I had a telephone call from this fellow. "Grandma," he began, "did I ever pay back that money to you?"

Quite astonished to hear from him at this date, I replied, "No, actually you didn't."

"Are you sure?"

"Yes, I'm sure. Would you like to come over and talk about it?"

"I'll be right over," he answered and very shortly he was at the door. As we sat and talked he remembered what had happened, and handed me the equivalent of US$700. The best part, though, was the fellowship we now experienced in the Lord.

The surprises weren't over. On my last day in Taiwan a young couple invited me out to dinner in Taipei. After dinner the young man, one of the original boys in the Hope of China Class, got up from the table to stand beside me. "Grandma," he said, "I'll be at the airport tomorrow to see you off, but I want to say goodbye to you now." Then he shook my hand and in doing so left a wad of bills in my hand. I glanced at them quickly, assuming they were local currency — but in a second realized that they were the wrong color for New Taiwan dollars. I looked again — a very un-Chinese thing to do — and saw in my hand *five American one hundred dollar bills*.

"Oh, but you can't afford to do this!" I remonstrated seriously.

"I can't afford *not* to do it," he said just as seriously. "You are going to need wheels under you when you get to America, and maybe this will help to buy one wheel for you!" How do you react to such generosity!

Ironically, my flying date was American Independence Day — July 4, 1978. Rather than gaining my independence, however, I felt a new dependence on the Lord as I faced an unknown and untried future.

29
Still bar nothing

Questions bombarded my peace of mind as I headed for the United States. Where should I settle? Since both my parents had died while I was on the mission field, the old home no longer existed. I felt it wouldn't be right to inflict myself on relatives — nor did I feel ready for O.M.F.'s retirement home even though I was coming home because of illness — in fact, was supposed to be long dead! And when I did settle, what would I be able to do? Could I carry on a ministry of any kind? After more than thirty years away, would I be a misfit in America? How would I find the car I would most certainly be needing? The questions were threatening panic.

Yet, as I looked back over the years, I thought, *I am His*. Through thick and thin He had been teaching me just that. While He claimed His right to sovereignty in my life, He was no capricious despot but a kind and loving Father. With this assurance I committed myself to Him afresh.

I did wonder, though, how I would make ends meet, as everywhere I heard people talking about inflation in the U.S. Yet God had taken care of me in the wild inflation of my days in Nanking. *And look*, I told myself, *how He handled your being robbed of everything*. I felt rebuked and ashamed at my lack of faith as I knew full well that one's geographical position makes no difference to God.

In England on the way home the Lord again moved to reassure me. A friend handed me a card, remarking, "This is especially for you now." It was as though she had read my thoughts about the uncertainties of the future. A modern translation of Zephaniah 3:17, the card read, "He is silently planning for you in love." It was just the word I needed and have needed many times since. God Himself is working things out for me, even when I don't feel it. He is at work — not because I merit His favor, but because of His great love. This time God wasn't about to let me forget it either — two weeks later, while visiting a friend in another part of England, I found this verse in practically every room of the house. My prayer changed from "What should I do?" to "Show me Your plan!"

Actually my introduction back into life in America was somewhat catastrophic. Because my plane from England was late arriving in New York, I didn't even have time to take the shuttle bus to my connecting flight to Harrisburg, Pennyslvania. The only way was to take a taxi the very short distance to the other section of the airport. But then the cabby tried to cheat me. Though the meter read three dollars, he was demanding fifteen. With no time to argue, I handed him five, rattled something in Chinese while pointing to the meter, then picked up my bags and ran. Wearing a big steel brace and a surgical collar, I must have been an amusing sight, especially with the cabby running and shouting after me! *Is this what America is like now?* I groaned.

Completely breathless, I ran up to the counter just in time to check my bags. Then, huffing and puffing my way up the ramp and onto the plane, I plopped down in the only vacant seat, the last passenger to board. Some way to treat a lady who is supposed to be dying of cancer! Anyway, I made it.

In Harrisburg I was met by most of my family. How old they looked! Of course, it had been nine years since we had seen each other, and I guess we all had a reason to look a bit more decrepit. But, I found out later, they were no more impressed by my youthful vigor than I was by theirs. Some even wondered if I would make it the eighteen miles to my sister's house in Elizabethtown.

I went to pick up my baggage, only to discover that it had been lost — on the shortest flight of the whole trip! Was this American efficiency? No use to grumble. "I guess I'm supposed to learn the meaning of 'wash and wear'!" I laughed, after filling out a lot of forms at the airline desk.

The day after I arrived my sister Dorothy, who had driven up from Florida for my homecoming, fell and dislocated her right arm. Most of that day we spent in doctors' offices and trying to help her find a comfortable position. With her thus handicapped, I became her chauffeur. Fortunately I still had a valid Pennsylvania driver's license.

On my fifth day of "wash and wear", as Dorothy was feeling much better, we decided to drive from Elizabethtown to the U.S. headquarters of O.M.F.

in Robesonia, an easy drive through the rolling hills of Pennsylvania Dutch country. A talk with the Home Director made it clear that I was on retirement without furlough — which meant I was not to be asked to take meetings.

On the way home I hardly saw the fresh green fields of growing grain broken by clumps of dense woods in summer finery. I was standing up inside. I was not sick enough just to be left to vegetate! In fact I was feeling fine and raring to go. Being treated like an invalid stirred the rebellion again.

This time, however, quiet was quickly restored as the Lord spoke to me once more. No, He wouldn't let me vegetate, but I did need time to adjust.

Returning from our jaunt that day we learned one piece of good news: my baggage had been found. And when we went to pick it up the next morning, we found it in good condition. While grateful for my luggage and a fresh change of clothes, I had to smile, for up to this point it hadn't really appeared as if God was "planning for me in love." In fact, almost everything seemed to be going wrong. Such times a person just has to walk by faith.

One day we decided to go car shopping. Some days earlier a long-standing computer error had been rectified in my bank account, considerably fattening the balance, so along with the gifts of Chinese friends and the repaid debt I felt I had enough to buy a good used car. Reminding the Lord as we set out just how much money I had, I asked Him to please find me just the right vehicle within that amount.

The first and only place we went that day was to the dealer who had sold me Datsie in 1968. As we walked out to the used-car lot, I couldn't miss the bright yellow four-door Datsun compact answering all my specifications. The car had just been put on the lot before we arrived. Not only was the price right, but I knew its previous owner! Just as impressed with the car's rightness after the test-drive, I told the man I would take it.

When the dealer discovered I intended to pay cash for the car, he blurted in surprise, "No one ever does *that* anymore!"

"Well, I pay cash," I replied. "However, since I am paying cash, don't you think you could give me a reduction in the price?" Good Chinese bargaining!

He wasn't sure at first how to react. "I can't do that," he came back eventually. "But I'll tell you what I'll do — I'll pay the tax." So after I wrote out a check for the car, insurance and registration on the spot, I had a bit of money left over for initial running expenses. How's that for the Lord's provision! By the way, I call the little yellow Datsun "*Hephzibah*," because my delight is in her.

While on the surface life began to be more routine after those first ten days at home, I was discovering that I had a good bit of catching up to do. Even reading the newspaper left me at a loss. Not only had vocabulary been corrupted and expanded in my absence, but initials had sprouted like weeds. Editors obviously presumed everyone knew what IRA, IBM, ICBM, OPEC, SALT and many others stood for. I was stumped. Surely Chinese was a simpler language than English after all!

Watching television was hardly more enlightening. I couldn't understand the jokes. While others laughed, obviously tickled, I could not see anything funny in them at all — even after the jokes were explained to me.

Soon my friends and relatives despaired of me and gave up even trying to explain.

Those first few weeks I really struggled to become intelligent.

Shopping brought its own shock. I was horrified at the prices. My mind, still computing in terms of what things cost in Taiwan, was having trouble shifting gears. Places had changed too. Once familiar routes left me lost. Not only did the one-way streets confuse things, they seemed always to be going the wrong way! One day I struggled for hours trying to find a friend's home in Philadelphia, a city I thought I knew very well — after all, I had lived there for nearly eight years. Every time I got on what I thought was a street going in the right direction, I landed at Robin Hood Dell in Fairmont Park! After I had returned to that park by four different routes, I gave up and headed out of the city.

Before long I was tiring of living out of a suitcase. Everyone was asking me where I would settle, and when. How I longed to have the answer! I was praying for guidance, the unmistakable kind. I wanted the Lord to show me where *He* wanted me to live, for I did not feel that my commitment to Him had ended with my leaving Taiwan. The commitment that I made to the Master many years earlier was not just for China, but for life — to do His will wherever He chose. It was still ANYWHERE, ANYTIME, ANYHOW — BAR NOTHING. But I was growing impatient, reminding the Lord constantly of His promise to plan for me in love for all my future. *Please, Lord, hurry up!* was my silent P.S.

When at last my sister Dorothy was permitted to travel, I chauffeured her home to Florida. It was

October, a lovely time to travel south, and the weather was beautiful. Vivid autumn colors followed us until palm trees and citrus groves took over in northern Florida, then balmy breezes and well-peopled beaches until we reached Clearwater and the Imperial Gardens, where Dot lived.

Since Clearwater abounds in apartment complexes, we started looking at places to live. I wasn't really expecting to settle in Florida — I had my eye on the Boston area to be near Park Street Church, my supporting church — so we were looking more to get a idea of rental costs than anything else. And as I would be setting up an apartment from scratch, we also scouted around to see the range of furniture prices. The longer we looked, the more I began to joke about buying a tent and an army cot. Prices were staggering! I had no idea what any of this had to do with God's guidance.

Next thing on my agenda was a visit to Boston. I planned to spend four or five weeks renewing acquaintances at Park Street Church, meanwhile hoping that something would open up in the way of a place to live, and perhaps a ministry among international students. But apartments in Boston turned out to be extremely expensive, away over my head — and low-income apartments had long waiting lists. I did fill out application forms for the low-income housing, however, believing that if God wanted me in Boston He could open the way. Then I went about my affairs, trusting Him to do some unexpected wonder. He did!

A few days before I was to leave Boston, Dorothy called from Florida to say there was an apartment available in her complex, Imperial Gardens, if I wanted it. The manager needed to know my answer within two days. In my heart I knew at once that this was the answer to my prayers. All this time the Lord had indeed been silently working for me, so that while I had no personal desire to settle in Florida I was sure the Lord had a purpose and a plan for me there.

To arrive in Florida three days before Christmas seemed all wrong. But then I discovered that the year-end sales had begun, and things we had priced in October were now thirty to forty percent cheaper. With the Lord's planning, the gift for furnishings from Grace Church in Taichung just about covered my basic needs, and by Christmas Day my little apartment was quite livable. I was out of a suitcase at last!

Rumor had it among my new neighbors that I was a retired nun. No wonder these senior citizens were so obviously curious! In fact, a retired missionary wasn't much better, for most had never seen a real live missionary before, and it took time for the barriers to come down.

The last day of 1978 I took as a quiet day to assess the past and to renew my commitment to the Lord for the new year. As I examined my attitudes regarding retirement, the Lord showed me how much was still negative and challenged me whether I was going to throw in the sponge and give up, or reach out to new opportunities as long as I could. Surrounded by evidences of the Lord's loving care and provision as well as the love of many friends, I prayed, Lord, *I don't know how much time I have left* (the two or three months had already stretched to several years!) *but don't let me just fritter my time away in idleness or self-pity. Help me to buy up the opportunities that come my way and use them for Your glory.*

Opportunities began to open up from surprising sources. And as taking up one usually led to two more,

I soon found myself claiming in a new way the promise, "As thy days, so shall thy strength be."

For a long time people both in and out of the O.M.F. had been urging me to do some writing — even an autobiography. Feeling the inadequacy of memory without supporting source material, I had been dragging my feet. But then, going through some old things put in storage when our family home was sold I discovered practically all the letters that I had written my parents during my early years in China and Taiwan. There they were, carefully kept in chronological order, even tied with a red ribbon. I no longer had my no-source-material excuse.

Reading through those letters and other material, I could only stand in awe at God's lovingkindness to me. Then, while in Pennsylvania working out an outline for this book, I heard a sermon which summed up for me God's working in my life. I remember little about the speaker or how he developed his sermon — I was too busy doing my own developing of his delightful three points: He never let me go, He never let me down, and He never let me off.

HE NEVER LET ME GO. When God saved me on that mountain road as a suicidal ex-medical student, He promised me He would never let me go — that I was held by Him in His hand and was forever safe. I didn't always remember that truth, but looking back now I see how He has kept a tight hold on me and hasn't let me go. He didn't let me go over that cliff that hot August afternoon in 1938; rather He showed me my need and wooed me to Himself. Nor did He let me return home when I was so discouraged and felt so much a failure in Shanghai; instead He showed me the plowman and my responsibility. Neither did He let me go when I was disobedient and failed Him time and again; He was always there whenever I was willing to return and admit my failure and my need of Him.

HE NEVER LET ME DOWN. God promised to supply all my needs according to His riches in glory by Christ Jesus. He has never swerved from doing just that. He did not let me down when I was in danger or sick or when I had failed or was robbed and down to my last cent. He didn't let me down in times of wild inflation or when faced with exorbitant medical bills. Though He often kept me waiting until the last minute, His faithfulness didn't waver. Material, physical and spiritual needs — He has met them all as He promised He would. He certainly has never let me down.

HE NEVER LET ME OFF. This is a lesson I am still learning — that He has not and will not let me off the hook. I am committed to serve Him wherever and however He wills. It is a commitment that has nothing to do with my convenience. It is a life sentence, so to speak. It is a commitment not given begrudgingly but with joy. I am His, and He is my Sovereign Lord. I am retired as men see it; from God's viewpoint I am recycled. The sphere of service has changed, not the call. He still has work for me to do, perhaps not with the same flurry of activity as before, but work that is His will, whether it is simply offering a helpful hand or reaching out to the lonely with uncomplicated friend-liness. No, He is not about to let me off, not even in retirement.

Often I am asked, "Are you healed?" I reply, "I don't know, and I'm not going to have them cut me open again just to find out!" I just try to live to God's glory, greatly helped by these four verses:

Deuteronomy 33:25: "As your days, so shall your strength be."

Nehemiah 8:10: "The joy of the Lord is your strength."

Psalm 118:24: "This is the day which the Lord has made; let us rejoice and be glad in it."

Proverbs 17:22: "A cheerful heart is a good medicine, but a downcast spirit dries up the bones."

Eight years ago I was told that I had two, maybe three months to live; but I'm writing these lines now since God has chosen, rather, to keep me alive for a time.

This verse from the well-known hymn, *The Sands of Times are Sinking*, summarizes better than I can God's sovereign working in my life down through the years:

With mercy and with judgment
  My web of time He wove,
And, aye, the dews of sorrow
  Were lustered with His love;
I'll bless the hand that guided,
  I'll bless the heart that planned,
When throned where glory dwelleth,
  In Immanuel's land.

(Cousins-Rutherford)